The
JEFFERSON LIES

The
JEFFERSON LIES

Exposing the Myths You've Always
Believed about Thomas Jefferson

DAVID BARTON

THOMAS NELSON
Since 1798

NASHVILLE   DALLAS   MEXICO CITY   RIO DE JANEIRO

Published in Nashville, Tennessee, by Thomas Nelson. Thomas Nelson is a registered trademark of Thomas Nelson, Inc.

Thomas Nelson, Inc., titles may be purchased in bulk for educational, business, fund-raising, or sales promotional use. For information, please e-mail SpecialMarkets@ThomasNelson.com.

Unless otherwise noted, Scripture quotations are taken from THE ENGLISH STANDARD VERSION. © 2001 by Crossway Bibles, a division of Good News Publishers. Scripture quotations marked NIV are taken from HOLY BIBLE: NEW INTERNATIONAL VERSION®. © 1973, 1978, 1984 by International Bible Society. Used by permission of Zondervan Publishing House. All rights reserved. Scripture quotations marked KJV are taken from the King James Version of the Bible.

Library of Congress Cataloging-in-Publication Data

Barton, David, 1954-
   The Jefferson lies : exposing the myths you've always believed about Thomas Jefferson / David Barton.
      p. cm.
   ISBN 978-1-59555-459-8 (hardback)
   ISBN: 9781595554604 (eBook)
   1. Jefferson, Thomas, 1743-1826. 2. Presidents--United States--Biography. I. Title.
   E332.B295 2012
   973.4'6092--dc23
   [B]
                                                                                      2011051543

Printed in the United States of America

12 13 14 15 16 QGF 6 5 4 3 2 1

Contents

CONTENTS

Foreword

I recently learned that the United States government was actually trying to strip God out of a private homeless shelter for previously incarcerated women struggling in Colorado. That's right, Marilyn Vyzourek, the woman who runs an organization called Gospel Shelters for Women, was told that she could no longer offer Bible studies at her shelter. Why did they have that ability? Because our government, which happily funds all kinds of programs championed by the secular left, decided that the shelter's acceptance of two $25,000 federal grants made them subservient to their will.

It's not surprising. In fact, it's just the latest in a decades-old attempt by progressive secularists to keep religion entirely separate from the government. *Everyone* knows that's just what Thomas Jefferson intended when he penned the words "separation of church and state," right?

Well, not quite.

My friend, historian David Barton, takes on this long-held falsehood about the separation of church and state and proves once and for all that our Founding Father was no secularist. Not even close. Did you know, for instance, that when Jefferson was president in 1800 he helped start church services *inside* the US Capitol? Those services grew to include more than two thousand people attending each week, and it became one of the biggest churches in America at the time.

And that's just the beginning.

Why does the Left continue to misquote Jefferson, accuse him of being anti-God, and attribute evil deeds to him? Because they know that if they are able to discredit and dismiss Jefferson and our other Founders, then we are that much closer to surrendering our birthright and our natural freedoms. These myths have flourished in our educational institutions in recent years and have become accepted as truth. It's a poison in our nation's system that can only be flushed out by light and truth.

There are three things I've learned from Thomas Jefferson and have tried hard to apply in my own life: (1) Question with boldness, (2) Hold to the truth, and (3) Speak without fear. In *The Jefferson Lies*, David Barton boldly questions the myths about Jefferson and arms you with the well-researched truth. I ask you to read it, learn from it, and then to go speak without fear.

Oh, by the way, Marilyn Vyzourek refused to back down from the government's demands. The government may have stripped her of federal money, but that would not be the end of Gospel Shelters for Women. When I heard about her story I decided to replace the money they'd lost with a personal contribution. After all, sometimes questioning with boldness involves more than just words; it requires action.

I like to think Thomas Jefferson would have smiled just a little if he were still around.

GLENN BECK

Editors' Notes

Many early American historical quotes have been used in this book—quotes made at a time when grammatical usage and spelling were quite different from what is practiced today. In an effort to improve readability and flow, we have modernized all spellings and puncuations in the historical quotes used throughout this work, leaving the historical content unimpaired.

As an example of the very different colonial spelling of words, consider the opening language of the Pilgrims' Mayflower Compact of 1620 (the words misspelled by today's standards are underlined):

> We whose names are <u>underwriten</u>, the <u>loyall</u> subjects of our dread <u>soveraigne</u> Lord King James, by the grace of God, of Great <u>Britaine</u>, <u>Franc</u>, & Ireland king, defender of the faith, &c., <u>haveing</u> undertaken, for the <u>glorie</u> of God, and <u>advancemente</u> of the Christian faith, and <u>honour</u> of our king & <u>countrie</u>, a voyage to plant the first <u>colonie</u> in the <u>Northerne</u> parts of Virginia, <u>doe</u> by these presents solemnly & <u>mutualy</u> in the presence of God, and one of another, covenant & combine <u>our selves togeather</u> into a <u>civill</u> body <u>politick</u>.

The use of modern spellings will not change any meanings in the quotes. By referring to the sources in the footnotes, the reader will be able to examine the original spelling should he or she so desire.

Similarly distracting to today's readers is the early use of capitals and commas. For an example of the copious use of commas, refer to the previous example; to see the excessive use of capitals, notice this excerpt from a 1749 letter written by signer of the Declaration Robert Treat Paine (underlined words would not be capitalized today):

> I <u>Believe</u> the Bible to be the written word of God & to <u>Contain</u> in it the whole <u>Rule</u> of <u>Faith</u> & manners; I consent to the Assemblys <u>Shorter</u> Chatachism as being <u>Agreable</u> to the <u>Reveal'd</u> <u>Will</u> of God & to contain in it the <u>Doctrines</u> that are <u>According</u> to Godliness. I have for some time had a desire to attend upon the Lords Supper and to <u>Come</u> to that divine <u>Institution</u> of a <u>Dying</u> Redeemer, And I trust I'm now convinced that it is my <u>Duty</u> <u>Openly</u> to profess him least he be ashamed to own me <u>An Other</u> day; I humbly therefore desire that you would receive me into your <u>Communion</u> & <u>Fellowship</u>, & I beg your <u>Prayers</u> for me that <u>Grace</u> may be carried on in my soul to <u>Perfection</u>, & that I may live answerable to the <u>Profession</u> I now make which (God <u>Assisting</u>) I purpose to be the main <u>End</u> of all my <u>Actions</u>.

In a further effort to improve readability, the modern rules of capitalization and punctuation have also been followed in the quotes throughout this book. These changes will not affect or alter the meaning of the content in the quotes.

Finally, the author, a professing Christian, personally chooses to capitalize all nouns or pronouns referring to God, Biblical Deity, or the Bible as a sign of his personal respect for his Biblical faith.

Rediscovering Thomas Jefferson

When I speak at universities and law schools across the nation, schools full of America's best and brightest students, I like to display a slide of the famous painting of the signers of the Declaration of Independence that hangs inside the Rotunda of the US Capitol. While displaying that slide, I often comment that it is unfortunate that the Founding Fathers were a collective group of racists, bigots, and slaveholders. Almost always I receive nods of sad affirmation from the students.

I then ask them to identify which signers in the painting owned slaves. Everyone immediately points to Thomas Jefferson, but to date no one has ever pointed out a second example. They have been taught that the Founding Fathers were racists. They know that Jefferson owned slaves; apparently that is all that is necessary to prove that the rest of the fifty-six also owned slaves. Yet a large majority of the Declaration signers were antislavery, introduced or passed anti-slavery legislation, or founded or led antislavery societies (including Jefferson—something students are never told).

Because of the many modern disparagements, these students have no idea that very few individuals in history have received as many titles of honor as Thomas Jefferson, including "Apostle of Liberty,"[1] "Man of the People,"[2] "Pen of the Revolution,"[3] "father of the Declaration of Independence,"[4] "the defender of the rights of man and the rights of conscience,"[5] the "Sage of Monticello,"[6] and "the apostle of Democracy."[7]

Jefferson was truly a visionary and an innovator—a Renaissance man in the classical sense of the term. He was masterful and skilled in diverse areas, and his multidimensional abilities were profusely praised by those who knew him. For example:

- Marquis de Chastellux, a French general who served with Jefferson during the American Revolution, described him as "a musician, skilled in drawing, a geometrician, an astronomer, a natural philosopher, legislator, and statesman."[8]

- Dr. Benjamin Rush, one of Jefferson's fellow signers of the Declaration of Independence, said he was "enlightened at the same time in chemistry, natural history, and medicine."[9]

- John Quincy Adams knew him as "a man of very extensive learning and pleasing manners."[10]

- The Reverend Ezra Stiles, a military chaplain in the Revolution and the president of Yale, called him a "naturalist and philosopher, a truly scientific and learned man."[11]

- General Marquis de Lafayette considered him a "great statesman, zealous citizen, and amiable friend."[12]

- Alexis de Tocqueville, historian and political leader who penned the famous *Democracy in America* as a result of his visit to America in 1831, called Jefferson "the greatest [man] whom the democracy of America has as yet produced."[13]

Perhaps the best summation was given by President John F. Kennedy, who once quipped to a group of Nobel Prize winners dining with him at the White House:

I think this is the most extraordinary collection of talent, of human knowledge, that has ever been gathered together at the

White House, with the possible exception of when Thomas
Jefferson dined alone. Someone once said that Thomas Jefferson
was a gentleman of 32 who could calculate an eclipse, survey an
estate, tie an artery, plan an edifice, try a cause, break a horse,
and dance the minuet.[14]

Jefferson was a remarkable man, and it is an understatement to
say that his positive influence was enormous. He indisputably helped
shape America for the better, and he exerted a positive influence on
nations across the world. Wherever tyranny is opposed and freedom
pursued, Jefferson and his words are held forth as the embodiment
of liberty and limited government—a fact especially reaffirmed in the
latter part of the twentieth century.

For example, Chinese students who strove to force democratic
reforms under their totalitarian government regularly invoked
Jefferson, even as the world watched the Communist tyrants massacre
those students at Tiananmen Square.[15]

When Czechoslovakians rose to throw off forty years of Soviet
Communist tyranny, Czech leader Zdenek Janicek quoted Jefferson
and his words to encourage the revolting Czech workers,[16] and after
Vaclav Havel became the first president of the freed Czech Republic,
he, too, pointed to Jefferson and his governing philosophy as the standard for his new nation.[17]

During Poland's struggle for independence from the Soviet Union,
Jefferson was invoked so often that award-winning Polish author
Jerzy Kosinski observed, "In every Pole, there is Jefferson more than
anyone else."[18]

Reform-minded Soviet leader Mikhail Gorbachev spoke openly
of Jefferson's positive influence upon him, explaining: "For myself,
I found one thing to be true: having once begun a dialogue with
Jefferson, one continues the conversation with him forever."[19]

When the Soviet Union fell in 1991 and Russia became free from its Communist oppressors, Andrei Kozyrev, the foreign minister of the new Russian republic, openly acknowledged that he was indebted to Jefferson and his governing philosophy.[20]

This pattern has been repeated around the globe. As former prime minister of England Lady Margaret Thatcher affirmed, "[I]n the history of liberty, he's a great figure everywhere in the world."[21]

Jefferson and his ideas of liberty, freedom, limited government, and God-given inalienable rights literally changed the world, and historians across the generations consistently praised his contributions and influence.

> American history presents few names to its students more attractive and distinguished than that of Thomas Jefferson, and rarely has a single individual, in civil station, acquired such an ascendancy over the feelings and actions of a people.[22]
>
> —BENSON LOSSING, 1848

> Thomas Jefferson . . . [was] singled out to draft the confession of faith of the rising empire. He owed this distinction to . . . that general favor which follows merit, modesty, and a sweet disposition. . . . No man of his century had more trust in the collective reason and conscience of his fellow-men, or better knew how to take their counsel.[23]
>
> —GEORGE BANCROFT, "Father of American History," 1864

> [He] had a faith in humanity that never wavered. He aimed to secure for it law that should deal out equal and exact justice to all men, and he sought to lift all men up to their native dignity by life-long labor in the cause of education.[24]
>
> —RICHARD FROTHINGHAM, 1872

> Few men have exerted as much influence in establishing the free institutions of the United States as Thomas Jefferson.[25]
>
> —BENSON LOSSING, 1888

Of all the men of that time, there was, perhaps, none of wider culture or keener political instincts.[26]

—John Fiske, 1891

[O]ne of the finest traits of his character was his magnanimity. . . . His dearest aim was to bring down the aristocracy and elevate the masses.[27]

—Edward Ellis, 1898

Jefferson often made mistakes, but, as he said of Washington, he "erred with integrity." If he changed his mind, it was because he had new light or a clearer understanding; if he altered his course, it was because he believed he could accomplish greater good.[28]

—William Eleroy Curtis, 1901

Democracy has won in the United States, and the spirit of its founder lives in all our political parties. He has stamped his individuality on the American government more than any other man.[29]

—Henry William Elson, 1904

[Jefferson] is a kind of Rosetta Stone of the American experience, a massive, tectonic intelligence that has formed and rattled the fault lines of our history, our present moment, and, if we are lucky, our future.[30]

—Ken Burns, 1996

Regrettably, this once universal praise of Jefferson has diminished in recent years. Mention Jefferson today and most Americans who have been through American history classes since the 1960s will retort, "Yeah, he may have done some of those things, but he was also a racist and a bigot—a slaveholder. And he slept with his fourteen-year-old slave Sally Hemings and made her pregnant. And he hated religion so much that he founded the first secular university in America, even writing his own Bible from which he cut out scriptures with which he disagreed."

Why can today's Americans list so many negatives about Jefferson but so few positives?

The answer is found in five twentieth-century practices that now dominate the study of American history and its heroes: Deconstructionism, Poststructuralism, Modernism, Minimalism, and Academic Collectivism. Although these five *isms* might suggest that an ivory-tower discussion is about to commence, this is not the case. Once we go through each of the five, you may have an *aha!* moment and recognize how each has shaped your own view of Jefferson. In fact, if you now think poorly of Jefferson, I can promise you that you will almost assuredly hold a very different opinion at the end of this book—and such is its object: to reverse the effect of the five malpractices of modern history that have distorted not only the presentation of Jefferson in particular but of American history in general.

Deconstructionism

The first of the five methods by which Jefferson (and most traditional history) has been impugned is *Deconstructionism*. Deconstructionism "tends to deemphasize or even efface [malign and smear] the subject" by posing "a continuous critique" to "lay low what was once high."[31] It "tear[s] down the old certainties upon which Western Culture is founded"[32] and the foundations on which those beliefs are based.[33] In short, Deconstructionism is a steady flow of belittling and negative portrayals of Western heroes, beliefs, values, and institutions. Deconstructionists make their living by telling only part of the story and spinning it negatively, manipulating others into supporting their views and objectives.

Deconstruction of American heroes, values, and institutions—which especially occurs in today's classrooms—is the reason most Americans can recite more of what's wrong with our nation than what's right. They can identify every wart that has ever appeared on the face of America over the past four centuries, but not what has made America the envy of every people in the world—every people, that is, except Americans.

Recall the students in the beginning of this chapter who believed all the Founders in the painting were proslavery. When I ask those same students to point out in the painting notable religious signers such as Robert Treat Paine, Roger Sherman, Benjamin Rush, Francis Hopkinson, John Witherspoon, Lyman Hall, Charles Carroll, or others, they look at me quizzically and say they've never heard those names before. They can always point out only Jefferson and Franklin—the two least religious among the Founders—but not the others. Students are taught the exception rather than the rule. (Incidentally, even the religious views of Franklin and Jefferson are frequently inaccurately portrayed in today's academic settings.)

Under Deconstructionism students are similarly taught about the "intolerant" Christian Puritans who conducted the infamous witch trials. And while twenty-seven individuals died in the Massachusetts witch trials,[34] almost universally ignored is the fact that witch trials were occurring across the world at that time; in Europe, 500,000 were put to death,[35] including 30,000 in England, 75,000 in France, and 100,000 in Germany.[36] Additionally, the American witch trials lasted eighteen months, but the European trials lasted years.[37]

Furthermore, the Massachusetts witch trials were brought to a close when Christian leaders such as the Reverend John Wise, the Reverend Increase Mather, and Thomas Brattle challenged the trials because the Biblical rules of evidence and due process had not been followed in the courts, thus convincing civil leaders and the governor to end those trials.[38] Twenty-seven deaths in America but 500,000 in

Europe? Why emphasize the twenty-seven but ignore the 500,000? The answer is "Deconstructionism"—presenting a negative portrayal of American faith and values.

Rarely do students hear that it was these "despised" Puritans who instituted America's first elective forms of government, originated the practice of written constitutions,[39] constructed the first bills of rights to protect individual liberties,[40] instituted the free market economic system,[41] or began America's system of common, or public, schools.[42]

In short, Deconstructionists happily point out everything that can possibly be portrayed as a flaw—even if they have to distort information to do so—but they remain conspicuously silent about the multitude of reasons to be proud of America and its many successes and heroes. They have led Americans toward knowing everything that "lays low" American traditions, values, and heroes but virtually nothing that honors or affirms them.

Poststructuralism

The second historical device for attacking and pulling down what is traditionally honored is called *Poststructuralism*. Poststructuralism is marked "by a rejection of totalizing, essentialist, foundationalist concepts" such as the reality of truth or "the will of God."[43] Poststructuralism discards absolutes and is "a-historical" (that is, non- or anti-historical),[44] believing that nothing transcendent can be learned from history. Instead, meaning must be constructed by each individual for him- or herself, and historical meanings may shift and change based on an individual's personal views.[45] Poststructuralism is especially evident in the judiciary, where judges often interpret and ascertain the meaning of the Constitution for themselves, redefining even the simplest words with new and previously unknown meanings that the judge has supposedly discovered for him- or herself.

Poststructuralism also encourages citizens to "view themselves as members of their interest group first, with the concerns of their nation and the wider community coming second, thus encouraging individual anarchy against traditional national unifying values."[46] In the past, America was characterized by the Latin phrase on the Great Seal of the United States: *E Pluribus Unum*, meaning "out of many, one." This acknowledges that although there was much diversity in America, there was a common unity that overcame all differences. But Poststructuralism reverses that emphasis to become *E Unum Pluribus*—that is, "out of one, many," dividing the nation into separate groups and components with no unifying commonality between them. In short, Poststructuralism ignores traditional national unifying structures, values, heroes, and institutions and instead substitutes personally constructed ones.

American Exceptionalism

Regrettably, the greatest casualty of the joint influence of Deconstructionism and Poststructuralism is American Exceptionalism—the belief that America is blessed and enjoys unprecedented stability, prosperity, and liberty as a result of the institutions and policies produced by unique ideas such as God-given inalienable rights, individualism, limited government, full republicanism, and an educated and virtuous citizenry.

Americans are blessed. America *is* an exceptional nation. That exceptionalism encompasses her great diversity of race, ethnicity, and religion, and it has benefited every American. But now, following several decades of Deconstruction and Poststructural indoctrination in education and politics, American Exceptionalism is no longer recognized, understood, or venerated. To the contrary, many American political officials now feel compelled to apologize to the world for

America; they are conscious of our flaws but seem ignorantly oblivious to our matchless benefits and opportunities.

The two-headed monster of Deconstructionism and Post-structuralism allows nothing respected to stand untainted—including Thomas Jefferson. Hence, Americans can readily point out what they have been told are his multitude of unpardonable sins but can list nearly none of his invaluable and timeless contributions that changed the face of America, and even the world.

Modernism

A third common attack device is *Modernism*, which examines historical events and persons as if they occurred and lived today rather than in the past. It severs history from its context and setting, misrepresenting historical beliefs and events.

For example, Modernists would look at what American Methodists believe today, recognize that they are among the most socially liberal of Christian denominations, and then declare that John and Charles Wesley and George Whitefield were also socially liberal because they founded Methodism. Yet the Wesleys and Whitefield were characterized by numerous beliefs and practices that are anathema to most Methodist congregations today, including the overtly evangelical nature of the denomination at its founding, its outdoor camp meetings and revivals, and its tendency for demonstrative behavior that observers in that day described as emotionalism and fanaticism—behavior that would make many Methodists today extremely uncomfortable. In fact, it is highly unlikely that the Wesleys or Whitefield would ever be invited into the pulpits of modern Methodist churches. Modernists assume that everything is static—that as it is today, so it was then, but to accurately portray history, each group or individual must be measured not by today's modes of thinking, customs, and usage but rather by the context of their own times.

This is not to say that there is no absolute truth or that historical eras, movements, and individuals should not be judged by the immutable standards of right and wrong that transcend all generations—the standards that Jefferson and the Founding Fathers described in the Declaration of Independence. Indeed, all must be judged by immutable objective standards, as "the laws of nature and of nature's God." But just because those in previous generations often saw through a glass darkly does not mean they can be dismissed out of hand. Yet this is invariably what occurs when history is presented through the filter of Modernism. Too often today, Jefferson's life is wrongly judged and critiqued as if he were living now rather than two centuries ago—a practice that produces many flawed conclusions.

Minimalism

The fourth modern device used today is *Minimalism*, which is an unreasonable insistence on oversimplification—on reducing everything to monolithic causes and linear effects. Minimalism is easily recognizable in political campaign rhetoric: candidates take behemoth problems facing the nation—complicated difficulties that often have been decades in the making—and reduce them to one-line platitudes and campaign slogans. Minimalism is also apparent in the modern portrayal of history.

Our modern culture insists on easy answers, but the life of Jefferson does not accommodate that demand. He was an extremely complicated individual, not a man to be flippantly stereotyped or compartmentalized. In fact, he was probably much more complex than most other historic individuals from the same era. But many who write about him today try to conform him to a preshaped, preconceived, simplistic mold into which he does not fit. The image of Thomas Jefferson as presented by one modern writer will therefore often completely contradict the image presented by another, because each writer attempted to squeeze Jefferson into his or her own Minimalistic perception.

Minimalism is especially utilized by single-issue groups seeking to keep their issue at the forefront of public thinking—an especially difficult task in a culture already overloaded with single-issue organizations. Because such movements often lack widespread public support, they frequently attempt to bolster their standing by attaching someone of much broader public appeal to their narrow agenda, making that person appear to prove their objectives. Consequently, Minimalists portray Jefferson only as a racist, atheist, secularist, or whatever else they believe will help their agenda.

Academic Collectivism

The fifth and final device that undermines historical accuracy is *Academic Collectivism*, whereby writers and scholars quote each other and those from their peer group rather than consult original sources. This destructive and harmful tendency now dominates the modern academic world, with a heavy reliance on peer review as the almost exclusive standard for historical truth.

An excellent, if chilling example of this historical malpractice is evdent in a book called *The Godless Constitution*. In that work, Cornell professors Isaac Kramnick and Laurence Moore assert that the Founding Fathers were a group of atheists, agnostics, and deists who deliberately set out to create a secular government.[47] This text has become a staple in many universities across the country; law reviews, courts, and other professors now cite this work as an authoritative source to "prove" the Founding Fathers' lack of religious belief.[48]

Strikingly, however, at the end of the book, where footnotes customarily appear, the professors candidly acknowledge that "we have dispensed with the usual scholarly apparatus of footnotes."[49]

What a startling admission by two so-called academics with PhDs! They make sweeping and forceful claims about a supposed lack of faith among the Founding Fathers, and their peers in academia herald this book as a great scholarly achievement. But there is not a single academic citation in the book to any original source or primary document. Not even a student at a community junior college would be permitted to submit a research paper with the same lack of primary source documentation, but somehow it is acceptable for professors at a noted academic institution to do so in a nationally published book.

This type of "peer review" is incestuous, with one scholar quoting another, each recirculating the other's views, but with none of them consulting sources or ideas outside his or her own academic gene pool. The presence of a PhD after one's name today somehow suggests academic infallibility—but this view must change if truth, accuracy, and objectivity are ever again to govern the presentation of history and historical figures. Primary source documents and historical evidence are the proper standard for historical truth, not professors' opinions.

In the following chapters, we will embark on a search for historical truth. We will attempt to reclaim many of the puzzle pieces of the image of Thomas Jefferson that have been discarded and lost in the twentieth century. Specifically, we will delve into seven contemporary claims about Jefferson's faith and morals, answering these questions:

- Did Thomas Jefferson really have a child (or children) by his young slave girl, Sally Hemings?

- Did Jefferson found a secular university as a reflection of his own allegedly secular lifestyle and beliefs?

- Did Jefferson write his own Bible, excluding the supernatural parts of Christianity with which he disagreed?

- Was Jefferson a racist who opposed civil rights and equality for black Americans?

- Did Jefferson, in his pursuit of separation of church and state, advocate secularizing the public square and the expulsion of faith and religious expressions from the public arena?

- Did Jefferson hate the clergy?

- Did Jefferson repudiate religion? Was he an atheist, deist, or secularist, or was he a Christian?

Let's examine Jefferson's own words and the eye-witness testimony of those who knew him best on each of these questions.

Lie #1

Thomas Jefferson Fathered Sally Hemings' Children

In 1998 the journal *Science* released the results of a DNA inquiry into whether Jefferson had fathered any children through his slave Sally Hemings, specifically her first child, Thomas, or her fifth child, Eston.[1] In conjunction with the announcement, Pulitzer Prize–winning historian Professor Joseph Ellis wrote an accompanying article in the journal *Nature* declaring that the question was now settled—that DNA testing had conclusively proved that Thomas Jefferson had indeed fathered a Hemings child, thus scientifically affirming a two-centuries-old rumor.[2]

That 1998 announcement concerning early American history was actually relevant to events occurring at the time, for it came at the commencement of President Bill Clinton's impeachment proceedings for lying under oath to a grand jury about his sexual activities with a young intern inside the Oval Office. News reports immediately pounced on the fortuitous DNA announcement, arguing that if a man as great as Thomas Jefferson had engaged in sexual trysts, then President Clinton should not face questions about his sexual misbehavior. After all, such conduct had not diminished the stature of Jefferson, they argued, so it should not be allowed to weaken that of Clinton.

Professor Ellis agreed, candidly admitting, "President William Jefferson Clinton also has a vested interest in this [DNA] revelation."[3] Significantly, just weeks before Ellis' bombshell announcement about

Jefferson, he had added his signature as a cosigner of an October 1998 ad in the *New York Times* opposing the impeachment of Clinton.[4] Henry Gee, a staff writer for *Nature* who also wrote a piece as part of the initial revelation, acknowledged that the DNA report provided much-needed cover for President Clinton:

> The parallels between the story of Jefferson's sexual indiscretions and the travails of the current President are close. Thomas Jefferson came close to impeachment—but the scandal did not affect his popularity and he won the 1804 Presidential election by a landslide. And if President William Jefferson Clinton has cause to curse the invention of DNA fingerprinting, the latest report shows that it has a long reach indeed—back to the birth of the United States itself.[5]

Dr. David Mayer, professor of law and history, was a member of an independent "Scholars Commission" later convened over the Jefferson-Hemings issue. He agreed that the timing of the DNA article had not been by accident:

> Professor Ellis' accompanying article also noted, quite frankly, "Politically, the Thomas Jefferson verdict is likely to figure in upcoming impeachment hearings on William Jefferson Clinton's sexual indiscretions, in which DNA testing has also played a role." In television interviews following release of the article, Professor Ellis elaborated on this theme; and Clinton's apologists made part of their defense the notion that every President—even Jefferson—had his "sexual indiscretions."[6]

As far as Clinton defenders were concerned (especially his supporters in the media), the announcement of Jefferson's alleged moral failings was a gift from heaven. The entire nation was bombarded with the Jefferson paternity story for weeks; and the news of his moral failings was burned deeply into the consciousness of Americans. But many groups beyond Clinton supporters also welcomed the test results as useful to their particular agendas.

For example, the Jefferson-Hemings affair became the perfect platform for the feminist movement to discuss the nature of sexual relations. Many in that movement had already asserted that *any* type of sexual relations between a male and a female constituted rape,[7] but this development seemed especially to prove their point.[8] It was questioned whether any sex could be consensual if it was between individuals from different stations in life—such as Hemings and Jefferson. Many feminist writers, including Fawn Brodie, Barbara Chase-Riboud, and Annette Gordon-Reed, had even authored books about the older Jefferson and the younger Hemings.[9]

Another movement that benefited from the Jefferson-Hemings story included those who wished to keep open the racial wounds of previous generations. They pointed to Jefferson and his sexual exploitation of the slave Hemings as proof of how *all* African Americans were treated by *all* white Americans, not only in Jefferson's day, but also throughout much of the rest of American history.[10] The Jefferson announcement rekindled demands for restitutionary policies that would provide preferential treatment and elevation of status and opportunity as repayment for past wrongs committed.

However, only eight weeks after the initial blockbuster DNA story was issued, it was retracted quietly and without fanfare, with the scientific researcher who had conducted the DNA test announcing that it actually had *not* proven that Jefferson fathered *any* children with Hemings.[11] But this news exonerating Jefferson did not make the same splash in the national headlines, for it aided no agenda being advanced at that time. Since doing justice to Jefferson's reputation was not deemed to be a worthy national consideration in and of itself, the retraction story was simply buried or ignored.

Consider the damage done by this false reporting. Ask any adult today whether it has been scientifically proven that Jefferson fathered illegitimate children with Hemings, and they will likely answer with a resounding "Yes!" The nation certainly heard and still remembers the news barrage following the initial report, but the silence surrounding its retraction was deafening.

Yet notwithstanding the 1998 DNA testing results, the fact remains that charges of a Jefferson moral failure with Hemings had circulated for almost two centuries *before* the DNA testing was undertaken. Even without the DNA testing results, it is still appropriate to ask why such charges were originally leveled against Jefferson. Did he actually commit the sexual misbehavior with which he has long been charged? After all, we're often told that where there's smoke, there's surely fire; and if it had not been for the charges raised long ago, no one today would have even considered undertaking DNA testing.

Here is some background to this situation. Sally Hemings was a young slave girl who served Jefferson's daughters at the family home, Monticello. Jefferson had five daughters: Martha (nicknamed "Patsy"), Mary (nicknamed "Maria" but also called "Polly"), Jane (who died very young), Lucy Elizabeth I (who also died very young), and Lucy Elizabeth II. During the American Revolution Jefferson was frequently away from his beloved family, serving in the Virginia legislature, the Continental Congress, and as state governor.

In 1784, following the Revolution, Jefferson was sent by Congress as an ambassador to Paris. His wife had recently died, so he took Patsy, the oldest of his three remaining daughters, with him to France. The other two daughters, Mary and Lucy Elizabeth II, stayed behind with their aunt. But after Jefferson departed Monticello with Patsy, the toddler Lucy Elizabeth II unexpectedly died, so Jefferson sent for his only remaining daughter, Mary, to join him in France. Accompanying the eight-year-old Mary on the voyage as her companion was the fourteen-year-old Sally Hemings, whom Jefferson described as "Maria's maid."[12]

Critics charge that after the girls arrived in Paris, Jefferson began a sexual relationship with Hemings, who was nearly thirty years his junior and the same age as his oldest daughter, fourteen-year-old Patsy[13]—a relationship that produced some or all of Sally's children. (Most scholars believe that Hemings had five children.)[14]

Following the initial DNA testing announcement that Jefferson was the father of Hemings' fifth child, Eston, some historians, including many who had previously believed Jefferson to be innocent of the paternity charges, declared Jefferson guilty, and the two-century-old debate finally closed.[15] But the subsequent retraction certainly changed matters. Yet, regardless of the on-and-then-off DNA testing results about Eston, was there a sexual moral failure between Jefferson and Hemings?

The evidence against Jefferson may be divided into three categories:

1. The original 1998 DNA report. While this category of evidence is now discredited, it is important to understand the reason behind the retraction.

2. Oral tradition from two of Sally's children, the strongest of which involved Thomas Woodson, her first child. Two centuries ago, he claimed (and others repeated) that Sally Hemings was his mother and Thomas Jefferson his father. The fact that Sally had named the boy Thomas was used as evidence to confirm that he had indeed been fathered by Jefferson. Sally's fourth child, Madison, also made similar claims.

3. Published newspaper reports from Jefferson's day specifically charging him with fathering Hemings' children.

Consider the evidence.

Category 1: The DNA Evidence

To delve further into the story behind the retraction of the 1998 DNA testing results, begin with Professor Ellis' original announcement in *Nature,* which had declared:

> Almost two hundred years ago Thomas Jefferson was alleged to have fathered children by his slave Sally Hemings. The charges have remained controversial. Now, DNA analysis confirms that Jefferson was indeed the father of at least one of Hemings' children [Eston].[16]

In the two weeks following that announcement, 221 printed news articles repeated the claim, embedding it deeply in the minds of Americans.[17] Typical articles declared:

> Did the author of the Declaration of Independence take a slave for his mistress? DNA tests say yes. . . . The evidence here, in other words, removes any shadow of a doubt that Thomas Jefferson sired at least one son by Sally Hemings.
>
> —*U.S. News Online*[18]

> DNA Test Finds Evidence of Jefferson Child by Slave.
>
> —*New York Times on the Web*[19]

> Jefferson affair no longer rumor. . . . The DNA tests end nearly two centuries of speculation. . . . The evidence has shifted so startlingly that it now appears likely that Jefferson fathered four or five children by Hemings.
>
> —*USA Today*[20]

> [G]enetic testing almost certainly proves that our third president fathered at least one child by Sally Hemings.
>
> —*Washington Post*[21]

The opportunity to announce these results afforded many Deconstructionists in the media a welcome occasion to denigrate Jefferson. One national columnist gloated, "What a relief. Now Jefferson can be brought down off the god-like pedestal on which some have tried to elevate him."[22] He continued, "How are we to view Jefferson now? How about 'deadbeat dad'? That's what you call fathers who run away from their responsibilities to their children."[23]

Another described him as a "slave-owning, serial flogger, sex maniac."[24] Others portrayed him as a child molester, using an innocent adolescent girl for sex:

> We have recently learned through DNA testing that Jefferson was probably the father of Sally Hemings' youngest child, a boy, and maybe the father of the other four children as well. . . . He took her to Paris when she was 13, and when she returned two years later, she was pregnant.
>
> —*Washington Post*[25]

> What type of relationship could this have been, considering the profound power differences between master and slave? . . . [S]he was 13 or 14 and he was 43.
>
> —*Chicago Tribune*[26]

> In 1789, Sally Hemings returned with the Jefferson family to Virginia. By then, Sally was 16 or 17 and pregnant.
>
> —*New York Times on the Web*[27]

The hysterics against Jefferson became so great that some questioned why his image appeared on our coins;[28] others clamored for "the dismantling of the Jefferson Memorial" in Washington, DC, and "the removal of his face from Mount Rushmore."[29]

The DNA evidence as originally presented by Professor Ellis and reported by the media had seemed both unassailable and irrefutable, but there were several critical facts in the report that most Americans never heard.

For example, the original 1998 report contained a significant finding about which scholars and the media remained conspicuously silent:

> President Thomas Jefferson was accused of having fathered a child, Tom, by Sally Hemings. Tom was said to have been born in 1790, soon after Jefferson and Sally Hemings returned from France, where he had been minister. Present-day members of the African-American Woodson family believe that Thomas Jefferson was the father of Thomas Woodson, whose name comes from his later owner. . . . [But DNA testing shows] Thomas Woodson was *not* Thomas Jefferson's son.[30] (emphasis added)

So, the longest rumored charge against Jefferson, originally printed two centuries ago in publications of the day, was now proven wrong. Jefferson had been completely exonerated of that longstanding claim.

Additionally, when *Nature* issued its embarrassing retraction, it sheepishly confessed, "The title assigned to our study was misleading."[31] Why? Because *no* DNA sample from the Thomas Jefferson family line had been used in the testing—and the public was never told of this significant omission. It does seem that if someone wanted to test Jefferson's paternity that *his* DNA should be used.

Genetic DNA paternity testing requires the testing of a Y chromosome from a male descendant of the subject because the Y chromosome in males remains virtually unchanged from generation to generation. But Thomas Jefferson had no male descendants from which to take a DNA sample. His only son had died at birth. Since Jefferson had no surviving male descendants, the researchers therefore chose to test the Y chromosomes from the descendants of Field Jefferson, Thomas's uncle.

The researchers found that the configuration of the Y chromosomes in the descendants of Field Jefferson—a general configuration common to the entire Jefferson family—was indeed present in the descendants of Sally Hemings' youngest child, Eston. Therefore, on the basis of DNA testing, the most that researchers could conclusively say was that *some* Jefferson male—and there were twenty-six Jefferson males living in the area at the time—had a relationship with Sally Hemings that resulted in the birth of Eston. But which Jefferson was it?

A distinguished commission of noted authorities was convened to examine the matter, and it concluded:

> There are at least ten possible fathers for Sally Hemings' children who could have passed down genetic material that might produce children physically resembling Thomas Jefferson and who are thought to have visited Monticello regularly during the years Sally Hemings was having children.[32]

After investigating the ten possible fathers, the group concluded that the "case against some of Thomas Jefferson's relatives appears significantly stronger than the case against him."[33] It was these other nine unaddressed paternity alternatives that made the DNA testing announcement suspect. Thomas Jefferson's own DNA was not checked, and with the exception of Field Jefferson, the DNA was not checked for the rest of the Jefferson males living in the area. *World* therefore correctly reported:

> According to the genetic evidence, the father *could* have been Jefferson. Or it *could* have been his brother Randolph. Or one of Randolph's sons. Or, presumably, his uncle Field, or his son

George or one of his sons. . . . Any of these men had access to Monticello and could have been culpable.[34] (emphasis added)

National columnist Mona Charen accurately summarized the scope of the testing results:

The DNA data did rule Jefferson out as the father of Thomas Woodson, the eldest of Sally's sons, and shed no light on the rest. That leaves a scenario in which Jefferson's sexual liaison with his slave [that produced Eston] is estimated to have begun when he was 65 years old. Possible certainly, but likely? While the DNA data adds to our knowledge—it is clear that there was mixing of Hemings and Jefferson genes sometime in the past 200 years—they do not provide names or dates. They most definitely do not "prove" anything about Thomas Jefferson himself.[35]

Herbert Barger, the Jefferson family historian and genealogist who assisted in the DNA testing, explained:

My study indicates to me that Thomas Jefferson was NOT the father of Eston or any other Hemings child. The DNA study . . . indicates that Randolph [Thomas' younger brother] is possibly the father of Eston and maybe the others. . . . [T]hree of Sally Hemings' children, Harriet, Beverly, and Eston (the latter two not common names), were given names of the *Randolph* family.[36] (emphasis added)

Significantly, a blue-ribbon commission of thirteen leading scholars was assembled to examine the Jefferson paternity issue. Those scholars were all PhDs, and most were department heads from schools such as Harvard, the University of Virginia, the University of North Carolina, the University of Kentucky, Indiana University, and others.[37] The group was not composed of Jefferson supporters; in fact, many believed that Jefferson might indeed be the father of Hemings' children.[38] But after spending a year investigating the evidence, they *all* concluded that Randolph was indeed the most likely father, explaining:

> [T]he circumstantial case that Eston Hemings was fathered by the President's younger brother is many times stronger than the case against the President himself. Among the considerations which might point to Randolph are:
>
> In *Memoirs of a Monticello Slave*, former slave Isaac Jefferson asserts that when Randolph Jefferson visited Monticello, he "used to come out among black people, play the fiddle and dance half the night . . ." In contrast, we have not a single account of Thomas Jefferson spending his nights socializing with the slaves in such a manner. . . .
>
> [W]e have Jefferson's letter inviting Randolph (and presumably his sons as well) to come to Monticello shortly before Sally became pregnant with Eston. It was common for such visits to last for weeks.
>
> Pearl Graham, who did original research among the Hemings descendants in the 1940s and believed the story that Thomas Jefferson fathered Sally Hemings' children, wrote in a 1958 letter to a leading Jefferson scholar at Princeton University that a granddaughter of one of Sally Hemings' children had told her that Randolph Jefferson "had colored children" of his own.
>
> Until Fawn Brodie [recently] persuaded the descendants of Eston Hemings that President Jefferson was his father, their family oral history had passed down that Eston was fathered by "Thomas Jefferson's uncle." That is not possible, as both of his paternal uncles died decades before Eston was conceived. But [according] to Martha Jefferson Randolph [Jefferson's oldest daughter], who was generally in charge of Monticello during Eston Hemings'

entire memory there, her father's younger brother was "Uncle Randolph"—and he was referred to as such in family letters.

We don't know exactly when Randolph's first wife died, but we do know that he remarried—to a very controlling woman—shortly after Eston Hemings was born. About the same time, Thomas Jefferson retired from public office and spent the rest of his life at Monticello, where he could presumably have had access to Sally Hemings any night he wished. But Sally, although only in her mid-thirties, gave birth to no known children after Eston was born in 1808. Even the Thomas Jefferson Memorial Foundation report acknowledges that Sally's childbearing years may have corresponded to the years in which Randolph Jefferson was a widower.[39]

Significantly, in its retraction even *Nature* ruefully conceded, "It is true that men of Randolph Jefferson's family could have fathered Sally Hemings' later children."[40] But this scholars' report was just as widely ignored by the media as had been both the DNA testing results that exonerated Jefferson and the retraction of its initial errant announcement. In fact, PBS's *Frontline*, A & E's *Biography*, the *Washington Post*, and others actually had in their possession reports that tended to exonerate Jefferson but deliberately omitted that information from their reporting.[41]

Incidentally, Dr. Eugene Foster, who conducted the DNA testing, had been very clear about the limitations of his testing, but his findings were misrepresented by Joseph Ellis, historian and professor at Mt. Holyoke College. Ellis, who opposed what was happening to President Clinton at the time, had written the sensationalistic "announcement" for *Nature*, but his personal spin went well beyond Foster's scientific findings, making the story both inaccurate and unfactual. Perhaps this should not be surprising; four years later, in 2002, it was revealed that Ellis was also guilty of publicly lying to his classes on many occasions. (For example, he told students that he went to Vietnam as a platoon leader and paratrooper in the 101st Airborne and served on General Westmoreland's staff during the war; he did neither. He also said that he did active civil rights work in Mississippi during the Civil Rights Movement and was harassed by the state police for his efforts; again, neither was true. He claimed that he scored the winning touchdown in the last football game of his senior year in high school; it turns out he wasn't even on the team.[42]) As one columnist properly queried, "How can you trust a historian who makes up history?"[43]

In hindsight, looking back over the complete fiasco, the *Wall Street Journal* correctly noted of the unreported retraction, "[T]he back-tracking comes a little late to change the hundreds of other headlines fingering Jefferson."[44] The effect of the original news flood was toxic. One reporter who covered the story accurately noted, "[D]efective scholarship is difficult to recall."[45] The *Jewish World Review* therefore properly asked, "Was Jefferson libeled by DNA?"[46] The evidence answers "Yes!"

In short, the DNA testing did not show Jefferson to be guilty of *any* sexual liaison with Hemings. The so-called smoking gun turned out to be a waterlogged pea shooter.

Category 2: The Evidence of Oral Tradition

The second source of Hemings' evidence used against Jefferson is oral tradition, but the DNA findings significantly weakened this source. The strongest evidence in this category had long been the two-century-old charge that Jefferson had fathered Thomas Woodson, but the DNA findings were conclusive that no Jefferson—not any of the twenty-six Jefferson males—had fathered Woodson. That original test was later repeated by Dr. Foster with the same results.[47] Consequently, that oral tradition is now authoritatively disproved.

(Incidentally, DNA testing has been conducted on descendants from two of Hemings' five children. As already noted, testing on the Thomas Woodson branch was negative for any Jefferson genes. The Eston Hemings branch showed some Jefferson genes, but it did not show from which of the twenty-six Jefferson males they came. The remaining three branches of Hemings' progeny have so far declined to participate in DNA testing.)

The other major oral tradition challenging Jefferson's sexual morality came from Sally Hemings' son Madison (the fourth Hemings child, born in 1805). In an article published in an Ohio newspaper in 1873, Madison Hemings claimed that in France "my mother became Mr. Jefferson's concubine, and when he was called back home she was enceinte [pregnant] by him" with Thomas Woodson.[48] But the DNA testing disproved two of Madison's major claims: (1) there were no Jefferson genes in Sally's first child, Thomas; therefore, (2) Sally did not return home pregnant by Jefferson.

Several other of Madison's claims about Jefferson have also been shown to be erroneous—including his claim that Jefferson was not interested in agriculture.[49] Yet modern authors such as Annette Gordon-Reed, professor of law at New York University, believe that Jefferson was guilty of all that Madison charged him with; she dismisses outright all evidence to the contrary and even concocts evidence in her attempts to "prove" her claims.

For instance, in her book *Thomas Jefferson-Sally Hemings: An American Controversy*, she "reprinted" a letter written in 1858 by Ellen Randolph Coolidge (Thomas Jefferson's granddaughter) describing the rooms at Monticello. According to Reed, Coolidge had written:

His [Jefferson's] apartments had no private entrance not perfectly accessible and visible to all the household. No female domestic ever entered his chambers except at hours when he was known not to be in the public gaze.[50]

So, based on Reed's quotation of Jefferson's granddaughter, female domestics such as Hemings entered Jefferson's apartment only at hours when no one was watching.

Significantly, however, Coolidge's actual letter had said exactly the *opposite*:

> His [Jefferson's] apartments had no private entrance not perfectly accessible and visible to all the household. No female domestic ever entered his chambers except at hours when he was known not to be *there; and none could have entered without being exposed to* the public gaze.[51] (emphasis added)

The emphasized portion above is what Gordon-Reed omitted, thus completely reversing its message. Significantly, the granddaughter had actually said that (1) no one could have entered without being seen and that (2) *no* female staff entered his room unless he was *not* there. But Reed, in order to bolster her own arguments against Jefferson, twisted and rewrote what Jefferson's granddaughter had actually said.

Sadly, when someone dismisses Madison Hemings' claims because of their many provable and obvious inaccuracies, writers such as Gordon-Reed cry "Racism!" and lament that black witnesses from history are automatically given less credence.[52] Other writers such as Jan Lewis and Peter Onuf believe that those who do not accept the testimony of Madison Hemings carte blanche are simply racists.[53]

Such irrational refusals to consider the substantial evidence that contradicts Madison Hemings' claims indicates that personal predilections and political agendas have been placed above an honest search for the truth. Genuine scholars require verifiable documentation—something completely lacking in the case of Thomas Woodson's and Madison Hemings' oral testimonies. In fact, their oral testimonies are factually disprovable, which eliminates the second category of "evidence" used to "prove" Jefferson's paternity through Hemings.

Category 3: The Charges Published Two Centuries Ago

The earliest printed charges alleging Jefferson's paternity with Hemings appeared in newspaper articles written from 1801 to 1803 by James T. Callender (1758–1803).

Callender first rose to attention in 1792 in Scotland when he authored *The Political Progress of Great Britain*. That work, highly critical of the British government, led to his indictment for sedition. After being "oftimes called in court, he did not appear and was pronounced a fugitive and outlaw."[54] Facing prison, Callender and his family of young children fled to America for refuge in 1793, arriving with no means or prospect of support. American patriots, learning of Callender's plight, sympathetically embraced him as a man suffering British persecution. Many, including Thomas Jefferson, personally provided charitable contributions to help Callender and his children.

In 1796 Callender secured a job writing for a Republican (an Anti-Federalist, pro-Jefferson) newspaper in Philadelphia. Promising "a tornado as no government ever got before,"[55] Callender resumed the defamatory writing style that had landed him in trouble in Great Britain, only this time it was against prominent Federalist Americans such as Alexander Hamilton, John Adams, and George Washington. By attacking the Federalists, Callender considered himself to be the mouthpiece for Jefferson's Republican Party and believed he was rendering it a valuable service.

The Northern states tended to be Federalist while the Southern ones tended to be Anti-Federalist (Republican). Callender was therefore in a northern state writing against Federalist statesmen highly regarded in that region. His writings not only raised great ire but were so defamatory as to invite litigation even in that land of free speech. So, fearing legal punishment, Callender fled from Philadelphia to Richmond in 1799.

Arriving there, he took a job with another Republican newspaper where he continued his attacks on the Federalists. Because of his vicious writings, Callender was convicted under the federal Sedition Law in 1800, fined $200 (about $3,000 today), and imprisoned for nine months. Still he did not relent. While in prison he authored two more attack pieces in the same style that had so frequently caused him difficulty. Callender proved to be a troublesome hothead with no sense of discretion.

During this time, Jefferson was serving as vice president under President John Adams. Callender wrote Jefferson twenty-nine letters, but Jefferson largely ignored him, replying only five times in a two-year period. Because of Jefferson's lack of response, Callender complained to James Madison that he "might as well have addressed a letter to Lot's wife."[56] Jefferson avoided Callender but continued occasional charitable gifts for the support of Callender's young children.

When Jefferson became president in 1801, he declared the Sedition Law to be unconstitutional and pardoned everyone who had been prosecuted under it (about two dozen individuals).[57] Jefferson also ordered that the fines collected under that law be returned with interest. But the Federalist sheriff who had collected the $200 fine from Callender refused and even ignored direct orders from Secretary of State James Madison to refund the fine.

Callender, now free, was unaware of these difficulties with the sheriff and became infuriated against Jefferson, blaming him for not returning his $200. Secretary of State Madison reported to Virginia governor James Monroe, "Callender, I find, is under a strange error on the subject of his fine, and in a strange humor in consequence of it."[58]

Callender became enraged at Jefferson. Believing that Jefferson's party owed him something for what he considered his long "service" on their behalf, he demanded a presidential appointment as the US postmaster for Richmond—an appointment that both President Jefferson and Secretary of State Madison properly refused him.

Meanwhile, Jefferson, still unable to obtain the return of the fine from the Federalist sheriff, took steps to repay Callender's fine from private funds. As he told Governor Monroe:

> I think with you we had better refund his fine by private contributions. I enclose you an order on Gibson & Jefferson for $50, which I believe is one fourth of the whole sum.[59]

Only three days later, following a meeting in which Callender responded viciously against Jefferson's offer of personal help, the formerly sympathetic Jefferson understandably underwent a complete change of heart toward Callender. As he explained to Monroe:

> Since [my last letter, three days ago], Callender is arrived here. He did not call on me; but understanding he was in distress, I sent Captain [Meriwether] Lewis to him with $50 to inform him we were making some inquiries as to his fine, which would take a little time; and lest he should suffer in the meantime I had sent him &c. His language to Captain Lewis was very high-toned. He intimated that he was in possession of things which he could and would make use of in a certain case: that he received the $50 not as a charity, but a due, in fact as hush money; that I knew what he expected, viz. a certain office [Richmond postmaster], and more to this effect. Such a misconstruction of my charities puts an end to them forever. You will therefore be so good as to make no use of the order I enclosed you [to repay the fine by private funds].[60]

Jefferson's instructions to withhold further relief from Callender arrived too late. As Governor Monroe told Jefferson, "Your [letter] just received. It is to be regretted that Capt[ain] Lewis paid the money. . . . [Y]our resolution to terminate all communication with him is wise."[61]

On the same day Monroe wrote Jefferson, Madison wrote Monroe describing the outrageous nature of his own meeting with Callender:

> Callender made his appearance here some days ago in the same temper which is described in your letter. He seems implacable [bull-headed] towards the principle object of his complaints and not to be satisfied in any respect without an office. It has been my lot to bear the burden of receiving & repelling his claims. . . . It is impossible however to reason concerning a man whose imagination & passions have been so fermented [soured].[62]

Madison then explained to Monroe part of the reason why he believed Callender was so irrational:

> Do you know, too, that besides his other passions, he is under the tyranny of that of love? . . . The object of his flame is in Richmond. . . . He has flattered himself, and probably been flattered by others, into a persuasion that the emoluments [compensations] and reputation of a post office would obtain her in marriage. Of these recommendations, however, he is sent back in despair. With respect to the fine even, I fear that delays, if nothing more, may still torment him and lead him to torment others. . . . Callender's irritation, produced by his wants, is whetted constantly by his suspicion that the difficulties, if not intended, are the offspring of indifference in those who have interposed in his behalf [Jefferson].[63]

Five days later Governor Monroe responded to Madison's letter, telling him of his own meeting with Callender:

> I have your [letter] and have since seen Mr. Callender, with whom I had much conversation. . . . I dwelt particularly on the

remission of the fine. . . . Still he added that some little office
would greatly accommodate him, and without one he did not
know how he should subsist. That he was tired of the press
&c.[64]

But even while Jefferson was working to obtain the return of the
fine, Callender announced his intention to punish Jefferson. Having
obtained neither the postal appointment (or any other "little office")
nor the full return of his fine, he became incensed against Jefferson.
Complaining that Jefferson had turned his back on him, he grumbled
"I now begin to know what ingratitude is"[65] and issued the ominous
warning that he was "not the man who is either to be oppressed or
plundered with impunity."[66]

The disgruntled Callender who previously had written only for
Republican newspapers—that is, pro-Jefferson and Anti-Federalist
publications—actively sought a job with the *Recorder*, a Federalist
newspaper in Richmond that was openly critical of President Jefferson.
Callender then launched a series of virulent attacks against Jefferson
in articles written throughout 1801, 1802, and 1803, accusing him,
among other things, of "dishonesty, cowardice, and gross personal
immorality."[67] It was in these defamatory articles that Callender
charged that Jefferson had fathered a child by Hemings.

Callender's charge about Hemings received broad circulation
when the Federalists of Massachusetts—strident and vocal opponents of President Jefferson, who used every opportunity to attack
him—reprinted the charges about Jefferson and Hemings in a series
of articles entitled "Commonwealth of Massachusetts vs. Thomas
Jefferson."[68]

Significantly, the claims about Jefferson and Hemings were always
associated with partisan smear politics. Callender died less than a
year after publishing his charges. During that time he was constantly
drunk, and after threatening suicide on several occasions, he eventu-

ally drowned in three feet of water in the James River. A coroner's jury ruled his death accidental, due to intoxication.

Before his death, however, Callender acknowledged that his attacks against Jefferson had been motivated by his belief that Jefferson had refused to repay his $200 fine.[69] In fact, in his article that first "exposed" the Jefferson-Hemings "relationship," Callender confirmed his own personal, vindictive motivation by closing the article with these stinging words:

> When Mr. Jefferson has read this article, he will find leisure to estimate how much has been lost or gained by so many unprovoked attacks upon J. T. Callender.[70]

History has proved many of Callender's charges against Jefferson to be totally inaccurate. For example, in his initial article in which he first "revealed" the Jefferson-Hemings "affair," Callender had asserted:

> It is well known that the man whom it delighteth the people to honor [President Jefferson] keeps, and for many years past has kept as his concubine one of his own slaves. Her name is Sally. The name of her eldest son is Tom. His features are said to bear a striking, although sable [dark-skinned] resemblance to those of the president himself. The boy is ten or twelve years of age. His mother went to France in the same vessel with Mr. Jefferson.[71]

This story was widely circulated, and the "striking resemblance" hearsay was often repeated to point to Jefferson's guilt. For example, the 1802 *Frederick-Town Herald* declared:

> Other information assures us that Mr. Jefferson's Sally and their children are real persons. . . . Her son, whom Callender calls

president Tom, we also are assured, bears a strong likeness to Mr. Jefferson.[72]

Interestingly, the "striking resemblance" charge is still invoked today as "proof" that Jefferson fathered Hemings' children,[73] but since the recent DNA testing unequivocally proved that Sally's son Tom was not the son of Thomas Jefferson, Callender's allegations that Tom bore a "striking resemblance to the president himself" are completely meaningless.

Furthermore, Callender claimed that Jefferson and Sally "went to France on the same vessel," which was also wrong; they went on two separate vessels, one in 1784 and the other in 1787. Callender made many other similarly erroneous claims.

He also wrongly predicted that Americans—especially the Federalists—would widely embrace his charges against Jefferson as true. Only three weeks after his first article, he forewarned:

> More About Sally and the President. For two days after the publication of the *Recorder* of September 1st, the [Jefferson's supporters] were at a loss what to say or think. The Philistine priesthood were not more confounded when they saw their idol Dagon prostrate and broke to pieces [1 Samuel 5:1–4]. . . . Sally's business makes a prodigious [monumental] noise. . . . After this discovery, I do not believe that at the next election [of 1804], Jefferson could obtain two votes on the eastern side of the Susquehanna [the general location of Jefferson opponents], and I think hardly four upon this side of it [the area of Jefferson supporters]. He will, therefore, be laid aside [i.e., not reelected].[74]

But Jefferson was easily reelected. Even many of his Federalist opponents rejected Callender's ludicrous charges. For example,

David Humphreys of Philadelphia wrote in that city's newspaper, the *Aurora*, that he had "shown that the story of Sally was a falsehood,"[75] and General Henry Lee, an ardent Federalist, declared that "there is no foundation whatsoever for that story."[76]

Callender was also wrong when he believed that he could besmirch the character of Jefferson supporters. He made an absurd string of accusations against James Madison's character,[77] and he also proffered equally ridiculous claims against Presidents George Washington and John Adams. He charged Washington with filling the American governmental process with "confusion and iniquity" and with "corrupt[ing] the American judges."[78] He charged Adams with attempting to overthrow the Constitution, betraying the nation to foreign powers, committing voter fraud and ballot tampering, allowing the slaughter of Americans by the Indians, ruining American morals, and even wishing that the British had won the American Revolution.[79]

The charges Callender made against Washington, Adams, and Madison were so ridiculous that they were never believed by objective historians—or, for that matter, by thoughtful citizens. So why, then, have Callender's charges against Jefferson survived when his charges against all the others deservedly perished long ago?

Because a few Deconstructionist writers in recent years have revived the work of Callender (called the "single poisoned spring" of Jefferson history[80]), citing his allegations against Jefferson as if they were indisputably proved while failing to mention Callender's established and well-documented pattern of false reporting, as well as the scurrilous, self-serving motives behind his published accusations. As Pulitzer Prize–winning historian James Truslow Adams explained, "Almost every scandalous story about Jefferson which is still whispered or believed can be traced to the lies in Callender's book."[81]

Merrill Peterson, professor of history at the University of Virginia, holds the same opinion,[82] and Pulitzer Prize–winning historian Dumas Malone described Callender as "one of the most notorious scandal-mongers and character assassins in American history."[83] Stanford University historian John C. Miller describes Callender as "the most unscrupulous scandalmonger of the day . . . a journalist who stopped at nothing and stooped to anything."[84] He explains:

> Callender made his charges against Jefferson without fear and without research. He had never visited Monticello; he had never spoken to Sally Hemings; and he never made the slightest effort to verify the "facts" he so stridently proclaimed. It was "journalism" at its most reckless, wildly irresponsible, and scurrilous. Callender was not an investigative journalist; he never bothered to investigate anything. For him, the story, especially if it reeked of scandal, was everything; truth, if it stood in his way, was summarily mowed down.[85]

Even historian Benjamin Ellis Martin—a strident, nineteenth-century Jefferson-bashing critic who easily might have accepted Callender's charges—found no basis for believing them. To the contrary, he described Callender as a writer who did "effective scavenger work" in "scandal, slanders, lies, libels, scurrility" and one who excelled in "blackguardism" (unprincipled, vile writing).[86] Martin, a confirmed anti-Jeffersonian, therefore concluded:

> I am unable to find one good word to speak of this man. . . . He was a journalistic janizary [mercenary], his pen always for sale on any side, a hardened and habitual liar, a traitorous and truculent [malicious] scoundrel; and the world went better when he sank out of sight beneath the waters of the James River.[87]

Significantly, Jefferson's long political career had been characterized by numerous personal attacks launched against him, especially during his presidential election. Jefferson placed the number of attacks in the thousands,[88] of which Callender's had been just one. In fact, after surveying the charges published against Jefferson by his opponents, Pulitzer Prize–winning historian Charles Warren concluded that "no other presidential campaign in American history ever brought forth such vicious and scurrilous personal attacks."[89] And Pulitzer Prize–winning historian Dumas Malone similarly observed that Jefferson "suffered open personal attacks which, in severity and obscenity, have rarely if ever been matched."[90]

Jefferson knew that he could never rebut the falsehoods as rapidly as they could be concocted. So long before Callender leveled his charges against him, Jefferson had made it his standing personal policy to ignore all ridiculous claims made against him by his enemies.

He gave three reasons for this policy: First, any response he made might seem to dignify the charges.[91] Second, he was convinced that his personal integrity would eventually prevail over the false accusations made against him.[92] And third, Jefferson trusted the good judgment of the people.[93]

Jefferson acknowledged that he could have successfully taken libelers like Callender to court, but he refused to lower himself to that level, instead turning them over to the Judge of the universe to Whom they would eventually answer. As he explained:

> I know that I might have filled the courts of the United States with actions for these slanders, and have ruined perhaps many persons who are not innocent. But this would be no equivalent to the loss of [my own] character [by retaliating against them]. I leave them, therefore, to the reproof of their own consciences. If these do not condemn them, there will yet come a day when the false witness will meet a judge Who has not slept over his slanders.[94]

Amazingly, Jefferson's lifelong policy of refusing to answer false claims has today been translated into culpatory evidence against him. In fact, one prominent national news outlet pointed out that since Jefferson "never directly denied"[95] having an affair with Sally, it was proof that he *had* fathered her children! (Consider the unreasonableness of declaring that an individual is guilty of whatever he does not deny.)

Even though Jefferson's public policy was silence, on two occasions he privately took pen in hand to recount his relationship with Callender to two friends. One was a lengthy letter to Governor James Monroe in which Jefferson explained:

> I am really mortified at the base ingratitude of Callender. It presents human nature in a hideous form. . . . When the *Political Progress of Britain* first appeared in this country [in 1794] . . . I was speaking of it in terms of strong approbation to a friend in Philadelphia when he asked me if I knew that the author [Callender] was then in the city, a fugitive from prosecution on account of that work and in want of employ for his subsistence. This was the first of my learning that Callender was the author of the work. I considered him as a man of science fled from persecution, and assured my friend of my readiness to do whatever could serve him. . . . In 1798, I think, I was applied . . . to contribute to his relief. I did so. In 1799 . . . I contributed again. He had, by this time, paid me two or three personal visits. When he fled in a panic from Philadelphia to General Mason's [in Virginia], he wrote to me that he was a fugitive in want of employ. . . . I availed myself of this pretext to cover a mere charity [and sent him] fifty dollars. . . . I considered him still as a proper object of benevolence. The succeeding year, he again wanted money. . . . I made his letter, as before, the occasion of

giving him another fifty dollars. He considers these as proofs of my approbation [approval]. . . . Soon after I was elected to the government, Callender came on here, wishing to be made postmaster at Richmond. I knew him to be totally unfit for it; and however ready I was to aid him with my own charities (and I then gave him fifty dollars), I did not think the public offices confided to me to give away as charities. He took it in mortal offense. . . . This is the true state of what has passed between him and me.[96]

In the second private letter about the Callender situation, written to Abigail Adams, Jefferson substantially repeated what he had said in his letter to Monroe and then closed by telling her:

I am not afraid to appeal to the nation at large, to posterity, and still less to that Being Who sees Himself our motives, Who will judge us from His own knowledge of them.[97]

Jefferson repeatedly affirmed that he had nothing to hide.[98]

Therefore, *none* of the three sources of evidence often invoked against Jefferson (the DNA testing, oral tradition, or the early published claims of Callender) provide any credible basis for believing that Jefferson fathered any of Hemings' children. Nevertheless, Deconstructionist attempts to convict Jefferson continue and have even expanded into new venues.

For example, Jefferson is now being subjected to the tests of "psychohistory" in order to "prove" that he had an affair with Hemings. "Psychohistory" occurs when, rather than accepting what someone actually said, a psychological counteranalysis of that person's words is attempted in an effort to establish their "true" motives. In my opinion, the result of such an analysis is psychobabble. Fawn Brodie used this method in her book *Thomas Jefferson: An Intimate History* in order to extract an implied confession from Jefferson. She explains:

> The first evidence that Sally Hemings had become for Jefferson a special preoccupation may be seen in one of the most subtly illuminating of all his writings, the daily journal he kept on a seven-week trip through eastern France, Germany, and Holland in March and April of 1788. . . . Anyone who reads with care these twenty-five pages must find it singular that in describing the countryside between these cities he used the word "mulatto" eight times.[99]

Since Sally Hemings was mulatto, Brodie concludes that Jefferson's use of that word when describing Land proves that he had a sexual relationship with her. Yet *mulatto* is used by Jefferson—who was by profession a farmer, scientist, and botanist—in his diary to describe the composition and color of the soil.

Notice the examples Brodie provides—examples that she claims "prove" Jefferson's sexual infatuation with Hemings:

> "The road goes thro' the plains of the Maine, which are mulatto and very fine . . ."; "It has a good Southern aspect, the soil a barren mulatto clay . . ."; "It is of South Western aspect, very poor, sometimes gray, sometimes mulatto . . ."; "These plains are sometimes black, sometimes mulatto, always rich . . ."; ". . . the plains are generally mulatto . . ."; ". . . the valley of the Rhine . . . varies in quality, sometimes a rich mulatto loam, sometimes a poor sand . . ."; ". . . the hills are mulatto but also whitish . . ."; "Meagre mulatto clay mixed with small broken stones . . ."[100]

Since the word *mulatto* is used only in a racial sense today, Modernist Brodie concludes that it was only used this way two centuries ago. She therefore claims that her psychoanalysis of Jefferson's observation of soil in Europe is "proof" of an affair with Hemings, but by so doing, she shows herself unfamiliar with both agriculture and linguistic etymology. Consider a few examples of the word *mulatto* as commonly used in early American agriculture:

Land rich—very rich; a deep stiff *mulatto* soil.

—Texas, 1846[101]

Both the deep black soil of the uplands and the light colored or *mulatto* soil peculiar to the bluff deposit are alike noted for productiveness.

—Iowa, 1875[102]

The soil . . . is a sandy, *mulatto*-colored soil; it has been called the corn soil, though it produces wheat, cotton, tobacco, potatoes, etc.

—Tennessee, 1879[103]

Highland is in the center of a tract of dark, "*mulatto*" soil of exceptional fertility, whence comes a large amount of farming trade.

—Kansas, 1883[104]

[T]he soil is called a "*mulatto* soil," and is that kind best adapted to the raising of cotton. It is a loamy clay, composed largely also of vegetable mould.

—Arkansas, 1889[105]

According to Brodie's reasoning, apparently all of these farmers who reported on soil conditions in their state must have also had "a special preoccupation" and attraction for women of mixed race since they also used the word *mulatto* in an agricultural context.

As Jefferson biographer Willard Sterne Randall correctly notes, Brodie's entire supposition is farcical:

> [W]hen Jefferson used the term *mulatto* to describe soil during his French travels, Sally was still on a ship with Polly, accompanying her to France. If he [Jefferson] had ever noticed her or remembered her at all, Sally had been only ten years old when Jefferson last visited Monticello hurriedly in 1784. . . . She was only eight when Jefferson last resided at Monticello and was mourning his wife's death. Unless Brodie was suggesting that Jefferson consoled himself by having an affair with an eight-year-old child, the whole chain of suppositions is preposterous.[106]

Pulitzer Prize–winning historian Garry Wills similarly observed of Brodie's work:

> She has managed to write a long and complex study of Jefferson without displaying any acquaintance with eighteenth-century plantation conditions, political thought, literary conventions, or scientific categories—all of which greatly concerned Jefferson. She constantly finds double meanings in colonial language, basing her arguments on the present usage of key words [i.e., Modernism].[107]

In summary, there exists *no* evidence, either modern or ancient, that Thomas Jefferson fathered even one child with Sally Hemings, much less five. In fact, if Jefferson were alive today and if he were charged with a crime for allegedly having sex with the young Hemings, it would be an open-and-shut case: he would be acquitted.

Thomas Jefferson Founded a Secular University

Jefferson was involved in many educational endeavors, but his greatest, and certainly the one dearest to his heart, was his founding of the University of Virginia. If one accepts the modern mischaracterization that Jefferson was antireligious and hostile to Christianity, it then becomes logical to assert that he would promote the secular and oppose the religious in his educational endeavors—especially at his beloved university. Reflective of this proposition, modern academics claim:

> Jefferson also founded the first intentionally secularized university in America. His vision for the University of Virginia was for education finally free from traditional Christian dogma. He had a disdain for the influence that institutional Christianity had on education. At the University of Virginia there was no Christian curriculum and the school had no chaplain. Its faculty were religiously Deists and Unitarians.
>
> —Professor Daryl Cornett, Mid-America Theological Seminary[1]

> After Jefferson left the presidency in 1809, he embarked on . . . the University of Virginia. . . . A Deist and a secular humanist, Jefferson rejected the religious tradition that had provided the foundation for the colonial universities.
>
> —Professor Anita Vickers, Penn State University[2]

No part of the regular school day was set aside for religious worship. . . . Jefferson did not permit the room belonging to the university to be used for religious purposes.

—Professor Leonard Levy, Southern Oregon State University, Claremont Graduate School[3]

The university which Thomas Jefferson established at Charlottesville in Virginia was . . . distinctly and purposely secular.

—Professor John Brubacher, Yale University, University of Michigan; Professor Willis Rudy, Fairleigh Dickinson University[4]

Many others make similar declarations, and several of their recurring claims are worthy of investigation.

1. Did Jefferson have a disdain for the influence of Christianity on education?

2. Did he found the first intentionally secular university in America?

3. Did he hire only Deists and Unitarians for his faculty?

4. Did he exclude chaplains and religious curriculum from the school?

Most Americans would probably answer "yes" to these four questions, for they have been told repeatedly by many of today's writers, both academic and journalistic, that Jefferson was an ardent secularist. But what if this is wrong? What if Jefferson's own education, one that so thoroughly prepared him for the national and international scene, had been largely religious and personally satisfying to him? If such was the case, then it is illogical to assert that Jefferson would seek to exclude from others that which had benefited him; so let's begin with a look at Jefferson's own education.

Jefferson was born in 1743. As a youngster he attended the Anglican St. James' Church of Northam Parish with his family. The church was pastored by the Reverend William Douglass, and from 1752 to 1758 Jefferson attended the Reverend Douglass' school. In 1758 his family moved to Albemarle County and attended the Anglican Fredericksville Parish Church, pastored by the Reverend James Fontaine Maury, and from 1758 to 1760 Jefferson attended the Reverend Maury's school. In 1760, after having been trained in religious schools, the seventeen-year-old Jefferson entered William and Mary, another religious school directly affiliated with the Anglican Church.

Part of Jefferson's daily routine at the college included morning and evening prayers from the *Book of Common Prayer* with lengthy Scripture readings. Scottish instructor Dr. William Small, the son of a Presbyterian minister, was Jefferson's favorite instructor. Jefferson later acknowledged: "It was my great good fortune, and what probably fixed the destinies of my life, that Dr. William Small of Scotland, was then professor."[5]

Interestingly, many of the best instructors in early America were Scottish clergymen. As noted historian George Marsden affirmed, "[I]t is not much of an exaggeration to say that outside of New England, the Scots were the educators of eighteenth-century America."[6] These Scottish instructors regularly tutored students in what was known as the Scottish Common Sense philosophy—a method under which not only Jefferson but also other notable Virginia Founding Fathers were trained, including George Washington, James Madison, George Mason, Peyton Randolph, Richard Henry Lee, and Thomas Nelson. Gaillard Hunt, head of the manuscript division of the Library of Congress, reported:

One reason why the ruling class in Virginia acted with such una-nimity [during the Revolution] . . . was that a large proportion of them had received the same kind of education. This usually came first from clergymen.[7]

The Scottish Common Sense approach was developed by the Reverend Thomas Reid (1710–1796) to counter the skepticism of stridently secular European writers and philosophers such as Hume, Rousseau, Voltaire, and Malby. Reid's approach argued that common sense should shape philosophy rather than philosophy shaping common sense. He asserted that normal, everyday language could express philosophical principles in a way that could be understood by ordinary individuals rather than just so-called elite thinkers and philosophers.

The principle tenets of Scottish Common Sense philosophy were straightforward:

1. There is a God

2. God placed into every individual a conscience—a moral sense written on his or her heart (cf. Jeremiah 31:33; Romans 2:14–15; Hebrews 8:10; 10:16; etc.)

3. God established "first principles" in areas such as law, government, education, politics, and economics, and these first principles could be discovered by the use of common sense

4. There is no conflict between reason and revelation. Both come directly from God, and revelation fortifies and clarifies reason

This is the philosophy under which Jefferson was educated at William and Mary. After completing his studies there, Jefferson entered five years of legal training with distinguished attorney and judge George Wythe, who later became a signer of the Declaration of Independence. A central subject of Jefferson's legal studies was English jurist Sir William Blackstone's four-volume *Commentaries on the Laws of England* (1765–1769).

That work was an important legal textbook not only for Jefferson but for all American law students. Founding Father James Iredell, a ratifier of the US Constitution who was placed on the US Supreme Court by President George Washington, affirmed that *Blackstone's Commentaries* was "the manual of almost every student of law in the United States."[8] Jefferson affirmed that American lawyers used *Blackstone's* with the same dedication and reverence that Muslims used the Koran.[9]

In this indispensable legal text, Blackstone forcefully expounded the four prime tenets of Scottish Common Sense philosophy:

> Man, considered as a creature, must necessarily be subject to the laws of his Creator. . . . This will of his Maker is called the law of nature. . . . These are the eternal immutable laws of good and evil to which the Creator Himself in all His dispensations conforms, and which He has enabled human reason to discover so far as they are necessary for the conduct of human actions. . . . And if our reason were always . . . clear and perfect, . . . the task would be pleasant and easy; we should need no other guide but this. But every man now finds the contrary in his own experience: that his reason is corrupt and his understanding full of ignorance and error. This has given manifold occasion for the benign interposition of Divine Providence, which . . . hath been pleased at sundry times and in divers manners to discover and enforce its laws by an immediate and direct revelation. The doctrines thus delivered we call the revealed or Divine law, and they are to be found only in the Holy Scriptures. . . . Upon these two foundations, the law of nature and the law of revelation, depend all human laws; that is to say, no human laws should be suffered to contradict these.[10]

These same four Scottish Common Sense tenets were subsequently included by Jefferson in the Declaration of Independence.

Even though Jefferson's own personal education at the elementary, secondary, and postsecondary levels consistently incorporated religious instruction, today's writers repeatedly insist that it was the secular European Enlightenment rather than Scottish Common Sense that was the greatest influence on Jefferson's thinking. For example:

> In Europe, the Enlightenment centered around the salons of Paris and was famous for the "philosophes"—popular philosophers—such as Voltaire, Montesquieu, Diderot, Rousseau. . . . American political leaders like Jefferson . . . were heavily influenced by Enlightenment thinking.[11]

> The European Enlightenment was an intellectual movement that subjected theological, philosophical, scientific and political dogma to critical analysis. . . . Deism was popular among many Enlightenment thinkers, including Thomas Jefferson.[12]

> [T]he Declaration of Independence . . . remains the best example of Enlightenment thought.[13]

Far too many of today's writers, consumed by the spirit of Academic Collectivism, regularly regurgitate each other's claims that Jefferson's philosophy and the Declaration were products of the secular European Enlightenment. Yet Jefferson himself forcefully disagreed, and when some in his day had suggested that he based the Declaration on the writings of other philosophers, he responded, "[W]hether I had gathered my ideas from reading or reflection I do not know. I know only that I turned to neither book nor pamphlet while writing it."[14]

In fact, he specifically asserted that the Declaration of Independence was "an expression of the *American* mind"[15] (emphasis added) rather than a lexicon of European ideas. He even proclaimed that "the comparisons of our governments with those of Europe are like a comparison of heaven and hell."[16]

This is not to say that the Enlightenment had no influence in the American Founding; it certainly did. However, the crucial distinction regularly overlooked (or ignored) by many of today's writers and academics is the fact that Enlightenment writers can be divided into two distinct groups: those with an overtly Christian viewpoint (such as Baron Puffendorf, Hugo Grotius, Richard Hooker, and William Blackstone), and those with an overtly secular viewpoint (such as Voltaire, Denis Diderot, David Hume, Claude Adrien Helvetius, Jean-Jacques Rousseau, Sir Nicholas Malby, and Guillaume Thomas François Raynal).

It was primarily the Christian writers, not the secular ones, upon which Jefferson and the other Founders relied. In fact, political researchers have conclusively documented that the four Enlightenment writers cited most frequently during the Founding Era were Charles Montesquieu, William Blackstone, John Locke, and David Hume.[17] Of the four, only Hume is from the secular group.

But if the Founders relied primarily on Christian thinkers rather than secular thinkers, then why was Hume the fourth most cited? After all, unlike the other three, he openly declared, "I expected in entering on my literary course that all the Christians . . . should be my enemies."[18]

So why Hume? Because the Founders regularly cited him in order to *refute* his political theories rather than endorse them. John Adams described him as an atheist, deist, and libertine,[19] James Madison placed him among "bungling lawgivers,"[20] and John Quincy Adams denounced Hume as "the Atheist Jacobite."[21] Hume and his writings were also roundly criticized by other Founders, including John Witherspoon,[22] Benjamin Rush,[23] and Patrick Henry.[24]

But what about Jefferson? If Jefferson was indeed antireligious, then perhaps he would be drawn toward Hume as a kindred spirit.

Such was definitely not the case. To the contrary, Jefferson found Hume "endeavoring to mislead, by either the suppression of a truth or by giving it a false coloring."[25] He even regretted the early influence that Hume had once had upon him, candidly lamenting:

> I remember well the enthusiasm with which I devoured it [Hume's work] when young, and the length of time, the research, and reflection which were necessary to eradicate the poison it had instilled into my mind.[26]

Jefferson was similarly forthright in his criticism of other secular Enlightenment writers, including Guillaume Thomas François Raynal (known as Abbé Raynal). Jefferson described his works as "a mass of errors and misconceptions from beginning to end," containing "a great deal of falsehood"[27] and being "wrong exactly in the same proportion."[28] He even described Raynal as "a mere shrimp."[29] Such vehement denunciations of leading secular Enlightenment writers are certainly not consistent with a Jefferson who was supposedly greatly influenced by them.

So if secular Enlightenment writers were not a primary force in shaping Jefferson's thinking, then who was? Jefferson himself answered that question, declaring that "Bacon, Newton and Locke . . . [are] my trinity of the three greatest men the world had ever produced."[30]

Francis Bacon, a British philosopher, attorney, and statesman, called the "Father of Modern Science,"[31] is known for developing the process of inductive thinking and creating the scientific method. Historians have declared that "[T]he intellect of Bacon was one of the most powerful and searching ever possessed by man."[32] Bacon was by no means secular; rather, he was quite the opposite. In his noted work *De Interpretatione Naturae Prooemium* (1603), he declared that his threefold goal was to discover truth, serve his country, and serve the church. He asserted that the vigorous pursuit of truth would always lead one directly to God:

> [A] little philosophy inclineth man's mind to atheism; but depth in philosophy bringeth men's minds about to religion.[33]

Bacon was famous for penning many religious works, including *Essays, Ten in Number, Combined with Sacred Meditations and the Colors of Good and Evil* (1597); *The Proficiencies and Advancement of Learning, Divine and Human* (1605); *On the Unity in Religion* (1612); *On Atheism* (1612); *Of Praise* (1612); as well as a translation of some of the psalms (1625). This outspoken and famous Christian writer and philosopher who never separated God or religion from science or government was the first of Jefferson's triumvirate of the world's greatest individuals.

The second in his list was Isaac Newton, an English statesman, mathematician, and scientist, credited with birthing modern calculus and discovering the laws of universal gravitation. Newton did extensive work in physics, astronomy, and optics and was the first scientist to be knighted for his work. Strikingly, however:

> He spent more time on theology than on science; indeed, he wrote about 1.3 million words on Biblical subjects. . . . Newton's understanding of God came primarily from the Bible, which he studied for days and weeks at a time. . . . Newton's theology profoundly influenced his scientific method. . . . His God was not merely a philosopher's impersonal First Cause; He was the God in the Bible Who freely creates and rules the world, Who speaks and acts in history.[34]

Among Newton's many theological works were his *Observations Upon the Prophecies of Daniel and the Apocalypse of St. John* (1733) and *Notes on Early Church History* (c. 1680) among many others. And throughout his scientific works, Newton also maintained a distinctly Biblical Creationist view—such as in his 1687 *Principia* (considered "the greatest scientific book ever written"[35]) in which he stated:

> This most beautiful system of the sun, planets, and comets could only proceed from the counsel and dominion of an intelligent and powerful Being. And if the fixed stars are the centres of other like systems, these, being formed by the like wise counsel, must be all subject to the dominion of One.[36]

This Christian theologian and philosopher was the second of Jefferson's trinity of personal heroes.

The third was English philosopher and political theorist John Locke. Locke was intimately involved with politics in England and also played a large role in shaping America, including writing the 1669 constitution for the Carolina Colony.[37] He also penned numerous works on education, philosophy, government, empiricism, and religion.

Today's writers frequently describe Locke as a deist (or at least a follower of an early form of deism),[38] but historians of earlier generations described him as a Christian theologian.[39] After all, Locke wrote a verse-by-verse commentary on Paul's Epistles[40] and also compiled a topical Bible, called a *Common Place-Book to the Holy Bible*,[41] that listed verses by subject for easy study reference. And when antireligionists attacked Christianity, Locke defended it in his book *The Reasonableness of Christianity as Delivered in the Scriptures* (1695).[42] When attacks continued, Locke responded with *A Vindication of the Reasonableness of Christianity* (1695)[43] and then with *A Second Vindication of the Reasonableness of Christianity* (1697).[44] Furthermore, in his *Two Treatises of Government* (1689)—the work specifically relied upon by Jefferson and the other Founders as they drafted the Declaration[45]—Locke invoked the Bible over 1,500 times.[46]

Jefferson studied not only Locke's governmental and legal writings but also his theological texts. His own personal summation of Locke's view of Christianity clearly shows that he definitely did not consider Locke to be a deist. According to Jefferson:

> Locke's system of Christianity is this: Adam was created happy & immortal. . . . By sin he lost this so that he became subject to total death (like that of brutes [animals]) to the crosses & unhappiness of this life. At the intercession however of the Son of God this sentence was in part remitted. . . . And moreover to them who believed their faith was to be counted for righteousness [Romans 4:3, 5]. Not that faith without works was to save them; St. James, chapter 2 says expressly the contrary [v. 14–26]. . . . So that a reformation of life (included under repentance) was essential, & defects in this would be made up by their faith; i.e. their faith should be counted for righteousness [Romans 4:3, 5]. . . . [A]dding a faith in God & His attributes that on their repentance He would pardon them [1 John 1:9]; they also would be justified [Romans 3:24]. This then explains the text "there is no other name under heaven by which a man may be saved" [Acts 4:12], i.e., the defects in good works shall not be supplied by a faith in Mahomet, Fo [i.e., Buddha], or any other except Christ.[47]

Francis Bacon, Issac Newton, and John Locke—each an outspoken Christian thinker and philosopher—were described by Jefferson as "the three greatest men the world has ever produced."[48]

So, to the question of whether Jefferson rejected his own personal educational experience because it had been so thoroughly infused with religion, the answer is a clear "No!" Jefferson was involved with many educational endeavors throughout his life, and he consistently took deliberate actions to include religious instruction in each.

For example, when a grammar school was being established in Jefferson's area in 1783, he wrote to the Reverend Dr. John Witherspoon, the head of Princeton (a university that trained Presbyterians for Gospel ministry), to request one of Witherspoon's students as an instructor for the school.[49] In 1792 Jefferson again wrote the Reverend Witherspoon about another local school "in hopes that your seminary . . . may furnish some person whom you could recommend" to be the assistant to "the head of a school of considerable reputation in Virginia."[50]

What would Jefferson expect from students trained by the Reverend Dr. Witherspoon? Certainly not a secular approach to education. On the contrary, not only did Witherspoon teach the Scottish Common Sense philosophy, but he also specifically instructed his students:

> That he is the best friend to American liberty who is the most sincere and active in promoting true and undefiled religion, and who sets himself with the greatest firmness to bear down profanity and immorality of every kind. Whoever is an avowed enemy of God, I scruple not to call him an enemy to his country.[51]

When Jefferson needed teachers for schools in his area, he called on a leading religious educator to send him religiously trained instructors.

In 1794, after Jefferson had returned home from serving as secretary of state for President George Washington, he contacted a member of the Virginia legislature about bringing the Geneva Academy from Europe to Virginia. The Geneva Academy was established in 1559 by Reformation theologian John Calvin.[52] In this school, the Bible was an indispensable textbook and students from the school became missionaries all over Europe;[53] and Jefferson wanted to bring this famous religious school to his state.

In 1803, while serving as president, Jefferson met with Presbyterian minister Gideon Blackburn at the White House about opening a missionary school for Cherokees near Knoxville, Tennessee. The school was to include religious instruction as a primary part of its studies, and President Jefferson directed Secretary of War Henry Dearborn to give federal money to help the school achieve its objectives.[54]

In 1804 President Jefferson negotiated the purchase of the Louisiana Territory. With authority over that region transferring from the French to the Americans, those living there were uncertain as to what changes might result. Sister Therese Farjon, Mother Superior of a Catholic school and convent in New Orleans, therefore wrote President Jefferson asking what the status of their religious school would now be under American government. Jefferson responded:

> Your institution . . . by training up its young members in the way they should go [Proverbs 22:6], cannot fail to ensure it *the patronage [support] of the government* it is under. Be assured that it will meet with all the protection my office can give it.[55] (emphasis added)

In 1805 President Jefferson was elected head of the board of trustees for the brand new Washington, DC, public schools.[56] He told the city council that he would "willingly undertake the duties proposed to me—so far as others of paramount obligation will permit my attention to them";[57] that is, he would do what he could for the city schools with the caveat that his presidential duties came first. Robert Brent, therefore, served as head of the trustees, instead of Jefferson, but as trustee, Jefferson did contribute much to the new school system and is credited with being "the chief author of the first plan of public education adopted for the city of Washington."[58] When the first report of the Washington public schools was released to demonstrate the progress of the students in the new schools, it noted:

Fifty-five have learned to read in the Old and New Testaments and are all able to spell words of three, four, and five syllables; twenty-six are now learning to read Dr. Watts' *Hymns* and spell words of two syllables; ten are learning words of four and five letters. Of fifty-nine out of the whole number admitted [enrolled] that did not know a single letter, twenty can now read the Bible and spell words of three, four, and five syllables; twenty-nine read Dr. Watts' *Hymns* and spell words of two syllables; and ten, words of four and five letters.[59]

Additionally, during the same time that Jefferson was working with the DC public school system, the board on which he served approved two of the schools being run by ministers, the Reverend Robert Elliott and the Reverend Richard White.[60] The Reverend Elliott was also allowed to use the school building concurrently as a meeting place for his church.[61]

In short, Jefferson was involved with many educational endeavors prior to establishing the University of Virginia in 1819, and in none of them was there any attempt to exclude religious instruction. To the contrary—in each case he took intentional steps to include or preserve it. So with this background, what about the four oft-repeated claims about Jefferson excluding religion from the university he founded?

1. Was the University of Virginia Founded as a Secular University?

Three distinctive features characterized universities founded in America prior to Jefferson's University of Virginia. Those universities (1) were founded and controlled by one particular denomination, (2) housed theological seminaries for training ministers for that specific denomination, and (3) had prominent ministers from that denomination serving as president of the university.

Reflective of this pattern, in 1636 Harvard was founded by and for *Congregationalists* to train Congregationalist ministers (so, too, with Yale in 1701 and Dartmouth in 1769). In 1692 the College of William and Mary was founded by and for the *Anglicans* to train Anglican ministers (as was the University of Pennsylvania in 1740, Kings College in 1754, and the College of Charleston in 1770). In 1746 Princeton was founded by and for *Presbyterians* (as was Dickinson in 1773 and Hampden-Sydney in 1775). In 1764 the College of Rhode Island (now Brown University) was founded by and for the *Baptists*. In 1766 Queens College (now Rutgers) was founded by and for the *Dutch Reformed*. In 1780 Transylvania University was founded by and for the *Disciples of Christ*, and so on.

Departing from this pattern, Jefferson and his Board of Visitors (or regents) specifically founded the University of Virginia to be America's first transdenominational school—a school not affiliated with one specific denomination but rather one that would train students from all denominations. By so doing, Jefferson was actually implementing the plan advocated by evangelical Presbyterian clergyman Samuel Knox of Baltimore.

In 1799 the Reverend Knox penned a policy paper proposing the formation of a state university that would invite many denominations to establish multiple theological schools rather than just one, so they would work together in mutual Christian cooperation rather than competition.[62] Jefferson agreed with Knox's philosophy, and it was this model that he employed at his University of Virginia. (In fact, Jefferson invited the Reverend Knox to be the very *first* professor at the university,[63] but because of a miscommunication, Knox did not respond to the offer in a timely fashion, so his teaching slot was finally offered to someone else.[64])

With its transdenominational model, the University of Virginia did not incorporate the three features so commonly associated with other universities at that time. This has caused modern critics to claim that it was founded as a secular university—a claim that will be shown to be completely false. Nearly forty years earlier in 1779, Jefferson had already demonstrated his affinity for this type of interdenominational cooperation and Christian nonpreferentialism in his famous Virginia Statute of Religious Freedom, which disestablished the Anglican Church as the official denomination of Virginia and instead welcomed all denominations with equal legal standing.

The charter for the new university had been issued by the state legislature, so the school was required to conform to the denominational nonpreferentialism set forth not only in the Virginia Statute but also in the Virginia Constitution—another document that Jefferson had helped author. But many today wrongly misinterpret Jefferson's denominational nonpreferentialism to be secularism, and they also erroneously point to what Jefferson did with his own alma mater's Professor of Divinity as another alleged "proof" of his commitment to religion-free education.

In 1779, when Jefferson became governor of Virginia, he was placed on the board of William and Mary. At that time he introduced legislation to recast the school—an accomplishment known as the Jefferson Reorganization. According to Professor Leonard Levy of Oregon State University:

Jefferson's first proposal on higher education came in 1779. His Bill for the Amending of the Constitution of the College of William and Mary stated that the college consisted of "one school of sacred theology, with two professorships therein, to wit, one for teaching the Hebrew tongue, and expounding the Holy Scriptures; and the other for explaining the commonplaces of Divinity and controversies with heretics." . . . Jefferson

proposed to abolish . . . the school of theology with its professorships of religion.[65]

Did Jefferson indeed propose to abolish "the school of theology
with its professorships of religion"? Apparently so, for Jefferson
himself acknowledged:

I effected, during my residence in Williamsburg that year, a
change in the organization of that institution by abolishing . . .
the two professorships of Divinity.[66]

So it appears that Professor Levy was right—that Jefferson did
seek to secularize higher education. At least it appears that way until
one reads the rest of Jefferson's explanation, and then it becomes evident that his intention was exactly the opposite. Jefferson explained:

The College of William and Mary was an establishment purely
of the Church of England; the Visitors [i.e., Regents] were
required to be all of that Church; the professors to subscribe its
thirty-nine [doctrinal] Articles; its students to learn its [Anglican]
Catechism; and one of its fundamental objects was declared to be
to raise up ministers for that church [i.e., the Anglican Church].
The religious jealousies, therefore, of all the Dissenters [those
from other denominations] took alarm lest this might give an
ascendancy to the Anglican sect.[67]

Jefferson abolished the School of Divinity because it was solely an
arm of the state-established Anglican Church, and he wanted to open
the college to greater involvement by those from other Christian
denominations. Further evidence that his reorganization of the college was not secular was his stipulation that "[T]he said professors
shall likewise appoint from time to time a missionary of approved

veracity to the several tribes of Indians."[68] Jefferson took steps to ensure that the Gospel was promoted at William and Mary but not just according to the thirty-nine Anglican articles and that church's denominational catechism.

In the same manner Jefferson sought to ensure that the University of Virginia would also reflect denominational nonpreferentialism. He therefore invited the seminaries of many denominations to establish themselves on the campus, explaining:

> We suggest the expediency of encouraging the different religious sects [denominations] to establish, each for itself, a professorship of their own tenets on the confines of the university so near as that their students may attend the lectures there and have the free use of our library and every other accommodation we can give them. . . . [B]y bringing the sects [denominations] together and mixing them with the mass of other students, we shall soften their asperities [harshness], liberalize and neutralize their prejudices [prejudgment without an examination of the facts], and make the general religion a religion of peace, reason, and morality.[69]

Jefferson observed that a positive benefit of this approach was that it would "give to the sectarian schools of divinity the full benefit of the public [university] provisions made for instruction"[70] and "leave every sect to provide as they think fittest the means of further instruction in their own peculiar tenets."[71] Jefferson pointed out that another benefit of this arrangement was that students could "attend religious exercises with the professor of their particular sect,"[72] and he made clear that students would be fully *expected* to actively participate in some denominational school.[73]

Jefferson and the Visitors (regents) also decided that there should be no clergyman as president and no Professor of Divinity because it might give the impression that the university favored the denomination with which the university president or professor of divinity was affiliated.[74] But the fact that the school did not have a specific professor of divinity did not mean that it was secular.

In fact, Jefferson had actually increased the number of Professorships of divinity by encouraging each denomination to have "a professorship of their own tenets" at the school.[75] And the decision not to have just one exclusive professor of divinity also did not mean that the university would have no religious instruction. To the contrary, Jefferson personally directed that the teaching of "the proofs of the being of a God, the Creator, Preserver, and Supreme Ruler of the Universe, the Author of all the relations of morality and of the laws and obligations these infer, will be within the province of the Professor of Ethics."[76]

As he explained:

> [T]he relations which exist between man and his Maker, and the duties resulting from those relations, are the most interesting and important to every human being, and the most incumbent on his study and investigation.[77]

Jefferson simply transferred the responsibility of religious teaching from the traditional professor of divinity to the professor of ethics. All students would be given general Biblical teaching about man's obligations to God and the injunctions to observe Biblical morality. Jefferson also made clear that religious instruction would encompass the many religious beliefs on which Christian denominations agreed rather than just the few specific theological doctrines that distinguished each particular one.[78] Any instruction about specific narrow doctrines would occur in the various denominational schools attached to the university.

This nondenominational approach caused Presbyterians, Baptists,

Methodists, and others to give the university the friendship and cooperative support necessary to make it a success. Consider Presbyterian minister John Holt Rice as an example.

Holt was a nationally known evangelical leader with extensive credentials. He founded the Virginia Bible Society,[79] started the *Virginia Evangelical and Literary Magazine* to report on revivals across the country, was elected national leader of the Presbyterian Church, and offered the presidency of Princeton (but instead accepted the chair of theology at Hampden-Sydney College). Rice fully supported and promoted the University of Virginia,[80] but this would not have been the case had the university been perceived to have been affiliated with just one denomination. As Rice explained:

> The plan humbly suggested is to allow Jews, Catholics, Protestants, Episcopalians, Methodists, Baptists, any and all sects, if they shall choose to exercise the privilege, to endow professorships, and nominate their respective professors. . . . [T]he students shall regularly attend Divine worship, but in what form should be left to the direction of parents; or in failure of this, to the choice of the students. In addition to this, the professors in every case must be men of the utmost purity of moral principle and strictness of moral conduct.[81]

Furthermore, when construction of the university began, the special ceremony at the laying of its cornerstone included both the reading of Scripture and a prayer—activities specifically arranged by Jefferson and the Board of Visitors. Notice the desires expressed in the university's founding prayer:

> May Almighty God, without invocation to Whom no work of importance should be begun, bless this undertaking and enable us to carry it on with success. Protect this college, the object of

which institution is to instill into the minds of youth principles of sound knowledge, *to inspire them with the love of religion and virtue*, and prepare them for filling the various situations in society with credit to themselves and benefit to their country.[82] (emphasis added)

Clearly, then, Jefferson's own writings and the records of the university, along with the explanations given by ministers who supported the school, all absolutely refute any notion that the University of Virginia was a secular institution. Instead, it was the nation's first prominent transdenominational school.

2. Was Jefferson's Faculty Composed of Unitarians?

Jefferson established ten teaching positions at the university,[83] and *none* of the professors filling them was a Unitarian. In fact, when two of the original professors (George Tucker, professor of moral philosophy, and Robley Dunglison, professor of anatomy and medicine) were later asked whether Jefferson had sought to fill the faculty with Deists or Unitarians, Professor Dunglison succinctly answered:

I have not the slightest reason for believing that Mr. Jefferson was in any respect guided in his selection of professors of the University of Virginia by religious considerations. . . . In all my conversations with Mr. Jefferson, no reference was made to the subject. I was an Episcopalian, so was Mr. Tucker, Mr. Long, Mr. Key, Mr. Bonnycastle, and Dr. Emmet. Dr. Blaetterman, I think, was a Lutheran, but I do not know so much about his religion as I do about that of the rest. There certainly was *not* a Unitarian among us.[84] (emphasis added)

Professor Tucker agreed, declaring:

> I believe that all the first professors belonged to the Episcopal
> Church, except Dr. Blaetterman, who, I believe, was a German
> Lutheran. . . . I don't remember that I ever heard the religious
> creeds of either professors or Visitors [Regents] discussed or
> inquired into by Mr. Jefferson, or anyone else.[85]

Jefferson simply did not delve into the denominational affiliations or specific religious beliefs of his faculty; what he sought was
professors who were competent and qualified in knowledge and
deportment. As he once told his close friend and fellow educator Dr.
Benjamin Rush:

> For thus I estimate the qualities of the mind: 1. good humor; 2.
> integrity; 3. industry; 4. science. The preference of the first to
> the second quality may not at first be acquiesced in [given up],
> but certainly we had all rather associate with a good-humored,
> light-principled man than with an ill-tempered rigorist in
> morality.[86]

It was by applying such standards that Jefferson once invited
Thomas Cooper to be professor of chemistry and law,[87] but when
it became known that Cooper was a Unitarian, a public outcry arose
against him and Jefferson and the university withdrew its offer
to him.[88]

Obviously, this type of original primary-source evidence concerning Jefferson and the religious views of his faculty is ignored by
many of today's writers. But Professor Roy Honeywell of Eastern
Michigan University was a professor from a much earlier period who
actually *did* review the original historical evidence. He correctly
concluded:

In general, Jefferson seems to have ignored the religious affiliations of the professors. His objection to ministers was because of their active association with sectarian groups, in his day, a fruitful source of social friction. The charge that he intended the University to be a center of Unitarian influence is totally groundless.[89]

3. Did Jefferson Bar Religious Instruction from the Academic Program?

In 1818 Jefferson and the university Visitors publicly released their plan for the new school. In addition to announcing that it would be transdenominational and that religious instruction would be provided to all students, Jefferson took further intentional steps to ensure that religious training would occur.

For example, he directed the professor of ancient languages to teach Biblical Greek, Hebrew, and Latin to students so that they would be equipped to read and study the "earliest and most respected authorities of the faith of every sect [denomination]."[90] Jefferson also wanted the writings of prominent Christian authorities to be placed in the university library. In August 1824 he asked Visitor (or regent) James Madison to prepare a list of Christian theological writings to be included on its shelves.[91]

Madison returned his recommendations to Jefferson, which included the early works of the Alexandrian Church Fathers, such as Clement, Origen, Pantaenus, Cyril, Athanasius, and Didymus the Blind. He also included Latin authors such as Saint Augustine; the writings of Saint Aquinas and other Christian leaders from the Middle Ages; and the works of Erasmus, Luther, Calvin, Socinius, and Bellarmine from the Reformation era. Madison's list also contained more contemporary theologians and religious writers such as Grotius,

Tillotson, Hooker, Pascal, Locke, Newton, Butler, Clarke, Wollaston, Edwards, Mather, Penn, Wesley, Leibnitz, Paley, and others.[92]

In addition to religious instruction given by the professor of ethics and the professor of ancient languages, Jefferson personally ensured that religious study would also be an inseparable part of the study of law and political science. As he explained to a prominent judge:

> [I]n my catalogue, considering ethics as well as religion as supplements to law in the government of man, I had placed them in that sequence.[93]

Jefferson also approved of worship on campus, acknowledging "that a building . . . in the middle of the grounds may be called for in time in which may be rooms for religious worship."[94] He later ordered that in the university Rotunda, "one of its large elliptical rooms on its middle floor shall be used for . . . religious worship."[95] He further declared that "the students of the university will be free and *expected* to attend religious worship at the establishment of their respective sects"[96] (emphasis added).

Jefferson took many deliberate steps to ensure that religious instruction was an integral part of academic studies. Clearly, then, the claim that there was no Christian curriculum or instruction at the University of Virginia is demonstrably false and easily disproved by Jefferson's own writings.

4. Did the University of Virginia Have Chaplains?

The modern claim that the University of Virginia had no chaplains is also easily disproved by original documents, including early newspaper ads that the university ran to recruit students from surrounding areas.

In the Washington newspaper the *Globe*, the Reverend Septimus Tuston (identified in the ad as the *chaplain* of the university and who later became the chaplain of the US House of Representatives and then the US Senate) discussed religious life at the school, reporting:

> [I]n the original organization of this establishment [i.e., the University of Virginia], the privilege of erecting theological seminaries on the territory [grounds] belonging to the university was cheerfully extended to every Christian denomination within the limits of the state.
>
> In the present arrangement for religious services at the university, you have all the evidence that can with propriety be asked respecting the favorable estimate which is placed upon the subject of Christianity.
>
> The *chaplains*, appointed annually and successively from the four prominent denominations in Virginia [Episcopalian, Presbyterian, Baptist, and Methodist], are supported by the voluntary contributions of professors and students. . . .
>
> Beside the regular services of the Sabbath, we have . . . also a Sabbath School in which several of the pious students are engaged.
>
> The monthly concert for prayer is regularly observed in the pavilion which I occupy.
>
> In all these different services we have enjoyed the presence and the smiles of an approving Redeemer . . . [and i]t has been my pleasure on each returning Sabbath to hold up before my enlightened audience the cross of Jesus—all stained with the blood of Him that hung upon it—as the only hope of the perishing.[97] (emphasis added)

Another ad run by the university similarly noted:

Religious services are regularly performed at the University by a *chaplain*, who is appointed in turn from the four principal denominations of the state. And by a resolution of the faculty, *ministers of the Gospel and young men preparing for the ministry may attend any of the schools without the payment of fees to the professors.*[98] (emphasis added)

It was the custom of that day that university faculty members receive their salaries from fees paid by the students directly to the staff, but the University of Virginia waived those fees for students studying for the Gospel ministry. So, if the school was secular, as claimed by so many of today's writers, then why did it extend *preferential treatment* to students pursuing religious careers? Surely a truly secular university would have given preference to students who were not religiously oriented.

The University of Virginia did indeed have chaplains, albeit not in its first three years (the university opened for students in 1825). At the beginning, when the university was establishing its reputation as a transdenominational university, the school had no appointed chaplain for the same reason that there had been no clergyman as president and no single professor of divinity: an ordained clergyman in any of those three positions might send an incorrect signal that the university was aligned with a specific denomination. But by 1829, when the nondenominational reputation of the university had been fully established, President Madison (who became rector of the university after Jefferson's death in 1826) announced "that [permanent] provision for religious instruction and observance among the students would be made by . . . services of clergymen."[99]

The university therefore extended official recognition to one primary chaplain for all the students, with the chaplain position rotating annually among the major denominations that Jefferson identified as the Baptists, Methodists, Presbyterians, and Anglicans.[100] In 1829

Presbyterian clergyman Rev. Edward Smith became the first chaplain at the University of Virginia. It was an official university position—but unpaid. In 1833, after three-fourths of the students pledged their own money for the chaplain's support, Methodist William Hammett became the first paid chaplain. He led Sunday worship and daily morning prayer meetings in the Rotunda. In 1855 the university built a parsonage to provide a residence for the university chaplain. Many of the school's chaplains went on to religious careers of renown, including Episcopalian Joseph Wilmer; Presbyterians William White, William H. Ruffner, and Robert Dabney; and Baptists Robert Ryland and John Broaddus. Clearly, the University of Virginia *did* have chaplains.

In short, first-hand source documents, especially Jefferson's own writings, incontestably refute all four modern assertions about the alleged secular nature of the University of Virginia. If anyone examines the original sources and claims otherwise, they are, to use the words of early military chaplain William Biederwolf, just as likely to "look all over the sky at high noon on a cloudless day and not see the sun."[101]

There is one other aspect of Jefferson's philosophy toward religion in education that draws much attention from those who would paint him as an irreligious, atheistic man. In a highly publicized letter to his nephew Peter Carr, Jefferson tells him to "question with boldness even the existence of a God."[102] Taken out of context this admonition does seem condemning—which is why Deconstructionists and Minimalists have lifted just this one line from a very long Jefferson letter. They deliberately misrepresent the full letter in order to make it seem that Jefferson was recommending exactly the opposite of what he was actually telling his nephew.

Jefferson had raised Peter as the son he never had—his only son was stillborn in 1777. Peter's father, Dabney, was Jefferson's brother-in-law and one of Jefferson's closest friends. While Peter was still a young boy, Dabney died and was buried on the grounds at Monticello. Jefferson then stepped in to help raise the young Peter.

In 1785, when Peter was fifteen years old and Jefferson was on an overseas assignment, he began to write Peter from Europe. He addressed the direction that the young man's education should take, instructing him not only about the importance of character ("give up science, give the earth itself and all it contains, rather than do an immoral act"[103]) but also about diligently pursuing the study of history, philosophy, and poetry. He especially recommended that Peter read:

> Virgil, Terence, Horace, Anacreon, Theocritus, Homer; read also Milton's Paradise Lost, Shakespeare, Ossian, Pope's and Swift's works, in order to form your style in your own language. In morality, read Epictetus, Xenophontis Memorabilia, Plato's Socratic dialogues, Cicero's philosophies.[104]

The next year Peter was accepted to William and Mary (Jefferson's alma mater). The following year, 1787, George Wythe agreed to tutor him in Latin and Greek.[105] When Jefferson learned of this latter development, he was thrilled and told Peter: "I am sure you will find this to have been one of the most fortunate events of your life."[106] A year later Wythe accepted Peter as a law student, just as he had done with Jefferson some twenty-five years earlier.

The famous letter containing the phrase so abused today was written by Jefferson to his nephew in Peter's second year at William and Mary. The letter contains recommendations to Peter about his studies in four areas: Italian, Spanish, moral philosophy, and religion. The fourth section on religion was by far the longest in the letter, and it is in that part of his extensive epistle that Jefferson advised Peter to "question with boldness even the existence of a God."[107]

Secularist and antireligious authors have made this short phrase the sole focus of that long letter,[108] but the rest of the letter makes abundantly clear that Jefferson was actually instructing Peter in apologetics. The term *apologetics* originated in 1733 and indicates an intelligent presentation and defense of major traditional elements of religious faith.[109]

Jefferson believed that the time had come for the seventeen-year-old Peter to know not just *what* he believed but *why* he believed it—and to be able to defend his beliefs. Peter believed in God and Christianity, but Jefferson urged him to examine both sides of the question of the existence of God, study opposing arguments, and then come to a conclusion he could ably defend. (This is exactly what the Bible advises in 1 Peter 3:15: to be able to get the *reason* for one's belief.)

The Founding Fathers regularly encouraged their own children and other youth to learn and use apologetics, to learn *both* sides of a religious issue. This is apparent in many of their writings. For example, Elias Boudinot, a president of Congress and a framer of the Bill of Rights, wrote to his daughter, Susan, after Thomas Paine had attacked the Bible in his famous *Age of Reason*.[110] He assured her that an open-minded examination of the evidence easily proved the existence of God and the truth of the Bible.

> God in His infinite wisdom has given us sufficient evidence that the revelation of the Gospel is from Him. This is subject to rational inquiry and of conviction from the conclusive nature of the evidence; but when that fact is established, you are bound as a rational creature to show your full confidence in His unchangeable veracity and infinite wisdom by firmly believing the great truths so revealed.[111]

Founding Father John Witherspoon, a signer of the Declaration and the president of Princeton, agreed with the use of this type of apologetics.[112] And the Reverend Ezra Stiles, a conservative theologian and the president of Yale who had served as a chaplain during the American Revolution, also encouraged direct challenges to traditional religious beliefs. He was fully convinced that through apologetics one could withstand and answer all attacks. As he acknowledged:

> Religious liberty is peculiarly friendly to fair and generous disquisition [systematic inquiry]. Here, Deism will have its full chance; nor need Libertines [morally unrestrained individuals] more to complain of being overcome by any weapons but the gentle, the powerful ones of argument and truth. Revelation will be found to stand the test to the ten-thousandth examination.[113]

Jefferson, by telling his nephew Peter to "question with boldness even the existence of a God," was doing exactly what the leading theologians and educators of his day similarly encouraged. Yet, for making the same recommendation made by prominent religious leaders, Jefferson is somehow proved today to be an antireligious secularist? Ridiculous.

Jefferson was thoroughly convinced that the existence of God was so self-evident and irrefutable that it could be easily proved even apart from the Scriptures.[114] In fact, he believed that arguing the existence of God from a position of blind faith, without resort to the proofs of reason, actually hurt Christianity. As he explained:

> I think that every Christian sect [denomination] gives a great handle to atheism by their general dogma that without a revelation there would not be sufficient proof of the being of a God.... So irresistible are these evidences of an intelligence and powerful Agent, that of the infinite numbers of men who have existed thro' all time, they have believed in the proportion of a million at least to unit [i.e., a million to one] in the hypothesis of an eternal pre-existence of a Creator.[115]

Recall that Jefferson's education took the Scottish Common Sense approach. It attacked European skepticism, praised the compatibility of reason and revelation, and demonstrated the superiority of evidence in all challenges. Jefferson had been trained in this vein of apologetics and it was in that same spirit that he challenged Peter to question—that is, to examine—the evidence of God's existence. In light of this background, consider the now infamous section from Jefferson's letter.

Note first that the controversial religious section in Jefferson's letter to Peter is very lengthy. Therefore, in opposition to Minimalism (where everything is reduced to one-line platitudes that require no thought or reasoning), that portion of the letter will be fully presented here so that its context is clear. Second, notice that throughout the letter Jefferson attempted to take a neutral position on many religious issues. He set forth the popular arguments both for and against various religious doctrines, presenting the major arguments to which Peter would undoubtedly be subjected. Yet throughout the letter, Jefferson's bias in favor of his belief in God clearly comes through, despite his well-intentioned attempt to be position neutral.

Here is the section of the letter in question, in its entirety.

4. Religion. Your reason is now mature enough to examine this object. In the first place, divest yourself of all bias in favor of novelty and singularity of opinion. Indulge them in any other subject rather than that of religion. It is too important, and the consequences of error may be too serious. On the other hand, shake off all the fears and servile prejudices under which weak minds are servilely crouched. Fix reason firmly in her seat and call to her tribunal every fact, every opinion. Question with boldness even the existence of a God, because if there be One, He must more approve the homage of reason than that of blindfolded fear. You will naturally examine first the religion of your

own country. Read the Bible then, as you would Livy or Tacitus. The facts which are within the ordinary course of nature, you will believe on the authority of the writer, as you do those of the same kind in Livy and Tacitus. The testimony of the writer weighs in their favor in one scale, and their not being against the laws of nature does not weigh against them. But those facts in the Bible which contradict the laws of nature must be examined with more care and under a variety of faces. Here you must recur to the pretensions [claims] of the writer to inspiration from God. Examine upon what evidence his pretensions are founded and whether that evidence is so strong as that its falsehood would be more improbable than a change of the laws of nature in the case he relates. For example, in the book of Joshua we are told the sun stood still several hours. Were we to read that fact in Livy or Tacitus, we should class it with their showers of blood, speaking of statues, beasts, &c. But it is said that the writer of that book was inspired. Examine, therefore, candidly what evidence there is of his having been inspired. The pretension [claim] is entitled to your inquiry, because millions believe it. On the other hand, you are astronomer enough to know how contrary it is to the law of nature that a body revolving on its axis, as the earth does, should have stopped, should not, by that sudden stoppage, have prostrated animals, trees, buildings, and should after a certain time have resumed its revolution, and that without a second general prostration. Is this arrest of the earth's motion, or the evidence which affirms it, most within the law of probabilities? You will next read the New Testament. It is the history of personage called Jesus. Keep in your eye the opposite pretensions. 1. Of those who say He was begotten by God, born of a virgin, suspended and reversed the laws of nature at will, and ascended bodily into Heaven; and 2. Of those who say he was a man, of illegitimate birth, of a benevolent heart, enthusiastic mind, who set out without pretensions to Divinity, ended in believing them, and was punished capitally for sedition by being gibbeted according to the Roman law, which punished the first commission of that offence by whipping, and the second by exile or death *in furca*. See this law in the Digest, Lib. 48, tit. 19, 28. 3. and Lipsius, Lib. 2. *De Cruce*, cap. 2. These questions are examined in the books I have mentioned under the head of religion and several others. They will assist you in your inquiries, but keep your reason firmly on the watch in reading them all. Do not be frightened from this inquiry by any fear of its consequences. If it ends in a belief that there is no God, you will find incitements to virtue in the comfort and pleasantness you feel in its exercise, and the love of these which it will procure you. If you find reason to believe there is a God, a consciousness that you are acting under His eye and that He approves of you will be a vast additional incitement. If that there be a future state, the hope of a happy existence in that increases the appetite to deserve it; if that Jesus was also a God, you will be comforted by a belief of His aid and love. In fine, I repeat you must lay aside all prejudice on both sides, and neither believe nor reject anything because any other person or description of persons have rejected or believed it. Your own reason is the only oracle given you by Heaven, and you are answerable not for the rightness but uprightness of the decision. I forgot to observe when speaking of the New Testament that you should read all the histories of Christ, as well of those whom a council of ecclesiastics have decided for us to be pseudo-evangelists, as those they named Evangelists, because these pseudo-evangelists pretended to inspiration as much as the others, and you are to judge their pretensions by your own reason and not by the reason of those ecclesiastics. Most of these are lost. There are some, however, still extant, collected by Fabricius, which I will endeavor to get and send you.[116]

By way of note, Jefferson's reference to the "pseudo-evangelists" and "Fabricius" is almost completely foreign to today's Modernists and therefore is often wrongly assumed to be an attack on the Scriptures or the Epistles. It was not. The term *evangelists* was a concrete and well understood term in the Founding Era, often utilized in courts of law,[117] and specifically meant the four Gospels as written by Matthew, Mark, Luke, and John.[118] So what does "pseudo-evangelists" mean? Does it mean the writings of the other Apostles such as Paul and Peter? And who is Fabricius?

In 397 AD the Synod of Carthage met and canonized the books that formed the inspired Scriptures.[119] At that time many other books, including what were known as the Gnostic Gospels (such as the Gospel of Marcion, the Gospel of Apelles, the Gospel of Bardesanes, the Gospel of Basilides, and others) were rejected; it was determined that they were not Divinely inspired. They were thus considered to be written by "pseudo evangelists." In 1713 and 1723 German scholar Johann Albert Fabricius made compilations of the Gnostic Gospels, and just as Jefferson urged Peter to read the canonized Scriptures, he also encouraged him to read and investigate noncanonized books (such as those compiled by Fabricius) in order to understand the debate over which parts of the Bible were actually inspired.

Jefferson was not being antireligious in his letter to Peter; he was simply trying to be neutral so as to encourage Peter to reach his own conclusions. As Jefferson scholar Dr. Mark Beliles accurately points out:

> Since Jefferson used in the letter the words "some people believe" when expressing both orthodox and unorthodox opinions, it cannot be proven that he was personally in favor of either. Scholars often quote excerpts from it to prove his unorthodoxy, but one could just as easily quote Jefferson's phrase from this letter which said "Jesus . . . was begotten by God, born of a

virgin, suspended and reversed the laws of nature at will, and ascended bodily into heaven."[120]

And Jefferson historian Robert Healey points out what he sees as a positive bias toward faith in the letter, explaining that "after saying to Peter Carr, 'Question with boldness even the existence of a God,' he writes a few lines further on, 'Your own reason is the only oracle *given you by heaven*'" (emphasis added).[121] Additionally, in the section of the letter immediately preceding his advice on religion, Jefferson told Peter:

> He Who made us would have been a pitiful bungler if He had made the rules of our moral conduct a matter of science. . . . The moral sense, or conscience, is as much a part of man, as his leg or arm.[122]

This is a clear declaration by Jefferson that man was created by God and endowed by Him with a conscience—two of the primary tenets of Scottish Common Sense. His statement that our reason was given us by Heaven is yet another of its four precepts. And, as already shown above, Jefferson had no personal doubts about the existence of God; to him, it was self-evident that God existed; it was also a belief held worldwide by what he called a margin of a million to one. So while Jefferson attempted to remain neutral in setting forth the possible options of belief to Peter (and largely succeeded), he definitely held a strong, personal, pro-God position.

Jefferson's advice to Peter about discovering and confirming for himself the foundation for his religious beliefs might just as easily have come from today's leading Christian apologists, whether Josh McDowell, Ray Comfort, Lee Strobel, or Ravi Zacharias. These apologists similarly advise Christians to know *what* they believe, *why* they believe it, and *how* to defend those beliefs.

In summary, Jefferson's letter to Peter definitely does *not* prove irreligion on the part of Jefferson, nor can it be used to show Jefferson was promoting secular education among his own family members. Jefferson has a long record of deliberately, purposefully, and intentionally including religious instruction in all educational endeavors in which he took part, and this is especially true concerning his beloved University of Virginia.

Thomas Jefferson Wrote His Own Bible and Edited Out the Things He Didn't Agree With

The notion that Jefferson so disliked Christianity and the Scriptures that he made his own Bible is commonly bandied about in both secular and religious circles.

Hunched over his desk, penknife in hand, Thomas Jefferson sliced carefully at the pages of Holy Scripture, excising select passages and pasting them together to create a Bible more to his liking. The "Jefferson Bible." A book he could feel comfortable with. What didn't make it into the Jefferson Bible was anything that conflicted with his personal worldview. Hell? It can't be. The supernatural? Not even worth considering. God's wrath against sin? I don't think so. The very words of God regarded as leftover scraps.[1]

Jefferson . . . wrote his own Bible that excluded all references to miracles, wonders, signs, virgin birth, resurrection, the God-head, and whatever else conflicted with his own religious thought.[2]

Jefferson . . . rejected the superstitions and mysticism of Christianity and even went so far as to edit the Gospels, removing the miracles and mysticism of Jesus.[3]

> Thomas Jefferson . . . actually took scissors to the Gospels and
> cut out all references to anything supernatural.[4]

Many others make similar claims.[5] Are they accurate?

Logic would tell us that if Jefferson wrote his own Bible, he would
do so only if he were thoroughly dissatisfied with the traditional Bible,
especially its inclusion of the supernatural. Evidence definitively shows
that this was *not* Jefferson's view. As noted in previous chapters of
this book, Jefferson made frequent, positive use of Bible references
and passages in his own writings.[6]

Perhaps even more important, Jefferson was an active member of
the Virginia Bible Society.[7] This was an organization that distributed the full, unedited text of the Bible, including all its supernatural
references. He also gave Bibles as gifts to members of his family,
including his grandchildren,[8] and contributed liberally to the distri-
bution of the full Bible. In fact, during a period of personal economic
crisis so severe that he arranged a personal loan[9] and even offered
to sell his own cherished private library to Congress to raise additional funds,[10] he made a very generous contribution to the Virginia
Bible Society, explaining:

> I had not supposed there was a family in this State not possess-
> ing a Bible. . . . I therefore enclose you cheerfully an order . . .
> for the purposes of the Society.[11]

Furthermore, in 1798 Jefferson personally helped finance the
printing of one of America's groundbreaking editions of the Bible.[12]
That Bible was a massive, two-volume folio set that was not only
the largest Bible ever published in America to that time, but it was
also America's first hot-pressed Bible.[13] President John Adams, several signers of the Constitution and Declaration, and other major
Founders joined with Jefferson to help fund that Bible.[14]

Jefferson personally possessed and studied many complete Bibles, including some exceptionally famous ones, such as:

- the Eliot Bible, printed in 1661 in the Algonquin Indian language by John Eliot, the apostle to the Indians (the first Bible printed in America in any language)
- the Bible in the Nattick Indian language (1666)
- the earliest Latin Bible printed in England (1580)
- the earliest French Geneva Bible printed in England (1687)

Jefferson owned many other full, uncut Bibles.[15]

And if we continue to follow the financial trail, we find that he also volunteered to help finance the 1808 publishing of Thomson's Bible—the first American translation of the Greek Septuagint into English.[16] Upon receiving the finished work, Jefferson told Thomson that he was thrilled with it and would "use it with great satisfaction," grateful for "the aid you have now given me"[17] through his scholarly translation of the Bible. Recall Jesus' axiom in Luke 12:34 that "where your treasure [money] is, there will your heart be also." Jefferson spent and offered to spend significant amounts of money on the full Bible, thus providing a glimpse into his heart and into what he felt was important.

So . . . Jefferson owned *many* Bibles, belonged to a Bible society and contributed to it, gave out copies of the full, unedited text of the traditional Bible, and assisted in publishing and distributing Bibles. In each of these situations, Jefferson had opportunity to indicate his personal displeasure with the Bible or at least to refrain from participating, but he did not do so.

Then what is the so-called Jefferson Bible that has received so much attention?

There actually is *no* Jefferson Bible, but modern spin is usually directed at one of two religious works that Jefferson prepared about Jesus. He compiled the first in 1804 and the second around 1820. Jefferson assigned an explicit title to each, accurately describing its scope and purpose. Neither was a "Bible," and Jefferson would have strenuously objected to that characterization. In his mind each was nothing more than what he said it was in its title.

Jefferson's title for his 1804 work about Jesus was:

> *The Philosophy of Jesus of Nazareth, being Extracted from the Account of His Life and Doctrines Given by Matthew, Mark, Luke and John; Being an Abridgement of the New Testament for the Use of the Indians, Unembarrassed [Uncomplicated] with Matters of Fact or Faith beyond the Level of their Comprehensions.*[18]

Notice several important points. First, this work was prepared for the use of Indians. Second, it was a work about Jesus drawn solely from the four Gospels. Third, it was not a Bible but rather an abridgment of the major doctrines of Jesus in the Gospels, and as will be seen below, it included *many* references to the miraculous and supernatural.

It is not surprising that Jefferson should have prepared such a work for Indians. For years preceding its compilation, Jefferson had shown a keen interest and taken an active role in promoting Christianity among various tribes. Recall that he owned several Bibles in differing Indian languages, and from 1798 to 1800 he corresponded with religious leaders and ministers such as the Reverend William Linn and the Reverend Samuel Miller on the subject of promoting Indian missions.[19] In 1802 while president, he signed a law authorizing the Society of the United Brethren to "propagat[e] the Gospel among the Heathen" in which he provided federal funds for churches, missionaries, and Christian schools among the Indians in the Northwest Territory.[20]

Shortly after signing that act, Edward Dowse, one of Jefferson's longtime friends, sent him a copy of a sermon preached in Scotland by the evangelical minister Reverend William Bennet in which he addressed the importance of promoting Christian knowledge among Indians of North America.[21] The Reverend Bennet advocated teaching Christianity to Indians by using just the simple teachings of Jesus—that is, using *only* Jesus' words and avoiding the many doctrines that caused conflict between groups of Christians. Concerning that sermon, Dowse, who knew Jefferson well, told him:

> [I]t seemed to me to have a claim to your attention. At any rate, the idea struck me that you will find it of use and perhaps may see fit to cause some copies of it to be reprinted, at your own charge, to distribute among our Indian missionaries.[22]

Jefferson replied to Dowse, telling him, "I . . . perused it with attention" and "I concur with the author."[23] Of this exchange between the two, one scholar accurately observed:

> Mr. Dowse apparently understood Jefferson's interest in Christian missions to the Native Americans in a way that many modern scholars have dismissed as irrelevant. This dismissal has led to the misunderstanding of Jefferson's motives for his compilation of Christ's teachings. Jefferson had a deep, genuine commitment to missionary efforts among the Indians. His account books show that he consistently donated his own money to missionaries and to societies that distributed Bibles to both Americans and Indians.[24]

In 1803 President Jefferson signed a treaty with the Kaskaskia tribe to provide them Christian ministry and teaching.[25] Of that treaty US Supreme Court Chief Justice William Rehnquist explained:

Jefferson's treaty with the Kaskaskia Indians . . . provided annual cash support for the Tribe's Roman Catholic priest and church. . . . The treaty stated in part: "And whereas the greater part of said Tribe have been baptized and received into the Catholic church, to which they are much attached, the United States will give annually for seven years one hundred dollars towards the support of a priest of that religion . . . [a]nd . . . three hundred dollars to assist the said Tribe in the erection of a church."[26]

In 1804 President Jefferson signed yet another federal act for "propagating the Gospel" among Indians.[27]

Clearly, over an extended period of years, Jefferson had repeatedly demonstrated his interest in bringing Christianity to Indians. So, in 1804 he prepared for them a work using nothing but Jesus' own words, just as had been recommended in the 1799 sermon that he applauded. He took two Bibles he had in the White House, cut from them words of Jesus in the Gospels, and then pasted those words into a separate folio, arranging them so that Indians could read the teachings of Jesus in a nonstop, end-to-end fashion.

According to Jefferson, that work was a "digest of His [Jesus'] moral doctrines, extracted in His own words from the Evangelists, and leaving out everything relative to His personal history and character."[28] In essence, this work was made up of the "red letters" of Jesus compiled into a short, pithy work to be read by Indians.

While this work is sometimes called the "Jefferson Bible," it is actually and only what Jefferson said it was: an *abridgement* of the four Gospels for the use of Indians. For centuries abridgments of the Bible have been a significant and an accepted part of the Bible market, popular for use among the young and new learners.[29]

No original copy of that work survives, but what does remain is Jefferson's title page for the work, his handwritten list of the passages he included, and the two White House Bibles from which he clipped the Gospel passages. In 1983 historian Dickinson Adams took those documents and reconstructed Jefferson's *Philosophy of Jesus . . . for the Use of the Indians*,[30] as did Charles Sanford in 1984[31] and Mark Beliles in 1993.[32] From those three reconstructions, it is clear that Jefferson definitely *did* include the subjects below:

> Miracles such as the healing on the Sabbath in Luke 14:1–6, and the commission of Jesus to His disciples in Matthew 10 to go and heal the sick and raise the dead. It includes Jesus' teaching about the resurrection of the dead, about His own second coming, about His role as judge of all men at the end of time, and about His place as Son of God and Lord of a heavenly kingdom. He is also shown forgiving the sins of men and women in a manner reserved for God alone.[33]

That abridgement also contained the miraculous resurrection of Jarius's daughter (Matthew 9:18–25), the healing of the bleeding woman (Matthew 9:20–22), and the healing of two blind men (Matthew 9:27–31), all of which are clearly acts of a miraculous or supernatural character.[34]

Numerous other passages also contained mentions of the Divine, the miraculous, Heaven, Hell, and other supernatural elements, including Mark 14:61–62 (Jesus saying He is the Son of God); Matthew 11:4–5 (Jesus healing the blind, lame, lepers, and deaf, and raising the dead); Matthew 10:28 (Jesus' teaching about Hell); Luke 15:7, 10 (Jesus' teaching about Heaven and angels); and Matthew 19:29 (Jesus' teaching on eternal life). It also included many other passages referring to Heaven, Hell, the resurrection, and other supernatural subjects (Matthew 13:40–42; Luke 14:14; Matthew 22:29–32; Matthew 25:31–34, 41, 46; Matthew 13:49–50; and so on). In light of this, it is obvious that the charge that

Jefferson clipped the supernatural or miraculous from this work is blatantly false.

Jefferson understood that the words of Jesus would change Native Americans just as they had changed other Americans and the rest of the world. And even though it took Jefferson "the work of one or two evenings only"[35] to prepare this work for Indians, Pulitzer Prize–winning Jefferson biographer Dumas Malone nevertheless observed that "it is a notable fact that this chief of state devoted even that time to such a task."[36]

So, since the 1804 work does not fit the modern description of a so-called Jefferson Bible, then how about Jefferson's 1820 work? Could that be the alleged Jefferson Bible that demonstrates a dismissal of Jesus' supernatural works?

With the 1820 work Jefferson took a much different approach than he did in the earlier one. He spent several years planning and preparing the later version; but like the 1804 work, it, too, had a specific purpose. He titled it *The Life and Morals of Jesus of Nazareth*; and on numerous occasions he said that the sole purpose of the work was to collect and present the major moral teachings of Jesus in one short, simple collection—teachings that on numerous occasions Jefferson declared surpassed those from all other sources.

It is a little-known fact that Jefferson spent literally decades of his life studying and comparing the moral teachings of dozens of history's most famous teachers and leaders, including Ocellus, Timæus, Pythagoras, Aristides, Cato, Socrates, Plato, Epicurus, Cicero, Xenophon, Seneca, Epictetus, Antoninus, and many others whose names are probably completely unknown to today's readers. Jefferson read and critiqued the moral teachings of each of these leaders and then compared them against the moral teachings of Jesus, finding those of Jesus to be far superior.

In today's shallow academic climate of Minimalism and Modernism, Jefferson's preoccupation with the study of morals seems eccentric and out of the ordinary. It is usually dismissed as nothing more than what critics consider to be a thinly veiled subterfuge masking his true hatred of the Bible. After all, those modern critics surely wouldn't have undertaken such an arduous study of morals across the millennia, so they can't imagine that Jefferson would have done so. But the subject of morality was indeed a genuine theme of concentrated academic inquiry—not only for Jefferson but for most Americans. It was even a required, stand-alone course in nearly every American university during the Founding Era.

For example, Princeton University had a dedicated Professor of Moral Philosophy,[37] and its president, John Witherspoon, a signer of the Declaration, delivered to students systematic "Lectures on Moral Philosophy."[38] Harvard had a Professor of Natural, Intellectual, and Moral Philosophy[39] as well as a Professor of Christian Morals. Even Jefferson's own university had a Professor of Moral Philosophy,[40] and similar moral instruction was common in other major colleges in the Founding Era.[41]

In Jefferson's day works addressng morals were written by individuals from a broad spectrum of professions, ranging from economists such as Adam Smith in his *Theory of Moral Sentiments* (1759)[42] to ministers such as the Reverend Richard Price with his *Review of the Principal Questions in Morals* (1757).[43] Many prominent Founding Fathers also wrote full works on morality[44] or offered lengthy declarations about the importance of morality,[45] and morals were a frequent object of legislation during the Founding Era.[46]

Now let us examine in detail Jefferson's comparisons between the moral teachings of ancient leaders and those of Jesus, especially his reasons for finding those of Jesus superior to all others. Chief among those reasons was because Jesus "pushed His scrutinies into the heart of man; erected His tribunal in the region of his thoughts, and purified the waters at the fountain head."[47] If Jefferson had felt that Jesus' teachings were somehow lacking embarrassing enough to warrant the slashing and reconstituting of the Bible, then why declare His moral superiority over and over again?

In the excerpt below Jefferson critiqued the moral teachings of eight different leaders, finding them deficient to those of Jesus:

> I consider the genuine (not the imputed) doctrines of Epicurus as containing everything rational in moral philosophy which Greece and Rome have left us. Epictetus indeed has given us what was good of the Stoics, all beyond of their dogmas being hypocrisy and grimace. Their great crime was in their calumnies [deliberate falsehoods] of Epicurus and misrepresentations of his doctrines, in which we lament to see the candid character of Cicero engaging as an accomplice—diffuse, vapid, rhetorical, but enchanting. His prototype Plato, eloquent as himself, dealing out mysticisms incomprehensible to the human mind. . . . Of Socrates we have nothing genuine but in the Memorabilia of Xenophon. . . . Seneca is indeed a fine moralist, disfiguring his work at times with some stoicisms and affecting too much of antithesis and point, yet giving us on the whole a great deal of sound and practical morality. But the greatest of all the reformers of the depraved religion of His own country was Jesus of Nazareth. . . . Epictetus and Epicurus give laws for governing ourselves; Jesus a supplement of the duties and charities we owe to others.[48]

How many of today's most educated scholars even recognize these ancient names, much less have read their works and compared them with those of Jesus? Certainly few have, but Jefferson had. He was genuinely and sincerely focused on the issue of morality in a way that few in this era can comprehend—a way that Modernists,

Deconstructionalist, Minimalist, and Academic Collectivists flatly dismiss.

During Jefferson's first term as president, as was dealing with various national issues affected by morality, he began expressing his desire to compile a work on the morals of Jesus. He explained:

> I should first take a general view of the moral doctrines of the most remarkable of the ancient philosophers, of whose ethics we have sufficient information to make an estimate—say Pythagoras, Epicurus, Epictetus, Socrates, Cicero, Seneca, Antoninus. I should do justice to the branches of morality they have treated well, but point out the importance of those in which they are deficient. I should then take a view of the deism and ethics of the Jews and show in what a degraded state they were, and the necessity they presented of a reformation. I should proceed to a view of the life, character, and doctrines of Jesus. . . . [H]is system of morality was the most benevolent and sublime probably that has been ever taught, and consequently more perfect than those of any of the ancient philosophers.[49]

Jefferson thought that his work should contrast the morals of Jesus not only with those of ancient leaders but also with several Christian movements of his day. (Interestingly, a number of Christian groups in Jefferson's time distinguished themselves by their attempts to combine the morality of some ancient philosopher with that of Jesus.) Jefferson explained:

> We must dismiss the Platonists and Plotinists, the Stagyrites and Gamalielites, the Eclectics, the Gnostics and Scholastics, their essences and emanations, their Logos and Demiurgos, Aeons and Daemons, male and female, with a long train of etc. etc. etc. or, shall I say at once, of nonsense. We must reduce our volume

to the simple Evangelists; select even from them the very words only of Jesus . . . There will be found remaining the most sublime and benevolent code of morals which has ever been offered to man.[50]

Jefferson believed that the moral teachings of Jesus needed nothing added from any other philosopher, whether Christian or Pagan. He declared:

The doctrines which flowed from the lips of Jesus Himself are within the comprehension of a child; but thousands of volumes have not yet explained the Platonisms [i.e., teachings of Plato] engrafted on them—and for this obvious reason: that nonsense can never be explained.[51]

Jefferson regularly and repeatedly effused about the superiority of Jesus' teachings,[52] and it was never his intention for his proposed work to do anything except investigate *only* the morals of Jesus and *nothing* else—a point he made clear for years.[53] In 1813 he finally began compiling the work about which he had so often spoken, reporting to his friend John Adams:

We must reduce our volume to the simple Evangelists [the Gospels], select even from them the very words only of Jesus. . . . There will be found remaining the most sublime and benevolent code of *morals* which has ever been offered to man. I have performed this operation for my own use by cutting verse by verse out of the printed book. . . . The result is an octavo of forty-six pages of pure and unsophisticated doctrines such as were professed and acted on by the unlettered Apostles, the Apostolic Fathers, and the Christians of the first century.[54] (emphasis added)

Two years later, in 1815, he told his close friend and famous Virginia evangelical leader, the Reverend Charles Clay, about his work:

> Probably you have heard me say I had taken the four Evangelists [Gospels], had cut out from them every text they had recorded of the *moral* precepts of Jesus, and arranged them in a certain order; and although they appeared but as fragments, yet fragments of the most sublime edifice of *morality* which had ever been exhibited to man.[55] (emphasis added)

The next year, in 1816, he wrote Christian theologian and fellow Founding Father Charles Thomson, who had earlier produced the Septuigent (Greek translation) Bible that Jefferson so admired. Thomson had just published his famous *Synopsis of the Four Evangelists* in which he had taken all the passages from each of the four Gospels and arranged them chronologically. The result was something like one long Gospel with all Jesus' words and acts arranged sequentially.

Having seen Thomson's newest work, Jefferson told him of his own project—"a wee little book . . . which I call the Philosophy of Jesus; it is a paradigma [example] of His doctrines made by cutting the texts out of the book [the Bible], and arranging them on the pages of a blank book in a certain order of time or subject."[56] Jefferson added, "If I had time, I would add to my little book the Greek, Latin, and French texts in columns side by side."[57] (Jefferson read seven languages: Greek, Latin, French, Italian, Spanish, German, and English.[58]) Four years later, in 1820, Jefferson did indeed add those languages and columns to his "wee little book," thus completing his *Life and Morals of Jesus of Nazareth* as a four-language polyglot.

Today's critics of Jefferson who claim that this is the "Jefferson Bible" from which he excluded the supernatural are either ill informed or ill intentioned. Jefferson did not produce and had no intention of producing a theological work. Rather, it was a work in which he compiled some fifty different moral teachings of Jesus. But inexplicably, many of today's alleged scholars refuse to allow that work to be just what he said it was. Instead, they insist on converting it into a supposed Jefferson attack against the Bible and the supernatural.

But the 1820 work, like the 1804 one before it, contained numerous passages on the miraculous and the supernatural, including Jesus' teachings about:

- healing on the Sabbath (Matthew 12:10–12; John 7:23)

- Hell (Luke 12:4–5; Matthew 10:28; Matthew 13:37–41, 50; Matthew 23:33; Matthew 5:29–30; Matthew 18:8–9; Matthew 25:46; Luke 16:23)

- Heaven (Luke 16:22–30; Matthew 19:16–26; Matthew 25:34; John 18:36–37; Luke 12:33; Luke 15:7)

- Angels (Matthew 13:39, 41, 49; Luke 15:10; Matthew 22:30)

- the Devil (Matthew 13:39)

- eternal life (Luke 10:25–28; Matthew 19:16; Matthew 25:46)

- the Holy Spirit (Luke 11:13)

- resurrection of the dead (Matthew 22:28–30; Luke 14:14)

- the Second Coming of Christ (Matthew 24:20–44; Matthew 25:31–34)

Many similar passages can found in that 1820 work.

Modern claims that Jefferson deleted the miraculous and supernatural, whether in reference to the 1804 or the 1820 work are erroneous. Neither of the two works fits the critics' description of the alleged "Jefferson Bible."

But if the 1804 work was prepared for the use and edification of

Indians, then who was the intended audience for his 1820 work? The answer to that question was provided by Jefferson's beloved eldest grandson, Thomas Jefferson Randolph:

> [H]e [my grandfather] left two codifications of the morals of Jesus—*one for himself*, and another for the Indians; the first of which I now possess: a blank volume, red morocco, gilt, letters on the back, "The Morals of Jesus"—into which he pasted extracts in Greek, Latin, French, and English, taken textually from the four Gospels and so arranged that he could run his eye of the reading of the same verse in four languages. . . . His codification of the *Morals of Jesus* was not known to his family before his death, and they learnt from a letter addressed to a friend that he was in the habit of *reading nightly from it* before going to bed.[59] (emphasis added)

This, then, is another problem with the modern description that this work was a "Jefferson Bible." It was *not* for public use, and Jefferson would never have allowed it to have been described as a "Bible." It was only a personal assemblage of Jesus' moral teachings from the Gospels for his own study. So how did this private work—a work unknown even to his family—become public?

In 1886 Cyrus Adler, the librarian for the Smithsonian, located the original that had been in the hands of Jefferson's grandson and arranged for its purchase by Congress in 1895. In 1900 US representative John Lacey of Iowa was so inspired by Jefferson's compilation of the moral teachings of Jesus that he brought the work to national attention through a newspaper article widely reprinted across the country.[60] In 1902 Lacey sponsored a congressional resolution that the government reprint *Jefferson's Morals of Jesus of Nazareth* for use by the nation's senators and representatives.[61] Lacey described Jefferson's work to Congress:

[It] is a consolidation of the beautiful, pure teachings of the Savior in a compact form . . . and the opportunity is given, plain and unadorned, to compare these teachings with Marcus Aurelius's and other pagan "morals." They are in striking contrast to Plutarch's "morals" (or rather his immorals). No greater practical test of the worth of the tenets of the Christian religion could be made than the publication of this condensation by Mr. Jefferson. . . . A verse of John is combined with a verse of Matthew with no interlineations, but is blended into a harmonious whole. . . . The work was intended to place the morals of Jesus in a form where, simple and alone, they could be contrasted with the teachings of the pagan philosophers. In doing this work, Mr. Jefferson has builded . . . this beautiful little volume in a form to be accessible to the Christian world.[62]

Congress passed Lacey's resolution and printed nine thousand copies at government expense.[63] For the next fifty years, a copy of *The Life and Morals of Jesus of Nazareth* was given to every senator and representative at his or her swearing in.[64]

So what is the origin of the modern charge that Jefferson hated the traditional Bible and therefore made his own? A contemporary researcher who investigated this claim concluded:

Unfortunately, all those who have published the "Jefferson Bible" since 1903 have been almost universally either Unitarian or rationalist and secular in their approach, and their introductions to the book have . . . misrepresented Jefferson's motivations and beliefs to conform to their own theological assumptions or agendas.[65]

In summary, there is *no* "Jefferson Bible," and Jefferson did *not* produce any work for the purpose of deleting the miraculous and supernatural. He did, however, make two works that compiled the teachings of Jesus—one for use as a beginning reader for Indians and the other for his own personal use. Each was exactly and only what Jefferson said it was. Two centuries ago Jefferson told his close evangelical friend, Dr. Benjamin Rush: "My views . . . [are] very different from that anti-Christian system imputed to me by those who know nothing of my opinions,"[67] and that declaration certainly remains true today.

So the next time someone refers to a so-called Jefferson Bible, ask them to identify the specific work about which they are talking; most won't be able to do so. Then ask them where they got their information. The chances are high that it was some recent Deconstructionist, Minimalist, Modernist, or Academic Collectivist source but certainly not any original documentary source—for the very simple reason that no such source exists.

LIE # 4

Thomas Jefferson Was a Racist Who Opposed Equality for Black Americans

In the past, leading civil rights advocates, both black and white, regularly invoked Jefferson as an inspiration for their own efforts, pointing to his lengthy record of legislative proposals and writings on the subject of emancipation and civil rights. But modern portrayal of Jefferson's views on these issues is just the opposite and is often deliberately misstated. Modern writers claim:

> Thomas Jefferson was demonstrably a racist—and a particularly aggressive and vindictive one at that. . . . His flaws are beyond redemption. . . . Jefferson is a patron saint far more suitable to white supremacists than to modern American liberals.[1]

> Jefferson . . . did not believe that all were created equal. He was a racist.[2]

> Jefferson was a racist. There is no question about that.[3]

Stephen Lyons, a writer for major national newspapers, adds even another charge:

> The venerable Thomas Jefferson has been the subject of a recent rash of bad publicity, including [Garry] Wills' *Negro President.* The book is an expansion of three lectures Wills gave

at Northwestern University in which he examines the influence on Jeffersonian politics by the infamous "three-fifths slave vote." . . . The infamous three-fifths vote, or "federal ratio," a non-negotiable ratification compromise insisted on by the South at the Constitutional Convention, counted each slave as 60 percent of a person. [4]

Before unequivocally demonstrating that Jefferson was not a racist, Lyons' charge concerning the Three-Fifths Clause of the Constitution must be addressed.

Fortunately, the discussion by the Founding Fathers concerning the Three-Fifths Clause is readily available, even online.[5] It will be evident to anyone reading that discussion that the clause did not deal with the innate worth of any individual. No individual, whether black, white, brown, purple, green, polka-dot, or any other color, was ever considered three-fifths of a person. To the contrary, the Three-Fifths Clause addressed federal representation, not human worth. And it was an antislavery provision inserted by the North (not the proslavery South, as Lyons and others wrongly claim) as a means of reducing the number of proslavery representatives in Congress.

In the Constitution, each state was to receive one federal representative to Congress for every 30,000 inhabitants in the state.[6] Since slaves accounted for much of the Southern population (almost half the inhabitants of South Carolina and 40 percent of Georgia),[7] Southern states planned to count their slaves as though they were free inhabitants, thereby using slaves to send more proslavery representatives to Congress.

The antislavery Founders from the North strenuously objected. They wanted only free residents to be counted, thus not only limiting proslavery members from the South but also providing them an incentive for emancipation. If the South wanted more representatives to Congress, it should free its slaves. Governor Morris, a strong opponent of slavery and "The Penman of the Constitution," argued:

> Upon what principle is it that the slaves shall be computed in the representation? Are they men? Then make them citizens and let them vote. . . . [But t]he admission of slaves into the representation . . . comes to this: that the inhabitants of Georgia and South Carolina . . . shall have more votes in a government instituted for protection of the rights of mankind than the citizens of Pennsylvania or New Jersey who view with a laudable horror so nefarious [wicked] a practice.[8]

Constitutional Convention delegate Luther Martin similarly argued that if the South was going to count its so-called property (that is, its slaves) in order to get more proslavery representation in Congress, then the North would count its "property" (that is, its "horses, cattle, mules, or any other [type of property]"[9]) in order to get more antislavery representation in Congress. Of course, the South objected just as strenuously to this proposal as the North objected to counting slaves.

The final compromise was that only 60 percent of the total slave population (that is, only three-fifths) would be counted to calculate the number of representatives to Congress.[10] This would reduce the number of representatives to Congress from Southern states with large slave populations. The Three-Fifths Clause had nothing to do with the worth of any individual; in fact, Free Blacks in the North and South often were extended the full rights of a citizen, including the right to vote.[11] The clause had to do only with calculating representation.[12]

Because previous generations actually read the debates surrounding that clause rather than just quoting some modern author's mischaracterization of it, black civil rights leaders such as Frederick Douglass identified the Three-Fifths Clause as one of the antislavery provisions of the Constitution.[13] But Deconstructionist scholars and writers are determined to twist that clause into a tool by which to bash the Founding Fathers—specifically Jefferson, as Lyons has done.

While the modern charge abounds that Jefferson was a blatant, unrepentant racist, an examination of his actual writings and actions on civil rights will demonstrate just how ridiculous these claims are. It will also make evident why civil rights leaders in previous generations praised Jefferson for his efforts on emancipation.

America in Jefferson's day, as today, was not homogenous, whether in business, religion, or culture. Many differences were distinguishable by geographic regions. This was especially true on the subject of slavery and civil rights.

In the Northern colonies (Massachusetts, Connecticut, Rhode Island, New Hampshire, etc.), slavery was generally abhorred; blacks were elected to public office (Wentworth Cheswill in New Hampshire in 1768, Thomas Hercules in Pennsylvania in 1793, and others). Blacks also distinguished themselves for their exploits in military service during the Revolution (Peter Salem, Lemuel Haynes, Prince Estabrook, Prince Whipple, and others); and both blacks and whites voted in elections.[14] Blacks could be found pastoring or preaching to largely white churches and congregations (Lemuel Haynes, Richard Allen, Harry Hoosier, and others); and in many churches, blacks and whites attended and worshipped together. While there definitely was some racism in the North, it was largely the exception rather than the rule. In the North, both ministers and political leaders were boldly and unapologetically outspoken for civil rights, and the general stance was for immediate emancipation and equality. Abolition societies abounded and exerted significant influence.

The Southern colonies (North Carolina, South Carolina, and Georgia) were almost polar opposites. Racism was institutionalized. Churches where both blacks and whites worshipped together, such as those pastored by black minister Andrew Bryan of Georgia, were the exception rather than the rule. The possibility of blacks holding office or voting was virtually nonexistent, and political leaders who spoke out against slavery were attacked. Freedom for slaves? Never! Equality for blacks? Unthinkable! This was the dominant view with only a few individual exceptions, such as Founding Father John Laurens of South Carolina. Abolition societies were rare, and the ones that existed were impotent.

The Middle colonies (Virginia, Maryland, and Delaware) were somewhat a mix of the two other regions, but they were much closer in philosophy to the Southern colonies than the Northern ones. The majority strongly supported slavery, but there were definitely vocal minority groups advocating civil rights. Institutionalized racism was present but not as rigidly enforced as in the Southern colonies. Many ministers and a few civil leaders—such as Jefferson, George Washington, Richard Bland, George Mason, Richard Henry Lee, William Hooper, William Few, and others—spoke openly for emancipation. But when doing so they often received a cold and sometimes even a hostile reception yet usually not with the virulent reaction and intolerance so common in the Southern colonies.

While the Northern colonies wanted emancipation immediately and the Southern colonies not at all, the Middle colonies believed that if emancipation was to occur, it must be gradual with relocation. Thus the Middle colonies had colonization societies rather than abolition societies. They sought emancipation for slaves, and then planned to transport them back to Africa from whence so many had originally been stolen. This Middle colony approach acknowledged that slavery was wrong, but it also recognized that blacks had greater freedom and opportunity in Africa than in the prejudice-filled Middle and Southern colonies.

The different views in each region required that differing political tactics be used. That is, abolition laws introduced in the North would never have seen the light of day in the South; and the colonization approach of the Middle would have been unacceptable to the other two regions, although each would have opposed it for opposite reasons. Therefore, those wishing to change the national culture on slavery had to start at different levels, depending on the region in which they lived.

It is evident that Jefferson was acutely aware of these distinct regional differences. A 1785 exchange he had with the Reverend Richard Price of England demonstrates this. Price had sided with America during the Revolution and written several pro-American pieces. He sent one of his pamphlets on the American Revolution to South Carolina where it met a very cold reception. Political leaders there condemned it "because it recommend[ed] measures for . . . abolishing the Negro trade and slavery."[15] Based on their reaction, Price was concerned that he had misread American intentions toward liberty, and he asked Jefferson whether South Carolina was representative of the other states.

Jefferson reassured Price that South Carolina was not representative of the country on the issue of slavery and then explained to him the three different reactions his pamphlet would likely receive. From the Southern colonies, Jefferson affirmed what Price had already discovered: "Southward of the Chesapeake, it will find but few readers concurring with it in sentiment on the subject of slavery."[16] The Chesapeake is the large bay between Maryland and Virginia, so "southward of the Chesapeake" means the colonies below or south of Virginia.

Concerning the Middle colonies, Jefferson told him: "From the mouth of the head of the Chesapeake [the Middle colonies], the bulk of the people will approve it in theory, and it will find a respectable minority ready to adopt it in practice."[17]

Regarding the Northern colonies, Jefferson explained:

Northward of the Chesapeake, you may find here and there an opponent to your doctrine as you may find here and there a robber and murderer, but in no greater number. In that part of America, there being but few slaves, they can easily disencumber themselves of them; and emancipation is put into such a train that in a few years there will be no slave northward of Maryland.[18]

Jefferson therefore reassured Price: "Be not therefore discouraged. What you have written will do a great deal of good. . . . I wish you to do more, and wish it on assurance of its effect."[19]

Jefferson explained these geographic distinctions to others as well. He lamented to the Reverend David Barrow, who had lived in Virginia but moved to Kentucky and founded the Kentucky Abolition Society, that emancipation would be slower in the Southern and Middle colonies than the Northern ones.

Where the disease [slavery] is most deeply seated, there it will be slowest in eradication. In the Northern states, it was merely superficial and easily corrected. In the Southern, it is incorporated with the whole system and requires time, patience, and perseverance in the curative process.[20]

Jefferson was optimistic about change in Virginia, but as he had acknowledged to the Reverend Price his own desire to abolish slavery had placed him in the "respectable minority" in his own state.

But before chronicling Jefferson's many emancipation declarations and actions, the elephant in the room must be addressed: if Jefferson was indeed so antislavery, then why didn't he release his own slaves? After all, George Washington allowed for the freeing of his slaves on his death in 1799, so why didn't Jefferson at least do the same at his death in 1826? The answer is Virginia law. In 1799 Virginia allowed owners to emancipate their slaves on their death; in 1826 state laws had been changed to prohibit that practice.

As previously acknowledged, Virginia was rigid in its proslavery laws and had been so for more than a century before Jefferson. As early as 1692, it began placing significant economic hurdles in the way of those wanting to emancipate slaves, requiring:

> [N]o Negro or mulatto slave shall be set free—unless the emancipator pays for his transportation out of the country within six months.[21]

Subsequent laws imposed even harsher restrictions, mandating that a slave could not be freed unless the owner guaranteed a full security bond for the education, livelihood, and support of the freed slave.[22] Then, in 1723 a law was passed that forbade the emancipation of slaves under *any* circumstance—even by a last will and testament. The only exceptions were for cases of "meritorious service" by a slave, a determination that could be made only by the state governor and his council on a case-by-case basis.[23]

But in 1782, for a very short time, Virginia began to move in a new direction. An emancipation law was passed, declaring:

> [T]hose persons who are disposed to emancipate their slaves may be empowered so to do and . . . it shall hereafter be lawful for any person, by his or her last will and testament, . . . to emancipate and set free his or her slaves.[24]

It was as a result of this law that George Washington was able to free his slaves in his last will and testament in 1799.

But in 1806 Virginia repealed much of that law.[25] It technically retained emancipation but placed an almost impossible economic burden on emancipators, requiring that freed slaves who were young, old, weak, or infirm "shall respectively be supported and maintained by the person so liberating them, or by his or her estate."[26] The law even allowed a wife to reverse an emancipation made by her husband in his will.[27] Furthermore, the law required that a freed slave promptly depart the state or else reenter slavery, thus making it almost impossible for an emancipated slave to remain near his or her spouse, children, or family members who had not been freed. Many, therefore, preferred to remain in slavery with their families rather than become free and be separated from them.[28]

It was under these laws that Jefferson was required to operate. In 1814 he lamented to an abolitionist minister friend in Illinois that in Virginia "[t]he laws do not permit us to turn them loose."[29] And even if Jefferson had done so, he certainly did not have the finances required by law to provide a livelihood and support for each of his freed slaves. Jefferson had received the bulk of his slaves—187 of them—through inheritance[30] and had done so at a very young age. As he acknowledged: "[A]t fourteen years of age, the whole care and direction of myself was thrown on myself entirely without a relation or friend qualified to advise or guide me."[31] He did not have the economic means to conform to that oppressive state law. Recall that at one point his own personal economic shortages had caused him to approach Congress about buying his cherished library in order to generate much-needed operating cash.[32]

Part of Jefferson's cash shortage was caused by a major devaluation of money. After placing large amounts of money in the loan office during the American Revolution, those funds were returned "back again at a depreciation out to him of one for forty."[33] That is, the amount he received back was worth only 2.5 percent of what it had been worth when he placed it into the government loan office.

Jefferson's economic hardship was also exacerbated by his practice, unlike other slave owners, of paying his slaves for the vegetables they raised, meat obtained while hunting and fishing, and for extra tasks performed outside normal working hours. He even offered a revolutionary profit-sharing plan for the products that his enslaved artisans produced in their shops.[34]

Despite the fact that Jefferson was unable to free his slaves under the requirements of state law, he nevertheless remained a local, national, and even a global voice advocating emancipation. He helped steadily turn the culture in a direction that would allow equal civil rights to eventually be secured for all Americans regardless of race. For this reason, early blacks viewed Jefferson in a much more favorable light than they did many other leaders from the South. In fact, one of the earliest black Americans to acknowledge Jefferson's relatively advanced views on race—at least when compared to the dominant views of others in the Middle and Southern colonies—was Benjamin Banneker, whom Jefferson hired to survey the brand-new city of Washington, DC.

Banneker was a highly accomplished and self-taught mathematician and astronomer. The scientific almanac he prepared was in high demand because of his accurate predictions for sunsets, sunrises, eclipses, weather conditions and even for his calculation of the recurrence of locust plagues in seventeen-year cycles. Banneker sent a handwritten copy of his almanac to Jefferson, beginning his letter by acknowledging that Jefferson had secured a reputation of favoring civil rights:

> [I] hope I may safely admit in consequence of the report which hath reached me that you are a man far less inflexible in sentiments of this nature than many others—that you are measurably friendly and well-disposed towards us and that you are willing to lend your aid and assistance for our relief from those many distresses and numerous calamities to which we are reduced.[35]

Banneker then appealed to Jefferson to further exert himself in behalf of blacks and throw off any remaining prejudice he might hold:

Now, sir, if this is founded in truth, I apprehend you will readily embrace every opportunity to eradicate that train of absurd and false ideas and opinions which so generally prevails with respect to us; and that your sentiments are concurrent with mine, which are that one universal Father hath given being to us all, and that He hath . . . made us all of one flesh [Acts 17:26]. . . . Sir, if these are sentiments of which you are fully persuaded, I hope you cannot but acknowledge that it is the indispensable duty of those who maintain for themselves the rights of human nature and who possess the obligations of Christianity to extend their power and influence to the relief of every part of the human race from whatever burden or oppression they may unjustly labor under.[36]

Having thus expounded to Jefferson on the unequal position of blacks across much of the nation, Banneker then returned to his original purpose in writing Jefferson, presenting him "a copy of an almanac which I have calculated for the succeeding year . . . in my own handwriting."[37] Jefferson responded:

I thank you sincerely for your letter of the 19th instant and for the almanac it contained. Nobody wishes more than I do to see such proofs as you exhibit—that nature has given to our black brethren talents equal to those of the other colors of men, and that the appearance of a want [lack] of them is owing merely to the degraded condition of their existence both in Africa and America. . . . I have taken the liberty of sending your almanac to Monsieur de Condorcet, Secretary of the Academy of Sciences at Paris and member of the Philanthropic Society, because I considered it as a document to which your whole color had a right for their justification against the doubts which have been entertained of them. I am with great esteem, sir, your most obedient humble servant.[38]

When Jefferson sent the almanac to Marquis de Condorcet, a leading antislavery voice in France, he told him:

> I am happy to be able to inform you that we have now in the United States a Negro . . . who is a very respectable mathematician. . . . [H]e made an almanac for the next year, which he sent me in his own handwriting, and which I enclose to you. I have seen very elegant solutions of geometrical problems by him. Add to this that he is a very worthy and respectable member of society. He is a free man. I shall be delighted to see these instances of moral eminence so multiplied as to prove that the want [lack] of talents observed in them [blacks] is merely the effect of their degraded condition, and not proceeding from any difference in the structure of the parts on which intellect depends.[39]

Many of those today who call Jefferson an unrepentant racist also claim that he believed blacks were inferior to whites. For example, in the true spirit of Academic Collectivism:

> Jefferson . . . was convinced . . . blacks had to be seen as lower beings because of their inferiority.[40]

> Jefferson . . . believed . . . blacks were inferior to whites in body and mind.[41]

> Thomas Jefferson . . . thought black people intellectually inferior to whites.[42]

> Thomas Jefferson was not interested in abolition. . . . Thomas Jefferson considered blacks inferior.[43]

To "prove" this charge, such writers point to comments Jefferson made in his *Notes on the State of Virginia* (1781) in which he expressed not only his ardent desire for the emancipation of slaves but also twice lightly questioned whether blacks *might* be inferior.[44] But the callous conclusion reached by modern Minimalist writers is possible *only* if they cite just those two Jefferson comments and ignore the rest of the lengthy emancipation treatise from which those statements are cut.

In fact, in order to mitigate his own two comments, Jefferson openly acknowledged that his personal experience with blacks had been limited almost exclusively to the context of slavery—that is, his personal dealings had been with oppressed blacks who had been denied education. Very few analysts, either then or now, would dispute that under such conditions blacks might well appear inferior in intellectual abilities, for they had absolutely no opportunity to prove otherwise. Jefferson candidly acknowledged his own subjective situation and his lack of objective data on which to base any fixed opinion. He even openly lamented:

> To our reproach, it must be said that though for a century and a half we have had under our eyes the races of black and of red men, they have never yet been viewed by us as subjects of natural history. I advance it, therefore, as a *suspicion only* that the blacks . . . are inferior to the whites in the endowments both of body and mind.[45] (emphasis added)

He also explained that "[i]t will be right *to make great allowances* for the difference of condition, of education, of conversation, of the sphere in which they move"[46] (emphasis added). Jefferson understood that slavery was certainly *not* a favorable condition in which to compare intellectual abilities. He therefore eagerly invited and even sought outside evidence to disprove what he had called his "suspicion only." Recall that he told Banneker:

> Nobody wishes more than I do to see such proofs . . . that nature has given to our black brethren talents equal to those

of the other colors of men, and that the appearance of a want [lack] of them is owing [due] merely to the degraded condition of their existence both in Africa and America.[47]

And he had similarly told Condorcet that "I shall be *delighted* to see [that] . . . the want [lack] of talents observed in them is merely the effect of their degraded condition, and not proceeding from any difference in the structure of the parts on which intellect depends."[48]

Jefferson made the same point to Henri Gregoire, a Catholic priest, ardent abolitionist, and leader in the French Revolution. Gregoire had prepared and sent Jefferson a book with the literary compositions of blacks, designed to demonstrate their equal intellectual capacity. Jefferson told him:

> Be assured that no person living wishes more sincerely than I do to see a complete refutation of the doubts I have myself entertained and expressed on the grade of understanding allotted to them by nature, and to find that in this respect they are on a par with ourselves. My doubts were the result of personal observation on the limited sphere of my own state, where the opportunities for the development of their genius were not favorable, and those of exercising it still less so. I expressed them therefore with great hesitation; but whatever be their degree of talent, it is no measure of their rights. Because Sir Isaac Newton was superior to others in understanding, he was not therefore lord of the person or property of others.[49]

Decades after Jefferson had made his two 1781 comments, he lamented to his old friend Joel Barlow, an American diplomat who had served with Jefferson during the American Revolution, about how some had taken his casually expressed "suspicions" and tried to misrepresent them. He pointed to his exchange with Gregoire as an example:

> He wrote to me also on the doubts I had expressed five or six and twenty years ago in the *Notes of Virginia* as to the grade of understanding of the Negroes. . . . It was impossible for doubt to have been more tenderly or hesitatingly expressed than that was in the *Notes of Virginia*, and nothing was or is farther from my intentions than to enlist myself as the champion of a fixed opinion where I have only expressed a doubt.[50]

In my opinion, for today's writers and academics to convert Jefferson's loosely held and cautiously and rarely expressed "suspicions" into unwavering resolute racism is a complete misrepresentation.

Now let us move from the question of Jefferson's perception of innate value in black Americans to his actions and writings advocating emancipation and equality—actions and writings largely ignored today.

In 1769 at the age of twenty-six, Jefferson began his political career as a member of the Virginia legislature. Shortly after entering that body, he approached respected senior legislator Richard Bland and proposed that the two of them undertake an "effort in that body for the permission of the emancipation of slaves."[51] Colonel Bland offered the motion and Jefferson seconded it, but it was resoundingly defeated. In fact, for even proposing that measure, Bland was vehemently "denounced as an enemy of his country" by the other legislators "and was treated with the grossest indecorum."[52] Jefferson lamented that as long as Virginia remained a British colony, no emancipation proposal "could expect success"[53]—a condition that he hoped would change.

In 1770 Jefferson represented a slave in court, arguing for his freedom. Jefferson explained:

> Under the law of nature, all men are born free. Everyone comes into the world with a right to his own person, which includes the liberty of moving and using it at his own will. This is what is called personal liberty, and is given him by the Author of Nature.[54]

Jefferson lost the case. In 1772, he also argued a similar case.[55]

In 1773 and 1774 a number of American colonies, including Rhode Island, Connecticut, and Pennsylvania, passed antislavery laws, all of which were struck down by the king in 1774.[56] That year Jefferson penned "A Summary View of the Rights of British America." His purpose was to remind the British that legitimate American concerns were being ignored—one of which was the king's veto of American antislavery laws.

> The abolition of domestic slavery is the great object of desire in those colonies where it was unhappily introduced in their infant state [by Britain]. But previous to the enfranchisement of the slaves we have, it is necessary to exclude all further importations from Africa. Yet our repeated attempts to effect this . . . have been hitherto defeated by His Majesty's negative [veto].[57]

In 1776 Jefferson wrote a draft of the original state constitution for Virginia and included a provision that "[n]o person hereafter coming into this country [Virginia] shall be held in slavery under any pretext whatever."[58] That provision was rejected by the state convention.

Later in 1776, as a member of the Continental Congress, Jefferson drafted the Declaration of Independence. Among the grievances impelling America's separation from Great Britain, Jefferson listed the fact that the king would not allow individual colonies to end slavery or the slave trade, even when they wished to do so:

> He [King George III] has waged cruel war against human nature itself, violating its most sacred rights of life and liberty in the persons of a distant people which never offended him, captivating & carrying them into slavery in another hemisphere, or to incur miserable death in their transportation thither. . . . He has . . . determin[ed] to keep open a market where men should be bought and sold.[59]

Unfortunately, Jefferson's antislavery clause was deleted from the Declaration "in complaisance to South Carolina and Georgia, who had never attempted to restrain the importation of slaves, and who, on the contrary, still wished to continue it."[60]

Although Jefferson's clause was not included in the Declaration, the grievance was very real. Following the separation from Great Britain, many individual states were finally able to begin abolishing slavery. Pennsylvania and Massachusetts did so in 1780; Connecticut and Rhode Island in 1784; Vermont in 1786; New Hampshire in 1792; New York in 1799; and New Jersey in 1804.[61]

In 1778 Jefferson introduced a bill in the Virginia legislature to at least ban the importation of slaves into Virginia from other countries. According to Jefferson, "This passed without opposition and stopped the increase of the evil by importation, leaving to future efforts its final eradication."[62]

In 1779 Jefferson became governor and undertook the next step toward what he had called slavery's "final eradication" by introducing a measure to "emancipate all slaves born after passing the act."[63] That measure was not successful,[64] but Jefferson held firm to his personal conviction that "[n]othing is more certainly written in the book of fate than that these people are to be free."[65]

In 1781 Jefferson penned answers to twenty-two questions posed him by the secretary of the French delegation to America. Those responses became the book *Notes on the State of Virginia* (1781) in which Jefferson declared:

> The whole commerce between master and slave is . . . the most unremitting despotism on the one part, and degrading submissions on the other. . . . And with what execrations [denunciations] should the statesman be loaded who permit[s] one half the citizens thus to trample on the rights of the other. . . . And can the liberties of a nation be thought secure when we have removed their only firm basis—a conviction in the minds of the people that these liberties are of the gift of God? . . . Indeed I tremble for my country when I reflect that God is just, that His justice cannot sleep forever. . . . [T]he way, I hope, [is] preparing under the auspices of Heaven for a total emancipation.[66]

In 1784 Jefferson returned to service in the Continental Congress where he introduced a provision to end slavery in every territory that would eventually become a state in the nation. His proposal stated that "after the year 1800 of the Christian era, there shall be neither slavery nor involuntary servitude in any of the said states."[67]

Jefferson's law fell one vote short of passage. As he explained:

> There were ten states present. Six voted unanimously for it, three against it, and one was divided. And seven votes being requisite to decide the proposition affirmatively [i.e., to pass the measure under the Articles of Confederation], it was lost. . . . Thus we see the fate of millions unborn hanging on the tongue of one man, & heaven was silent in that awful moment! But it is to be hoped it will not always be silent & that the friends to the rights of human nature will in the end prevail.[68]

In 1786, while Jefferson was serving as American ambassador in France, he responded to an article in a French encyclopedia written by French official Louis Dominique de Meunier stating that Virginia did not allow the emancipation of slaves. Jefferson wanted to make sure that de Meunier knew not only that he had wanted it otherwise but also that someday it *would* be otherwise:

> We must await with patience the workings of an overruling Providence & hope that it is preparing the deliverance of these our suffering brethren. When the measure of their tears shall be full—when their groans shall have involved Heaven itself in darkness—doubtless a God of justice will awaken to their distress.[69]

In 1788 Jacques Pierre de Warville, a leader in the French Revolution, started an antislavery society and invited Jefferson to become a member. Jefferson declined because he was in France as "a public servant" of America, therefore making it inappropriate for him to undertake something of a personal nature.[70] But he wished hearty blessings on their efforts, reaffirming his private commitment to their goals:

> You know that nobody wishes more ardently to see an abolition not only of the trade but of the condition of slavery, and certainly nobody will be more willing to encounter every sacrifice for that object.[71]

In 1789 the federal Congress took Jefferson's antislavery proposal from 1784 and included it in the Northwest Ordinance, thereby causing Minnesota, Ohio, Michigan, Illinois, Indiana, and Wisconsin to enter the United States as antislavery states.

In 1805, after nearly forty years of efforts to end slavery,

Jefferson bemoaned that it had become a task much more difficult than he had ever imagined, lamenting the national stalemate over the issue:

> I have long since given up the expectation of any early provision for the extinguishment of slavery among us. [While] there are many virtuous men who would make any sacrifices to affect it, many equally virtuous persuade themselves either that the thing is not wrong or that it cannot be remedied.[72]

In 1807 President Jefferson signed a law long anticipated by antislavery citizens across the nation. Article I, Section 9 of the Constitution had included a provision whereby Congress could ban the importation of all slaves after "the year one thousand eight hundred and eight." At the time the Constitution was written and ratified, it was believed that within twenty years, the Southern states would be ready to relinquish slavery, and this law would pave the way.

Jefferson happily signed that law, telling a group of Quakers:

> Whatever may have been the circumstances which influenced our forefathers to permit the introduction of personal bondage into any part of these states . . . we may rejoice that such circumstances and such a sense of them exist no longer. . . . I sincerely pray with you, my friends, that all the members of the human family may, in the time prescribed by the Father of us all, find themselves securely established in the enjoyment of life, liberty, and happiness.[73]

In 1808 President Jefferson sent a message to the Reverend James Lemen, an old friend from Virginia who in 1786 had moved to the Northwest Territory at Jefferson's suggestion to work to ensure that it would be antislavery.[74] Ohio was first organized from that territory, then Indiana—both as antislavery territories. In 1808, when Illinois was on the verge of becoming the third official territory, President Jefferson privately contacted Lemen, who explained:

> I received Jefferson's confidential message on October 10, 1808, suggesting . . . the organization of a church on a strictly anti-slavery basis for the purpose of heading a movement to finally make Illinois a free state. . . . I acted on Jefferson's plan and . . . the anti-slavery element formed a Baptist church . . . on an anti-slavery basis.[75]

In 1814 Jefferson corresponded with Edward Coles, private secretary to President Madison. Coles, a Virginia planter, lamented to Jefferson that he wanted to free his slaves but that Virginia law made it impossible. He then asked Jefferson to head a new antislavery movement, to which Jefferson responded:

> Your [letter] was duly received and was read with peculiar pleasure. . . . Mine on the subject of slavery of Negroes have long since been in possession of the public, and time has only served to give them stronger root. The love of justice and the love of country plead equally the cause of these people, and it is a moral reproach to us that they should have pleaded it so long in vain and should have produced not a single effort—nay, I fear not much serious willingness to relieve them & ourselves from our present condition of moral & political reprobation . . . [but] the hour of emancipation is advancing; in the march of time, it will come.[76]

But citing his advanced age of seventy-one, Jefferson declined to take the helm of the new movement proposed by Coles. He explained,

"This enterprise is for the young—for those who can follow it up and bear it through to its consummation," but he promised that his greatest contributions to the fight would be his fervent "prayers—and these are the only weapons of an old man."[77] He therefore encouraged Coles to take the lead:

> I hope . . . you will come forward in the public councils, become the missionary of this doctrine truly Christian, insinuate & inculcate it softly but steadily through the medium of writing and conversation, associate others in your labors, and when the phalanx [large battalion] is formed, bring on and press the proposition perseveringly until its accomplishment. . . . That your success may be as speedy and complete . . . I shall as fervently and sincerely pray.[78]

Five years later, in 1819, Coles packed up everything, including his slaves, left Virginia, and moved into the "to the country North West of the River Ohio"[79] (recall that in 1789 Congress had adopted Jefferson's 1784 provision to make that territory antislavery). When Coles arrived, he settled in the Illinois territory, emancipated all his slaves, gave them each 160 acres, and then joined with the Reverend James Lemen in his antislavery endeavors. Coles later became governor of Illinois.[80]

In 1815 Jefferson corresponded with the Reverend David Barrow, the Virginian who moved to Kentucky and became a cofounder of the Kentucky Abolition Society. Barrow had penned an antislavery work and sent it to Jefferson, who responded:

> The particular subject of the pamphlet you enclosed me [emancipation] was one of early and tender consideration with me; and had I continued in the councils [legislatures] of my own state, it should never have been out of sight. . . . We are not in

a world ungoverned by the laws and the power of a Superior Agent. Our efforts are in His hand and directed by it; and He will give them their effect in His own time. . . . That it may finally be effected and its progress hastened will be [my] last and fondest prayer.[81]

By 1820 only a little antislavery ground had been gained nationally. In 1789 Congress banned slavery from the Northwest Territory; in 1794 it banned the exportation of slaves from America; in 1808 it banned the importation of slaves into America. But in 1820 Democrats gained control of Congress for the first time. They enacted the Missouri Compromise, thus reversing the 1789 policy and allowing slavery into some federal territories where it had been previously prohibited.[82] For the first time slavery was being not just tolerated but officially expanded by the federal government.

The Missouri Compromise was strenuously opposed by the few Founding Fathers still alive at that time. Elias Boudinot, a president of Congress during the Revolution and a framer of the Bill of Rights, warned that this new pro-slavery direction by Congress would bring "an end to the happiness of the United States;"[83] a frail John Adams feared that lifting the slavery prohibition would destroy America;[84] James Madison confessed that the new policy "fills me with no slight anxiety," and foreseeing what would become the Civil War, he worried that pitting slave states against free states would result in "awful shocks against each other."[85] But perhaps no one from that generation was as greatly distressed as the elderly seventy-seven-year-old Jefferson, who was dismayed, frustrated, and even depressed by the passage of that law and the retreat from emancipation that it represented. He lamented, "In the gloomiest moment of the Revolutionary War, I never had any apprehensions equal to what I feel from this source."[86]

Jefferson confided to a fellow political leader:

I had for a long time ceased to read newspapers or pay any attention to public affairs, confident they were in good hands, and
content to be a passenger in our bark [small ship] to the shore
from which I am not distant [death]. But this momentous question,
like a fire bell in the night, awakened and filled me with terror. I
considered it at once as the knell [funeral bell] of the Union. . . . I
regret that I am now to die in the belief that the useless sacrifice of
themselves by the generation of 1776 to acquire self-government
and happiness to their country is to be thrown away by the unwise
and unworthy passions of their sons. . . . [This is an] act of suicide
on themselves, and of treason against the hopes of the world.[87]

He concluded with a reaffirmation of his desire to end slavery and
his frustration at America not having already done so:

I can say with conscious truth that there is not a man on earth
who would sacrifice more than I would to relieve us from this
heavy reproach in any practicable way. The cession of that kind
of "property," for so it is misnamed, is a bagatelle [an insignificant trifle] which would not cost me a second thought if
in that way a general emancipation and expatriation could be
effected. . . . But as it is, we have the wolf by the ears and we can
neither hold him nor safely let him go.[88]

In 1825 Jefferson corresponded with Frances Wright, a young,
energetic antislavery enthusiast. Frances first met Jefferson in 1824
when the famous American hero French general Marquis de Lafayette
returned to America for his farewell tour, bringing with him Frances,
whom he considered an adopted daughter. When Lafayette returned
to France, Frances stayed behind to become an American citizen and
help fight slavery. She eventually founded Nashoba, Tennessee, as a
model to illustrate Jefferson's plan of emancipation. Writing a very

elderly Jefferson (who would die the next year), she asked him to help her with the effort. Jefferson replied:

> At the age of eighty-two, with one foot in the grave and the other uplifted to follow it, I do not permit myself to take part in any new enterprises, even for bettering the condition of man— not even in the great one which is the subject of your letter and which has been through life that of my greatest anxieties. . . . I leave its accomplishment as the work of another generation, and I am cheered when I see that one on which it is devolved taking it up with so much good will and such minds engaged in its encouragement. The abolition of the evil is not impossible; it ought never therefore to be despaired of. Every plan should be adopted, every experiment tried, which may do something towards the ultimate object.[89]

In 1826, just two weeks before his death, Jefferson reiterated:

> On the question of the lawfulness of slavery (that is, of the right of one man to appropriate to himself the faculties of another without his consent), I certainly retain my early opinions.[90]

With such a clear and unbroken train of words and actions against slavery and in favor of emancipation and civil rights, it is no surprise that previous generations of abolitionists and civil rights leaders regularly invoked Jefferson's words in their own efforts. Sadly, these words and actions are deliberately ignored today by those from all five groups of historical malpractice who decry Jefferson as an unrepentant racist.

But among those early leaders who favorably cited Jefferson was President John Quincy Adams, called the "Hell Hound of Abolition" for his relentless pursuit of that object. In a famous 1837 speech, he told the crowd gathered before him:

The inconsistency of the institution of domestic slavery with the principles of the Declaration of Independence was seen and lamented by all the southern patriots of the Revolution; by no one with deeper and more unalterable conviction than by the author of the Declaration himself [Jefferson]. . . . Such was the undoubting conviction of Jefferson to his dying day. In the *Memoir of His Life*, written at the age of seventy-seven, he gave to his countrymen the solemn and emphatic warning that the day was not distant when they must hear and adopt the general emancipation of their slaves.[91]

Daniel Webster, whose efforts in the US Senate to end slavery paralleled those of John Quincy Adams in the US House, similarly invoked Jefferson in order to bolster his efforts. In 1845 he issued an address to the nation, reminding them:

No language can be more explicit, more emphatic, or more solemn than that in which Thomas Jefferson, from the beginning to the end of his life, uniformly declared his opposition to slavery. "I tremble for my country," said he, "when I reflect that God is just—that His justice cannot sleep forever." "The Almighty has no attribute which can take side with us in such a contest." . . . [T]o show his own view of the proper influence of the spirit of the Revolution upon slavery, he proposed the searching question: "Who can endure toil, famine, stripes, imprisonment, and death itself in vindication of his own liberty, and the next moment . . . inflict on his fellow men a bondage, one hour of which is fraught with more misery than ages of that which he rose in rebellion to oppose?"[92]

Abraham Lincoln likewise cited Jefferson to support his own crusade to end slavery and achieve civil rights and equality for blacks, specifically in 1854, when the Democratically controlled Congress passed the Kansas-Nebraska Act. In 1820, when Congress expanded the federal territories in which slavery was permitted through passage of the Missouri Compromise, they had retained a ban on slavery in the Kansas-Nebraska territory (which included not only Kansas and Nebraska but also Wyoming, Montana, Idaho, North Dakota, and South Dakota). But the 1854 Kansas-Nebraska Act changed those restrictions, allowing slavery into even more territories. Lincoln invoked Jefferson to condemn that act, explaining:

> Mr. Jefferson . . . conceived the idea of taking that occasion to prevent slavery ever going into the northwestern territory . . . and in the first Ordinance (which the acts of Congress were then called) for the government of the territory, provided that slavery should never be permitted therein. . . . Thus, with the author of the Declaration of Independence, the policy of prohibiting slavery in new territory originated. . . . But now [in May 1854], new light breaks upon us. Now Congress declares this [law constructed by Jefferson] ought never to have been.[93]

Black abolitionists, such as Fredrick Douglass also regularly invoked Jefferson to assist their own efforts. Douglass had lived in slavery until he escaped to New York, later going to work for the Massachusetts antislavery society and also serving as a Zion Methodist Church preacher. During the Civil War Douglass helped recruit the first black regiment to fight for the Union and advised Abraham Lincoln on the Emancipation Proclamation. Following the war he received presidential appointments from four Republican presidents. Concerning Jefferson, Douglass declared:

> It was the Sage of the Old Dominion [Virginia] that said—while speaking of the possibility of a conflict between the slaves and

slaveholders—"God has no attribute that could take sides with the oppressor in such a contest. I tremble for my country when I reflect that God is just and that His justice cannot sleep forever." Such is the warning voice of Thomas Jefferson, and every day's experience since its utterance until now confirms its wisdom and commends its truth.[94]

At a speech in Virginia following the Civil War, Douglass declared:

I have been charged with lifelong hostility to one of the cherished institutions of Virginia [i.e., slavery]. I am not ashamed of that lifelong opposition. . . . It was, Virginia, your own Thomas Jefferson that taught me that all men are created equal.[95]

And describing Jefferson's dealings with Banneker, Douglass reminded an audience:

Jefferson was not ashamed to call the black man his brother and to address him as a gentleman.[96]

On numerous other occasions Douglass invoked Jefferson as an authority in his crusade to end slavery and achieve full equality and civil rights.[97] Additional civil rights crusaders who invoked Jefferson in a similarly positive manner included Henry Highland Garnet,[98] Dr. Martin Luther King Jr.,[99] Colin Powell,[100] and others.

Was Jefferson impeccable on race and civil rights? Certainly not. He recognized and admitted that he had some prejudices, but he also openly acknowledged that he wanted to be proven wrong concerning those views. Yet despite his self-acknowledged weaknesses, Jefferson faithfully and consistently advocated for emancipation and civil rights throughout his long life, even when it would have been easier and better for him if he had remained silent or inactive.

Had Jefferson been free from the laws of his own state—that is, had he lived in a state such as Massachusetts, New Hampshire, or Connecticut—he likely would be universally hailed today as a bold civil rights leader, for his efforts and writings would certainly compare favorably to those of great civil rights advocates in the Northern states. In fact, if Jefferson had proposed his various pieces of legislation in those states, they would certainly have passed, and he would have been deemed a national civil rights hero. But his geography and circumstances doomed him to a different fate. Modern writers now refuse to recognize what previous generations openly acknowledged: Jefferson was a bold, staunch, and consistent advocate and defender of emancipation and civil rights.

Thomas Jefferson Advocated a Secular Public Square through the Separation of Church and State

Many of the lies about Jefferson, from education to the Bible, have been made to support one key overarching premise: Jefferson was secular and therefore his overall goal was a public sphere devoid of religion and from which religious expressions had been expunged. Typical of this oft-repeated charge is the claim that "Jefferson's Presidential administration was probably the most purely secular this country has ever had."[1]

But before determining whether Jefferson really was a secularist, it is important to define that term—a term that did not exist until modern times. By definition, *secularist* means:

- holding a system of political or social philosophy that rejects all forms of religious faith and worship

- embracing the view that public education and other matters of civil policy should be conducted without the introduction of a religious element[2]

- having indifference to, or a rejection or exclusion of, religion and religious considerations[3]

- believing that religious considerations should be excluded from civil affairs[4]

From what has thus far been presented from Jefferson's own writings and actions, it is indisputable that he was not a secularist by the first three definitions. And this chapter will demonstrate that Jefferson definitely did not embrace the fourth point, that religious considerations should be excluded from civil affairs.

But for those who maintain otherwise, since they already believe that he was a secularist it is logical to further assert that Jefferson was also the father of the modern separation of church and state doctrine. In fact, they actually believe that Jefferson personally placed the separation of church and state into the First Amendment of the Constitution in order to secure public secularism. Consequently, these modern proponents claim:

> Jefferson can probably best be considered the founding father of separation of church and state.[5]

> Jefferson . . . is responsible for the precursor to the First Amendment that is almost universally interpreted as the constitutional justification for the separation of church and state.[6]

> [T]he First Amendment was Jefferson's top priority.[7]

> Thomas Jefferson—the Father of the First Amendment.[8]

Others similarly claim that Jefferson is responsible for the First Amendment,[9] and many modern courts also espouse this position—a trend that began in 1947 when the US Supreme Court asserted:

> This Court has previously recognized that the provisions of the First Amendment, in the drafting and adoption of which . . . Jefferson played such [a] leading role.[10]

In subsequent cases the Court even described Jefferson was indeed "the architect of the First Amendment."[11] So firmly does the Court believe this that, in the six decades following its 1947 announcement, in *every* case addressing the removal of religious expressions from the public square it used Jefferson either directly or indirectly as its authority.[12]

Interestingly, however, the current heavy reliance on Jefferson as the primary constitutional voice on religion and the First Amendment is a modern phenomenon *not* a historic practice.[13] Why? Because previous generations knew American history well enough to know better than to invoke Jefferson in such a manner.

Two centuries ago a Jefferson supporter penned a work foreshadowing modern claims by declaring Jefferson to be a leading constitutional influence. When Jefferson read that claim, he promptly instructed the author to correct that mistake, telling him:

> One passage in the paper you enclosed me must be corrected. It is the following, "and all say it was yourself more than any other individual, that planned and established it," i.e., the Constitution.[14]

What did Jefferson see wrong in stating the very claim repeated today? He bluntly explained:

> I was in Europe when the Constitution was planned and never saw it till after it was established.[15]

A simple fact unknown or ignored by many of today's writers and scholars is that Jefferson did *not* participate in framing the Constitution. He was not even in America when it was framed; so how could he be considered a primary influence on it? And he was also out of the country when the First Amendment and Bill of Rights were framed. As he openly acknowledged:

On receiving [the Constitution while in France], I wrote strongly to Mr. Madison, urging the want of provision [lack of provision] for the freedom of religion, freedom of the press, trial by jury, habeas corpus, the substitution of militia for a standing army, and an express reservation to the States of all rights not specifically granted to the Union. . . . *This is all the hand I had in what related to the Constitution.*[16] (emphasis added)

Jefferson's only role with the Constitution was to broadly call for a general Bill of Rights. While this is no insignificant thing, it was the same action taken by dozens of other Founders. So how can Jefferson be the father of the First Amendment if he never saw it until months after it was finished? Significantly, there were fifty-five individuals who framed the Constitution at the Constitutional Convention and ninety in the first federal Congress who framed the Bill of Rights; Jefferson was among neither group.

So why have so many courts and modern writers made him the singular go-to expert on religion clauses from documents in which he had no direct involvement? Why has he been given a position of "expert" that he himself properly refused? It is because he penned a letter containing the eight-word phrase "a wall of separation between church and state." Courts and modern scholars have found that simple phrase, when divorced from its context, useful in providing the appearance of historical approval for their own efforts to secularize the public square.

Historically speaking, Jefferson was a latecomer to the separation phrase. The famous metaphor so often attributed to him was introduced in the 1500s by prominent ministers in England. And throughout the 1600s it was carried to America by Bible-oriented colonists who planted it deeply in the thinking of Americans, all long before Jefferson ever repeated it. So what was the historic origin of that now-famous phrase?

Jefferson was familiar with the writings of the Reverends John Wise, Joseph Priestly, and many others who divided the history of Christianity into three periods. [17] In Peroid I (called the Age of Purity), the followers of Jesus did just as He had taught them and retained Bible teaching uncorrupted. In Period II (the Age of Corruption), State leaders declared themselves also to be the Church leaders and seized control of the Church, assimilating it into the State and thus merging the two previously separate institutions into one. But in Period III (the Age of Reformation), Bible-centered leaders began loudly calling for reinstating the Bible-ordained separation between the two entities.

In the Scriptures, God had placed Moses over civil affairs and Aaron over spiritual ones. The nation was one, but the jurisdictions were two with separate leaders over each. In 2 Chronicles 26, when King Uzziah attempted to assume the duties of both State and Church, God Himself weighed in; He sovereignly and instantly struck down Uzziah, thus reaffirming the separation He had placed between the two institutions.

Period III Christian ministers understood these Biblical precedents and urged a return to the original model. As early Methodist bishop Charles Galloway affirmed:

> The miter and the crown should never encircle the same brow.
> The crozier and the scepter should never be wielded by the same hand. [18]

Of the four items specifically mentioned—the miter, crown, crozier, and scepter—two reference the Church and two the State. Concerning the Church, the miter was the headgear worn by the high priest in Jewish times (see Exodus 28:3–4, 35–37) and later by popes, cardinals, and bishops. The crozier was the shepherd's crook carried by Church officials during special ceremonies. Pertaining to the State, the crown was the symbol of authority placed upon the heads of kings, and the scepter was held in their hand as an emblem of their extensive power (see the book of Esther). Therefore, the metaphor that "the miter and the crown should never encircle the same brow" meant that the same person should not be the head of the Church and the head of the State. Galloway's declaration that "the crozier and the scepter should never be wielded by the same hand" meant that authority over the Church and authority over the State should never be given to the same individual.

Galloway's phrases not only provided clear and easily understandable visual pictures, but also referenced specific historical incidents—as when Period II Roman Emperor Otto III (980–1002 AD) constructed his king's crown to fit atop the miter worn by Church officials.[19] This type of jurisdictional blending had been common in England before American colonization, as when the English Parliament passed civil laws stipulating who could take communion in the church or who could be a minister of the Gospel, thus governmentally controlling what should have been purely ecclesiastical matters.[20]

It is important to note that it was not secular civil leaders who emphasized a separation of the Church from the control of the State but rather Bible-based ministers. In fact, it was English Reformation clergyman Reverend Richard Hooker who first used the phrase during the reign of England's King Henry VIII, calling for a "separation of . . . Church and Commonwealth."[21] (Recall that Henry had wanted a divorce, but when the Church refused to give it, he simply started his own national church—the Anglican Church—and gave himself a divorce under his new state-established doctrines.[22])

Other Bible-centered ministers also spoke out against the intrusion of the State into the jurisdiction of the Church, including the Reverend John Greenwood (1556–1593) who started the church attended by many of the Pilgrims when they still lived in England.

Queen Elizabeth was head over both the State and the Church at that time, but Greenwood asserted "that there could be but one head to the church and that head was *not* the Queen, but Christ!"[23] He was eventually executed for "denying Her Majesty's ecclesiastical supremacy and attacking the existing ecclesiastical order."[24]

Then, when Parliament passed a law requiring that if "any of her Majesty's subjects deny the Queen's ecclesiastical supremacy . . . they shall be committed to prison without bail,"[25] most of the Pilgrims fled from England to Holland. From Holland they went to America where they boldly advocated separation of church and state, affirming that government had no right to "compel religion, to plant churches by power, and to force a submission to ecclesiastical government by laws and penalties."[26]

Many other reformation-minded ministers and colonists traveling from Europe to America also openly advocated the institutional separation of State and Church, including the Reverends Roger Williams (1603–1683),[27] John Wise (1652–1725),[28] William Penn (1614–1718),[29] and many others. In fact, they often did so in language even more articulate than the original Reformers.[30]

The entire history of the separation doctrine centered around preventing the State from taking control of the Church, and meddling with or controlling its doctrines or punishing its religious expressions. Throughout history, it had not been the Church that had seized the State but just the opposite. Furthermore, the separation doctrine had never been used to secularize the public square. As affirmed by early Quaker leader Will Wood, "The separation of Church and State does not mean the exclusion of God, righteousness, morality, from the State."[31]

Early Methodist bishop Charles Galloway agreed: "The separation of the Church from the State did not mean the severance of the State from God, or of the nation from Christianity."[32]

The philosophy of keeping the State limited and at arm's length from regulating or punishing religious practices and expressions was planted deeply into American thinking. Eventually, it was nationally enshrined in the First Amendment, which states, "Congress shall make no law respecting an establishment of religion, or prohibiting the Free Exercise thereof."

The first part of the Amendment is now called the establishment clause and the latter part, the free exercise clause. The language of both is clear; and both clauses were pointed solely at the State not the Church. Notice that the establishment clause prohibited the *State* from enforcing religious conformity, and the free exercise clause ensured that the *State* would protect—rather than suppress, as it currently does—citizens' rights of conscience and religious expression. Both clauses are prohibitions only on the power of *Congress* (i.e., the government), not on religious individuals or organizations.

This was the meaning of "separation of church and state" with which Jefferson was intimately familiar, and it was this interpretation, and not the modern perversion of it, that he repeatedly reaffirmed in his writings and practices. This is especially evident in his famous letter containing the separation phrase. Consider the background of that letter and why Jefferson wrote it.

When Jefferson, the head of the Anti-Federalists, became president in 1801, his election was particularly well received by Baptists. This political disposition was understandable, for from the early settlement of Rhode Island in the 1630s to the time of the writing of the federal Constitution in 1787, the Baptists had often found their free exercise limited by state-established government power. Baptist ministers had often been beaten, imprisoned, and even faced death by those from the government church,[33] so it was not surprising that they strongly opposed centralized government power. For this reason the predominately Baptist state of Rhode Island refused to send delegates to the Constitutional Convention;[34] and the Baptists were the only denomination in which a majority of its clergy across the nation voted against the ratification of the Constitution.[35]

Jefferson's election as an Anti-Federalist opposed to a strong central government elated the Baptists. They were very familiar with Jefferson's record not only of disestablishing the official church in Virginia but also of championing the cause of religious freedom for Baptists and other denominations.[36] Not surprisingly, therefore, he received numerous letters of congratulations from Baptist organizations.[37]

One of them was penned on October 7, 1801, by the Baptist Association of Danbury, Connecticut. Their letter began with an expression of gratitude to God for Jefferson's election followed by prayers of blessing for him. They then expressed grave concern over the proposed government protections for their free exercise. As they explained:

> Our sentiments are uniformly on the side of religious liberty— that religion is at all times and places a matter between God and individuals; that no man ought to suffer in name, person, or effects on account of his religious opinions; that the legitimate power of civil government extends no further than to punish the man who works ill to his neighbor. But sir, our constitution of government is not specific. . . . Religion is considered as the first object of legislation and therefore what religious privileges we enjoy (as a minor part of the State) we enjoy as favors granted and not as inalienable rights.[38]

These ministers were troubled that their "religious privileges" were being guaranteed by the apparent generosity of government.

Many citizens today do not grasp their concern. Why would ministers object to the State guaranteeing their enjoyment of religious privileges? Because to the far-sighted Danbury Baptists, the mere presence of governmental language protecting their free exercise of religion suggested that it had become a government-granted right (and thus alienable) rather than a God-given one (and hence inalienable). Fearing that the inclusion of such language in governing documents might someday cause the government wrongly to believe that since it had "granted" the freedom of religious expression it therefore had the authority to regulate it, the Danbury Baptists had strenuously objected. They believed that government should not interfere with any public religious expression unless, as they told Jefferson, that religious practice caused someone to genuinely "work ill to his neighbor."[39]

The Danbury Baptists were writing to Jefferson fully understanding that he was an ally of their viewpoint, not an adversary of it. After all, three years earlier in his famous Kentucky Resolution of 1798 Jefferson had already emphatically declared:

[N]o power over the freedom of religion . . . [is] delegated to the United States by the Constitution [the First Amendment].[40]

Jefferson believed that the federal government had *no* authority to interfere with, limit, regulate, or prohibit public religious expressions—a position he repeated on many subsequent occasions:

In matters of religion I have considered that its free exercise is placed by the Constitution independent of the powers of the general [federal] government.[41]

[O]ur excellent Constitution . . . has not placed our religious rights under the power of any public functionary.[42]

None of these or any other statements of Jefferson contain even the slightest suggestion that religion should be removed from the public square or that the square should be secularized, but rather only that the government could not limit or regulate it—which is what had concerned the Danbury Baptists. Understanding this, Jefferson replied to them on January 1, 1802, assuring them that they had nothing to fear: the government would not meddle with their religious expressions.

> Believing with you that religion is a matter which lies solely between man and his God; that he owes account to none other for his faith or his worship; that the legislative powers of government reach actions only and not opinions; I contemplate with sovereign reverence that act of the whole American people which declared that their legislature should "make no law respecting an establishment of religion or prohibiting the free exercise thereof," thus building a wall of separation between Church and State. Adhering to this expression of the supreme will of the nation in behalf of the rights of conscience, I shall see with sincere satisfaction the progress of those sentiments which tend to restore to man all his natural rights, convinced he has no natural right in opposition to his social duties. I reciprocate your kind prayers for the protection and blessing of the common Father and Creator of man, and tender you, for yourselves and your religious association, assurances of my high respect and esteem.[43]

The separation metaphor was a phrase already commonly used and well understood by the government-oppressed Baptists and their ministers, and Jefferson used it to assure them that the government would protect rather than impede their religious beliefs and expressions. As James Adams noted:

> Jefferson's reference to a "wall of separation between Church and State" . . . was not formulating a secular principle to banish religion from the public arena. Rather he was trying to keep government from darkening the doors of Church.[44]

The first occasion in which the US Supreme Court invoked the separation metaphor from Jefferson's letter was in 1878 when the Court affirmed that the purpose of separation was to protect rather than limit public religious expressions.[45] In fact, after reprinting lengthy portions of Jefferson's letter and reviewing its general prohibition against federal intrusion into religious beliefs and the free exercise of religion, the Court concluded:

> [I]t [Jefferson's letter] may be accepted almost as an authoritative declaration of the scope and effect of the Amendment thus secured. Congress was deprived of all legislative power over mere [religious] opinion, but was left free to reach actions which were in violation of social duties or subversive of good order.[46]

Then to affirm Jefferson's point that there were only a handful of religious expressions against which the federal government could legitimately interfere, the Court quoted from his famous Virginia Statute to establish that:

> [T]he rightful purposes of civil government are for its officers to interfere when principles break out into overt acts against peace and good order. In th[is] . . . is found the true distinction between what properly belongs to the Church and what to the State.[47]

Notice that in Jefferson's view, the only religious expressions that the government could hamper were acts "against peace and good order," "injurious to others," acts "subversive of good order," or acts by "the man who works ill to his neighbor."

That Court (and others[48]) then identified a handful of actions that, if perpetrated in the name of religion, the government did have legitimate reason to limit, including bigamy, concubinage, incest, child sacrifice, infanticide, parricide, and other similar crimes. But the government was *not* to impede traditional religious expressions in public, such as public prayer, public display of religious symbols, public use of Scriptures, acknowledgement of God in public events, and so on. In short, the separation of Church and State existed not to remove or secularize the free exercise of religion but rather to preserve and protect it, regardless of whether it was exercised in private or public.

This was the universal understanding of separation of Church and State—until the Court's landmark ruling in 1947 in *Everson v. Board of Education* in which it announced it would reverse this historic meaning.[49] In that case the Court cited only Jefferson's eight-word separation metaphor, completely severing the phrase from its historical context and the rest of Jefferson's clearly worded letter, and then expressed for the first time that the phrase existed not to protect religion in the public square but to remove it.

The next year, in 1948, the Court repeated its rhetoric of the previous year declaring:

> [T]he First Amendment has erected a wall between Church and State which must be kept high and impregnable.[50]

The Court again refused to reference Jefferson's full (and short) letter, and it again applied Jefferson's eight-word phrase in a religiously hostile manner, using it to enforce an ardent public secularism.

Amazingly, in that case the Court had ruled that a school in Illinois had made the egregious mistake of allowing voluntary religious activities by students, a practice that had characterized American education for the previous three centuries. The permitted religious activity had actually been so voluntary that students were allowed to participate only with the written consent of their parents.[51] But an atheist had objected not to what her own children were doing with religious expressions but to what other parents were letting their children do—attend a voluntary religious class. The Court therefore struck down those individual voluntary activities, demanding that the school remain aggressively and rigidly secular. It ruled that the school should no longer permit the constitutionally guaranteed free exercise of religion even for those who wished to enjoy it. For the first time the separation metaphor had become a rigid, callous phrase no longer allowing or accommodating voluntary religious activities in a public setting. The result of the Court's twisting of Jefferson's phrase was that the First Amendment was no longer a prohibition on the government but rather on individuals.

Courts have subsequently pushed that original misinterpretation of separation increasingly outward to the point where they have decided the First Amendment's injunction that "*Congress* shall make no law respecting an establishment of religion or prohibiting the free exercise thereof" now means:

- an *individual* student may not say a voluntary prayer at a football game,[52] graduation,[53] or any other school event[54]

- *cadets* at military academies may not engage in offering voluntary prayers over their meals[55]

- *a choir* may not sing a religious song as part of a school concert[56]

- *a school* may not place a Bible in a classroom library[57]

- *an individual student* may not write a research paper on a religious topic,[58] draw religious artwork in an art class,[59] or carry his personal Bible onto school grounds[60]

Significantly, none of these activities pertains to "Congress making a law," which is the *only* body and the *only* activity proscribed by the First Amendment. But ignoring that succinct stricture, the modern misapplication of the historic separation doctrine now routinely results in egregious decisions:

- A state employee in Minnesota was barred from parking his car in the state parking lot because he had a religious sticker on his bumper.[61]

- A five-year-old kindergarten student in Saratoga Springs, New York, was forbidden to say a prayer over her lunch and was scolded by a teacher for doing so.[62]

- A military honor guardsman was removed from his position for saying, "God bless you and this family, and God bless the United States of America" while presenting a folded flag to a family during a military funeral—a statement that the family requested be made at the funeral.[63]

- Senior citizens meeting at a community senior center in Balch Springs, Texas, were prohibited from praying over their own meals.[64]

- A library employee in Russellville, Kentucky, was barred from wearing her necklace because it had a small cross on it.[65]

- College students serving as residential assistants in Eu Claire, Wisconsin, were prohibited from holding Bible studies in their own private dorm rooms.[66]

- A third grader in Orono, Maine, who wore a T-shirt containing the words "Jesus Christ" was required to turn the shirt inside out so the words could not be seen.[67]

- A school official in Saint Louis, Missouri, caught an elementary student praying over his lunch; he lifted the student from his seat, reprimanded him in front of the other students, and took him to the principal, who ordered him to stop praying.[68]

- In cities in Texas, Indiana, Ohio, Georgia, Kansas, Michigan, Pennsylvania, California, Nebraska, and elsewhere citizens were not permitted to hand out religious literature on public sidewalks or preach in public areas and were actually arrested or threatened with arrest for doing so.[69]

And there are literally hundreds of similar examples.[70]

Is this what Jefferson intended? Did he want to prohibit citizens from expressing their faith publically? Was he truly a secularist who wanted a stridently religion-free public square? His words certainly do not indicate this to be his desire; but how about his actions? After all, actions speak louder than words.

Jefferson's actions in this area are completely consistent with his words. He has an extremely long and consistent record of deliberately and intentionally including rather than excluding religious expressions and activities in the public arena.

For example, in 1773, following the Boston Tea Party protest against oppressive British policy, Parliament retaliated with the Boston Port Bill to blockade the harbor and eliminate its trade, thus hoping to financially cripple the Americans and force them into submission. The blockade was to take effect on June 1, 1774. Upon hearing of this Jefferson introduced a measure in the Virginia legislature calling for a public day of fasting and prayer to be observed on that same day "devoutly to implore the Divine interposition in behalf of an injured and oppressed people"[71] He also recommended that legislators "proceed with the Speaker and the Mace to the Church . . . and that the Reverend Mr. Price be appointed to read prayers, and the Reverend Mr. Gwatkin to preach a sermon suitable to the occasion."[72] Additionally, Jefferson wrote home to his local church community in Monticello urging them also to arrange a special day of prayer and worship at "the new church on Hardware River"[73]—a service which Jefferson attended.[74]

In 1776, while serving in the Continental Congress, he was placed on a committee of five to draft the Declaration of Independence. He was the principal author of that document, and he incorporated four explicit, open acknowledgments of God, some made by his own hand and some added by Congress. Jefferson's Declaration was actually a dual declaration: of independence from Great Britain and dependence on God.

On July 4, 1776, Jefferson was placed on a committee of three to draft an official seal for the new American government. His recommendation was from the Bible: "The children of Israel in the wilderness, led by a cloud by day, and a pillar of fire by night."[75]

In 1779 Jefferson became the governor of Virginia and introduced several bills into the state legislature, including:

- A Bill for Punishing Disturbers of Religious Worship and Sabbath Breakers[76]

- A Bill for Appointing Days of Public Fasting and Thanksgiving[77]

- A Bill Annulling Marriages Prohibited by the Levitical Law and Appointing the Mode of Solemnizing Lawful Marriage[78]

- A Bill for Saving the Property of the Church Heretofore by Law Established[79]

Jefferson personally penned the language for each proposal, and there was no hint of public secularism in any of them; instead, it was just the opposite. For example, Jefferson's bill for preserving the Sabbath stipulated:

If any person on Sunday shall himself be found laboring at his own or any other trade or calling . . . except that it be in the ordinary household offices of daily necessity or other work of necessity or charity, he shall forfeit the sum of ten shillings for every such offence.[80]

His bill for public days of prayer declared:

[T]he power of appointing Days of Public Fasting and Thanksgiving may be exercised by the Governor. . . . Every minister of the Gospel shall, on each day so to be appointed, attend and perform Divine service and preach a sermon or discourse suited to the occasion in his church, on pain of forfeiting fifty pounds for every failure, not having a reasonable excuse.[81]

His bill for protecting marriage stipulated:

Marriages prohibited by the Levitical law shall be null; and persons marrying contrary to that prohibition and cohabitating as man and wife, convicted thereof in the General Court, shall be [fined] from time to time until they separate.[82]

Jefferson also introduced a Bill for Establishing General Courts in Virginia, requiring:

Every person so commissioned . . . [shall] take the following oath of office, to wit, "You shall swear. . . . So help you God."[83]

Clearly, Jefferson introduced many religious activities directly into civil law.

In 1780, while still serving as governor, Jefferson ordered that an official state medal be created with the religious motto "Rebellion to Tyrants is Obedience to God."[84] This phrase had been proposed to Congress in 1776 as part of the new national seal,[85] and Jefferson also placed it on his own personal seal.[86]

In 1789 Thomas Jefferson began his federal career as secretary of state to President George Washington. One of his early assignments was to oversee the layout and construction of Washington, DC.[87] The plan for the city was approved by Jefferson in 1791, and in 1793 construction began on permanent federal buildings such as the White House and the Capitol. Work proceeded rapidly, and by 1795 the structure had progressed far enough that Secretary Jefferson approved a special activity in the Capitol that was still under construction. Newspapers as far away as Boston happily reported:

City of Washington, June 19. It is with much pleasure that we discover the rising consequence of our infant city. Public worship is now regularly administered at the Capitol, every Sunday morning at 11 o'clock, by the Reverend Mr. Ralph.[88]

From 1797 to 1801 Jefferson served as vice president of the United States under President John Adams. During that time, on November 22, 1800, Congress moved into the new Capitol. Two weeks later, on December 4, 1800, with Theodore Sedgwick presiding over the House and Vice President Thomas Jefferson presiding over the US Senate, Congress approved a plan whereby Christian church services would be held each Sunday in the Hall of the House of Representatives,[89] the largest room in the Capitol building. The spiritual leadership for each Sunday's service would alternate between the chaplain of the House and the chaplain of the Senate, who would either personally conduct the service or invite an outside minister to preach.

It was in this most recognizable of all government buildings, the US Capitol, that Vice President Jefferson attended church.[90] This was a practice he continued throughout his two terms as president.[91] In fact, US congressman Manasseh Cutler, who also attended church at the Capitol, affirmed that "[h]e [Jefferson] and his family have constantly attended public worship in the Hall."[92] Mary Bayard Smith, another attendee at the Capitol services, confirmed, "Mr. Jefferson during his whole administration, was a most regular attendant."[93] She even noted that Jefferson had a designated seat at the Capitol church: "The seat he chose the first Sabbath, and the adjoining one, which his private secretary occupied, were ever afterwards by the courtesy of the congregation left for him and his secretary."[94]

For those services Jefferson rode his horse from the White House to the Capitol,[95] a distance of 1.6 miles and a trip of about twenty minutes. He made this ride regardless of weather conditions. Among Representative Cutler's entries is one noting that "[i]t was very rainy, but his [Jefferson's] ardent zeal brought him through the rain and on horseback to the Hall."[96] Other diary entries similarly confirm Jefferson's faithful attendance despite bad weather.[97]

President Jefferson personally contributed to the worship atmosphere of the Capitol church by having the Marine Band play at the services.[98] According to attendee Margaret Bayard Smith, the band, clad in their scarlet uniforms, made a "dazzling appearance" as they played from the gallery, providing instrumental accompaniment for the singing.[99] However, good as they were, they seemed too ostentatious for the services and "the attendance of the Marine Band was soon discontinued."[100]

Under President Jefferson Sunday church services were also started at the War Department and the Treasury Department,[101] which were two government buildings under his direct control. Therefore, on any given Sunday, worshippers could choose between attending church at the US Capitol, the War Department, or the Treasury Department, all with the blessing and support of Jefferson.

Why was Jefferson such a faithful participant at the Capitol church? He once explained to a friend while they were walking to church together:

No nation has ever yet existed or been governed without religion—nor can be. The Christian religion is the best religion that has been given to man and I, as Chief Magistrate of this nation, am bound to give it the sanction of my example.[102]

By 1867 the church in the Capitol had become the largest church in Washington.[103]

Other presidential actions of Jefferson include:

- Urging the commissioners of the District of Columbia to sell land for the construction of a Roman Catholic Church, recognizing "the advantages of every kind which it would promise" (1801)[104]

- Writing a letter to Constitution signer and penman Gouverneur Morris (then serving as a US senator) describing America as a Christian nation, telling him that "we are already about the 7th of the Christian nations in population, but holding a higher place in substantial abilities" (1801)[105]

- Signing federal acts setting aside government lands so that missionaries might be assisted in "propagating the Gospel" among the Indians (1802, and again in 1803 and 1804)[106]

- Directing the secretary of war to give federal funds to a religious school established for Cherokees in Tennessee (1803)[107]

- Negotiating and signing a treaty with the Kaskaskia Indians that directly funded Christian missionaries and provided federal funding to help erect a church building in which they might worship (1803)[108]

- Assuring a Christian school in the newly purchased Louisiana Territory that it would enjoy "the patronage of the government" (1804)[109]

- Renegotiating and deleting from a lengthy clause in the 1797 United States treaty with Tripoli[110] the portion that had stated "the United States is in no sense founded on the Christian religion" (1805)[111]

- Passing "An Act for Establishing the Government of the Armies" in which:

  > It is earnestly recommended to all officers and soldiers diligently to attend Divine service; and all officers who shall behave indecently or irreverently at any place of Divine worship shall, if commissioned officers, be brought before a general court martial, there to be publicly and severely *reprimanded by the President* [Jefferson]; if non-commissioned officers or soldiers, every person so offending shall [be fined][112] (1806) (emphasis added)

- Declaring that religion is "deemed in other countries incompatible with good government, and yet proved by our experience to be its best support"[113] (1807)

- Closing presidential documents with the appellation, "In the year of our Lord Christ"[114] (1801–1809; see inset)

There are many additional examples, and they all clearly demonstrate that Jefferson has *no* record of attempting to secularize the public square. Furthermore, all of his religious activities at the federal level occurred after the First Amendment had been adopted, showing that he saw no violation of the First Amendment in any of his actions. In fact, no one did—not even his enemies. No one ever raised a voice of dissent against Jefferson's federal religious practices; no one claimed that they were improper or that they violated the Constitution.

The only voice of objection ever raised was to complain that President Jefferson, unlike his predecessors George Washington and John Adams, did not issue any national prayer proclamations. This absence of a national prayer proclamation by Jefferson is cited by critics today as definitive proof of Jefferson's public secularism.

For example, Supreme Court Justices William Brennan and Thurgood Marshall noted in *Marsh v. Chambers* that:

> Thomas Jefferson . . . during [his] respective terms as President, refused on Establishment Clause [First Amendment] grounds to declare national days of thanksgiving or fasting.[115]

Justice Anthony Kennedy similarly noted in *Allegheny v. ACLU*:

> In keeping with his strict views of the degree of separation mandated by the Establishment Clause, Thomas Jefferson declined to follow this tradition [of issuing national proclamations].[116]

Yet these justices are completely wrong. Jefferson himself pointedly stated that his refusal to issue national prayer proclamations was not because of any First Amendment scruples about religion but rather because of his specific views of Federalism—that the Constitution specifically limited the federal government but not the states or other government entities. He explained:

I consider the government of the United States [the federal government] as interdicted [prohibited] by the Constitution from intermeddling with religious institutions, their doctrines, discipline, or exercises. This results not only from the provision that "no law shall be made respecting the establishment or free exercise of religion" [the First Amendment], but from that also which reserves to the states the powers not delegated to the United States [the Tenth Amendment]. Certainly, no power to prescribe any religious exercise or to assume authority in religious discipline has been delegated to the general [federal] government. It must then rest with the states, as far as it can be in any human authority. But it is only proposed that I should *recommend*, not prescribe [require] a day of fasting and prayer. . . . I am aware that the practice of my predecessors may be quoted. But I have ever believed that the example of state executives [governors issuing prayer proclamations] led to the assumption of that authority by the general government [the president issuing prayer proclamations] without due examination, which would have discovered that what might be a right in a state government was a violation of that right when assumed by another.[117]

Jefferson made very clear that his refusal to issue federal prayer proclamations did not spring from any concerns over religious expressions in general but rather only from his view of federalism and which was the proper governmental jurisdiction. He believed that there was a limitation on the federal government's ability to direct the states in which religious activities they could or should participate in, but he saw no such limitations on state or local governments. Actively encouraging public religious activities for citizens was well within their jurisdiction and completely appropriate and constitutional.

Because of his understanding of federalism, Jefferson refused to issue a presidential call for prayer, but he had certainly done so as a state leader. In addition to his 1774 Virginia legislative call for prayer,[118] he called his fellow Virginians to a time of prayer and thanksgiving while serving as governor in 1779, asking the people to give thanks "that He hath diffused the glorious light of the Gospel, whereby through the merits of our gracious Redeemer we may become the heirs of the eternal glory."[119]

He also asked Virginians to pray "that He would grant to His church the plentiful effusions of Divine grace and pour out his Holy Spirit on all ministers on the Gospel; that He would bless and prosper the means of education and spread the light of Christian knowledge through the remotest corners of the earth."[120]

And Jefferson had personally penned the state bill "Appointing Days of Public Fasting and Thanksgiving." He clearly was not opposed to official prayer proclamations, but he believed that this function was within the jurisdiction of governors, not presidents. Certainly, presidents before and after Jefferson did not agree with this view and regularly issued federal prayer proclamations, but the evidence shows that Jefferson's refusal to do so was not because of any notion of secularism on his part but rather because of his view of federalism.

Jefferson's record of including, advocating, and promoting religious activities and expressions in public is strong, clear, and consistent. He did not support a secular public square. The institutional separation of Church and State so highly praised by today's civil libertarians did not originate from Jefferson or even from secularists—nor did it have societal secularization as its object. To the contrary, it was the product of Bible teachings and Christian ministers. Its object was the protection of religious activities and expressions whether in public or private.

Jefferson's words and actions unequivocally demonstrate that he was not "a secular humanist,"[121] nor did he in any manner seek to secularize the public square. This is simply another of the many modern Jefferson lies that has no basis in history.

LIE # 6

Thomas Jefferson Detested the Clergy

Some claim that Jefferson had a dislike of Christian clergy and that this dislike was yet one more manifestation of his overall hostility to religion. They say:

> [H]e detested the entire clergy, regarding them as a worthless class living like parasites upon the labors of others.[1]

> Thomas Jefferson, in fact, was fiercely anti-cleric.[2]

> "The clergy" were one of his enemies who were trying to keep him from being elected President. Surely they would have wanted a devout, God-fearing Christian to be elected! So this is one more proof of Jefferson's religious beliefs.[3]

> Some of the Framers of the Constitution were anti-clerical— Thomas Jefferson, for example.[4]

By now, we have covered enough original source material from Jefferson to make these claims laughably, obviously incorrect. But let us proceed to put the final nails in the coffin of this lie and lay it permanently to rest. Of course, as noted in the last chapter, with the fact that Jefferson was *not* a framer of the Constitution despite what writers such as Austin Cline, the author of the latter quote and a leader in prominent secularist groups, continue wrongly to assert.

But notwithstanding that glaring historical inaccuracy, was Jefferson indeed anticlerical?

To unequivocally put this question to bed, it is important to place Jefferson within his own time rather than that of today, avoiding the mistakes that occur when Modernism is applied to historical inquiry.

Throughout the Colonial, Revolutionary, and early Federal periods, organized political parties were nonexistent. The people were divided as Whigs and Tories, Patriots and Loyalists, Monarchists and Republicans, but there was no political party affiliation. This changed during the administration of President George Washington. Widely differing viewpoints on the scope and power of the federal government emerged among his leadership. Individuals such as Secretary of Treasury Alexander Hamilton and Vice President John Adams sought for increased federal power, while others, such as Secretary of State Thomas Jefferson and Attorney General Edmund Jennings Randolph, sought for limited federal power.

Those led by Adams and Hamilton coalesced into what became known as the Federalist Party; those led by Jefferson coalesced into the Anti-Federalist Party. Anti-Federalists were also known as Republicans and then as Democratic-Republicans; by the time of Andrew Jackson, they had become the Democrats. The Northern colonies and New England provided the strongest base of support for the Federalists while the strength of the Anti-Federalists was from Pennsylvania southward. The Federalists tended to be stronger in populous areas already accustomed to more government at numerous levels. The Anti-Federalists were generally stronger in rural areas where people were more lightly governed.

Jefferson observed that those in the Northern regions had many good traits; they were "cool, sober, laborious, persevering . . . jealous of their own liberties and just to those of others" while those in the south had many negative traits, including being "voluptuary, indolent, unsteady, . . . zealous for their own liberties but trampling on those of others."[5] But Jefferson saw the religious characteristics of the two regions as generally reversed: "[I]n the north they are . . . chicaning, superstitious, and hypocritical in their religion" while "in the south they are . . . candid, without attachment or pretentions to any religion but that of the heart."[6] Religion was definitely important in all regions of early America, but as Jefferson noted, there was indeed a clear difference in the way it was practiced in Federalist and Anti-Federalist regions.

In the more populated North, churches abounded and participation was convenient; citizens were therefore frequent and regular in their attendance. John Adams, like so many others in New England, described himself as a "church-going animal."[7] The pastors of New England had frequent contact with their parishioners throughout the week and held much influence in the community.

With sparser population southward, churches were fewer and more distant from each other. Participation often required deliberate effort. For George Washington to attend church each Sunday, as was his habit, was a full day commitment. It was typically a two- to three-hour ride on horseback or carriage to his church ten miles from Mt. Vernon. A two-hour service was common, and the return ride home took another few hours, thus consuming the entire day. Ministers in the South were just as important as in the North, but they had fewer opportunities to influence their parishioners.

The presidential election of 1800 was America's first real partisan political contest, pitting Jefferson the Anti-Federalist against Adams the Federalist. New Englanders were fiercely loyal to their Federalist hero, John Adams; those southward strongly supported their Anti-Federalist champion, Thomas Jefferson. The campaign was vicious—probably the most venomous in American history with the Federalists taking a much nastier approach in their attacks against Jefferson than the Anti-Federalists did against Adams.

For example, Jefferson was accused by Federalist critics not only of being anti-Christian but also of being a murderer, an atheist, a thief, and a cohort of foreign convicts. It was reported that he was secretly plotting the destruction and overthrow of the Constitution. He was accused of defrauding a widow and her children. The nation was alerted that he planned to abolish the navy and starve the farmers, and citizens were warned that if Jefferson were elected, he would confiscate and burn every Bible in America.[8] This latter charge was so widely disseminated that in New England Bibles were actually buried upon Jefferson's election so that he could not find and burn them.[9]

Since one of the quickest ways to vilify and ostracize a person in New England was to claim that he was antireligious or lacked morals, Federalist ministers regularly accused Jefferson of both. Some of the most vicious attacks against him actually came from such ministers who preached notable sermons about him—sermons often containing blatant lies, gross distortions, and vile misrepresentations.

But John Adams was not exempted from similarly ill-intentioned attacks; he also was maligned and misrepresented by his Anti-Federalist opponents. Years later he recounted the maltreatment he had suffered to his close friend and fellow signer of the Declaration, Benjamin Rush:

> If I am to judge by the newspapers and pamphlets that have been printed in America for twenty years past, I should think that both parties believed me the meanest villain in the world.[10]

But however fierce the attacks on Adams, those on Jefferson were much more despicable. Regardless of what Jefferson said or did concerning religion, no matter how innocent or honest his actions or words might be, they were spun negatively and used against him by his enemies, especially by Federalist clergymen.

The Reverend Cotton Mather Smith of Connecticut provides an excellent example. Smith had served as a military chaplain during the American Revolution and delivered over four thousand sermons and messages in his lengthy career.[11] On one occasion he was visited by a friend of Jefferson, who subsequently reported:

> I called on and dined with the Revered Cotton Mather Smith of Sharon. . . . I found him an engaged *federal* politician; he soon found that my political feelings were not in unison with his and asked whether my good wishes would really extend Mr. Jefferson to the Presidential Chair [in the election of 1800]. I answered in the affirmative—on which, accompanied with much other malicious invective [vicious attack] and in presence of five men and two women, he said that you, Sir, "had obtained your property by fraud and robbery, and that in one instance you had defrauded and robbed a widow and fatherless children of an estate to which you were executor." . . . I told him with some warmth that I did not believe it. He said that "it was true" and that "it could be proved." . . . I thought it my duty, Sir, to communicate the assertion.[12]

Upon learning of that accusation, Jefferson replied to his friend:

> Every tittle of it is fable [i.e., a lie]. . . . I never was executor but in two instances. . . . In one of the cases only were there a widow and children: she was my sister. She retained and managed the estate in her own hands, and no part of it was ever in mine. . . . If Mr. Smith, therefore, thinks the precepts of the Gospel [are] intended for those who preach them as well as for others, he will doubtless someday feel the duties of repentance and of acknowledgment in such forms as to correct the wrong he has done.[13]

Despite Smith's blatant lie that Jefferson obtained his belongings by defrauding widows and orphans, the charge nevertheless roared across New England.

Similarly false charges were made by the Reverend William Linn of New York who pastored several churches, served as a military chaplain during the Revolution, became the first chaplain of the House of Representatives, and then a university president. Linn was also a staunch Federalist and close friend of Alexander Hamilton and thus a mortal political enemy of Jefferson.

Linn penned *Serious Considerations on the Election of a President* in which he warned that if Jefferson won the 1800 election, "[t]he effects would be to destroy religion, introduce immorality, and loosen all the bonds of society."[14]

The Reverend Linn concluded his pamphlet by telling the country that "Jefferson's opponent," John Adams, was "irreproachable." He then bluntly warned Americans that "it would be more acceptable to God and beneficial to the interests of our country to throw away your votes" than to vote for Jefferson.[15]

The Reverend John Mason was another New York Federalist pastor who detested Jefferson. He, too, was a close friend of Alexander Hamilton and actually attended Hamilton at his death after he was shot down in the famous duel with Aaron Burr. Mason authored *The Voice of Warning to Christians on the Ensuing Election* to warn Americans that Jefferson was a "confirmed" and "a hardened infidel" and one "who writes against the truth of God's Word; who makes not even a profession of Christianity; who is without Sabbaths, without the sanctuary, without so much as a decent external respect for the faith and worship of Christians."[16] Of course, as has already been shown, Jefferson had done exactly the opposite of what Mason claimed in each of these charges, including having written the law in Virginia that punished violators of the Sabbath. Nevertheless, Mason then solemnly warned voters:

If therefore an infidel [Jefferson] presides over our country, it will be your fault, Christians, and YOUR act—and YOU shall answer it! And for aiding and abetting such a design, I charge upon your consciences the SIN of striking hands in a covenant of friendship with the enemies of your Master's glory.[17]

The Reverend Nathanael Emmons of Massachusetts also raised a strident voice against Jefferson. Emmons had been an ardent patriot during the Revolution. He later established several missionary and theological societies and two hundred of his sermons were published and publicly distributed.

Emmons, a devoted Federalist, worked actively against Jefferson, but despite his best efforts, Jefferson was elected. In a famous sermon preached after Jefferson won, Emmons asserted that Jefferson was the American Jeroboam.

In the Bible, Jeroboam was the wicked leader who divided Israel following the death of Solomon. Taking ten tribes, Jeroboam became their king and led them away from God, ordaining pagan priests and pagan places of worship throughout the land, thus causing the ten tribes to eventually be conquered and destroyed.

In Emmons' two-hour sermon he compared the wise and Godly leader Solomon (whom he likened to John Adams) with the wicked and nefarious leader Jeroboam (whom he asserted was Thomas Jefferson). He then chastised voters for choosing Jefferson, telling them:

Solomon [John Adams] did a great deal to promote the temporal and eternal interests of his subjects; but Jeroboam [Jefferson] did as much to ruin his subjects both in time and eternity. . . . It is more than possible that our nation may find themselves in the hand of a Jeroboam who will drive them from following the Lord; and whenever they do, they will rue the day and detest the folly, delusion, and intrigue which raised him to the head of the United States.[18]

Years later, during the War of 1812, long after Jefferson had retired from his two terms as president, Emmons still couldn't let go of his hatred. In fact, he directly blamed Jefferson for the war. In an 1813 sermon he continued the odious tone of his sermon from more than a decade earlier, still chiding voters with a denunciation of their stupidity for having chosen the "wicked" Jefferson:

[W]hen [the nation] neglected their best men and chose the worst [Jefferson], their glory departed and their calamities began. Against the solemn warning voice of some of the best patriots in the Union, they committed the supreme power into the hands of Mr. Jefferson, who had publicly condemned the federal Constitution. This they did with their eyes wide open. . . . We deserved to be punished.[19]

Publicly condemned the Constitution? Jefferson? The War of 1812—a war that occurred years after Jefferson left office—was America's "punishment" for electing Jefferson? Such was the loathsome tone of sermons and publications of that era, and such was the caliber of lies issued against Jefferson by leading Federalist ministers. As Jefferson lamented:

[F]rom the [Federalist] clergy I expect no mercy. They crucified their Savior, Who preached that their kingdom was not of this world; and all who practice on that precept must expect the extreme of their wrath. The laws of the present day withhold their hands from blood, but lies and slander still remain to them.[20]

Early Jefferson historian Claude G. Bowers affirmed:

[I]n New England States, where the greater part of the ministers were militant Federalists, he was hated with an unholy hate. More false witness had been borne by the ministers of New England and New York against Jefferson than had ever been borne against any other American publicist.[21]

Noted political historian Saul Padover agreed.

They accused Jefferson of everything. If the sermons of the clergy were to be believed, there was no crime in the calendar of which Jefferson was not guilty and no unspeakable evil which he had not committed.[22]

With these types of reprehensible charges coming from Federalist clergy, it should not be surprising that the comments Jefferson made about these specific Federalist ministers might indeed seem anti-clergy. But the modern errant conclusion that then imputes those comments against all clergy instead of just Federalist ones can be reached only through Minimalism (ignoring complex situations in order to present an exaggeratedly simplistic conclusion). Minimalists, Academic Collectivists, and Deconstructionists regularly ignore Jefferson's scores of letters praising other clergymen. They also universally dismiss the countless Anti-Federalist (Republican) ministers and clergy who supported Jefferson with a zeal and fervor equal to that of the hatred shown him by the Federalists.

Among the many ministers and clergy who vociferously supported Jefferson was the Reverend John Leland of Massachusetts. Before the American Revolution Leland moved to Virginia where he pastored Baptist churches and became a good friend of Jefferson, working closely with him to disestablish the Anglican Church in the state. In 1788 Leland was selected as a Virginia delegate to ratify the US Constitution. In 1792 he moved back to Massachusetts, and in 1800 became a significant leader in organizing the Evangelicals in New England to support Jefferson for president.[23]

Following Jefferson's successful election Leland preached a sermon in which he effused:

> Heaven above looked down and awakened the American genius. . . . This exertion of the American genius has brought forth the *Man of the People*, the defender of the rights of man and the rights of conscience to fill the chair of state. . . . Pardon me, my hearers, if I am over-warm. I lived in Virginia fourteen years. The beneficent influence of my hero was too generally felt to leave me a stoic. . . . Let us then adore that God Who has been so favorable to our land and nation.[24]

Leland made a special trip from Massachusetts to the White House to bring his friend Jefferson a special gift: a giant cheese.

> Leland proposed that his flock should celebrate [Jefferson's] victory by making for the new Chief Magistrate the biggest cheese the world had ever seen. Every man and woman who owned a cow was to give for this cheese all the milk yielded on a certain day—only no federal cow must contribute a drop. A huge cider-press was fitted up to make it in, and on the appointed day, the whole country turned out with pails and tubs of curd, the girls and women in their best gowns and ribbons, and the men in their Sunday coats and clean shirt-collars. The cheese was put to press with prayer, and hymn-singing, and great solemnity. When it was well dried, it weighed 1,600 pounds. It was placed on a sleigh, and Elder John Leland drove with it all the way to Washington, It was a journey of three weeks. All the country had heard of the big cheese, and came out to look at it as the Elder drove along.[25]

The massive cheese had Jefferson's favorite motto etched into it: "Rebellion to Tyrants is Obedience to God."[26] Jefferson and Leland went inside the White House where Leland spoke in the East Room, declaring:

> We believe the Supreme Ruler of the Universe, Who raises up men to achieve great events, has raised up a Jefferson at this critical day to defend republicanism.[27]

Leland's visit to the White House occurred on Friday, January 1, 1802—the same day that Jefferson wrote Leland's fellow Baptists in Danbury, Connecticut, assuring them that because of "separation of church and state," they had nothing to fear from government limiting their religious practices or expressions. Two days later, on Sunday, January 3, Jefferson arranged for Leland to preach the sermon in the church at the Capitol. But didn't Jefferson understand the "separation" doctrine that he had just penned? Of course he did, and he understood that separation prohibited the government from *preventing* a religious expression, which is why having church in the Capitol was completely acceptable.

Members of Congress such as the Reverend Manasseh Cutler, a Federalist minister and a member of Congress from Massachusetts, also attended that church service. Cutler was disgusted by the Anti-Federalist Leland, complaining:

> Last Sunday, Leland the cheesemonger, a poor, ignorant, illiterate, clownish preacher (who was the conductor of this monument of human weakness and folly [the Republican cheese] to the place of its destination), was introduced as the preacher to both Houses of Congress.[28]

Cutler not only loathed Leland but was also revolted by his sermon. The text was:

"And behold a greater than Solomon is here" [Matthew 12:42]. The design of the preacher was principally to apply the allusion not to the person intended in the text, but to him who was then present [to Jefferson]. . . . Such an outrage upon religion, the Sabbath, and common decency was extremely painful to every sober thinking person present.[29]

Federalist ministers clearly did not like Anti-Federalist ministers doing to Jefferson the opposite of what they had inflicted upon him. But Jefferson was so moved by Leland's visit that when Leland left Washington to return to Massachusetts, Jefferson "gave Rev. Mr. Leland, bearer of the cheese, $200."[30]

Jefferson also arranged for other ministers to preach at the Capitol, including the Reverend James O'Kelly, another of his strong supporters. Originally a Methodist, O'Kelly later founded a movement known as the "Republican Methodists" because of the common beliefs they shared with Jefferson's political movement. He twice visited Jefferson at the White House, and Jefferson twice arranged for him to preach in the church at the Capitol.[31] Following one of those occasions, a newspaper editor reported that after O'Kelly's sermon, "Mr. Jefferson arose with tears in his eyes and said that while he was no preacher, in his opinion James O'Kelly was one of the greatest preachers living."[32]

Another Anti-Federalist evangelical minister with whom Jefferson was very close was his own pastor, the Reverend Charles Clay, an Anglican minister at St. Anne's parish in Fredericksville, where Jefferson attended. Clay had been greatly influenced by the religious revival known as the Great Awakening and was a thoroughly energetic and evangelical preacher. He was also a strong patriot, ministering during the Revolution both to the American forces from the area and to the captured British forces imprisoned there. Clay was a neighbor of Jefferson, became a justice of the peace, and even acted as Jefferson's attorney.

Recall that in 1774 because of the Boston Port Bill Jefferson had introduced and the legislature had passed a call for a statewide day of prayer, which included a call for attendance at a special legislative religious service. In addition to that service, Jefferson reported:

> We returned home, and in our several counties invited the clergy
> to meet assemblies of the people on the 1st of June to perform
> the ceremonies of the day and to address to them discourses
> [sermons] suited to the occasion.[33]

The Reverend Clay was a prominent part of the local service that Jefferson attended, offering both its sermon and the prayers.[34]

By 1777 the board of Reverend Clay's church had stopped paying his salary—perhaps because of his overt patriotism or possibly because of his evangelical tendencies. After being unable to secure the back pay, Jefferson worked with a group of citizens to start a new church that the Reverend Clay would pastor—the Calvinistic Reformed Church, which Jefferson called the Protestant Episcopal Church. Jefferson explained that they started that church in order to "derive to ourselves . . . the benefits of Gospel knowledge and religious improvement" and to "support those who have qualified themselves by regular education for explaining the Holy Scriptures."[35]

Jefferson and the others personally pledged the financial support necessary for the Reverend Clay and the new church. In fact, Jefferson himself drafted the public announcement setting forth the reason they were supporting Clay and how they planned to do it:

> Whereas by a late act of General Assembly, freedom of religious
> opinion and worship is restored to all, and it is left to the mem-
> bers of each religious society to employ such teachers as they
> think fit for their own spiritual comfort and instruction and to

maintain the same by their free and voluntary contributions. . . .
[A]pproving highly the political conduct of Revd. Charles Clay,
who early rejecting the tyrant and tyranny of Britain, proved his
religion genuine by its harmony with the liberties of mankind,
and conforming his public prayers to the spirit and injured rights
of his country, ever addressing the God of battles for victory to
our arms (while others impiously prayed that our enemies might
vanquish and overcome us), do hereby oblige ourselves, our
heirs, executors, and administrators to pay to the said Charles
Clay of Albemarle, his executors, or administrators the several
sums affixed to our respective names.[36]

Of the many who signed that pledge in 1777, Jefferson was by
far among the most generous financial contributors.

Two years after starting this church Jefferson also wrote a public
letter of commendation for the Reverend Clay in case he should ever
seek employment at another church:

The Reverend Charles Clay has been many years rector of this
parish and has been particularly known to me. During the
whole course of that time, his deportment has been exemplary,
as became a divine, and his attention to parochial duties unex-
ceptionable. . . . As he has some thought of leaving us, I feel
myself obliged, in compliance with the common duty of bearing
witness to the truth when called on, to give this testimonial of
his merit that it may not be altogether unknown to those with
whom he may propose to take up his residence.[37]

Jefferson also wrote such letters for other ministers, including the
Reverend James Fontaine, recommending him for a place in state
government.[38] He also penned a letter of enthusiastic praise for the
Rev. Mr. Glendye, who was moving to Baltimore.[39]

Jefferson closely attended many sermons of his republican clergy friends, and those sermons helped directly shape his political philosophy. For example, Jefferson was a close follower of the Reverend Clay's sermons. It is therefore not surprising to find that Jefferson's political language paralleled the language of Clay's sermons. As Jefferson scholar Dr. Mark Beliles noted:

> Given the close friendship and identification that Jefferson publicly made with Clay and his sermons, the language therefore that is found in these sermons is important because of its similarities with much of Jefferson's terminology in his public writings. The phrase "Providence" or "Divine Providence," used 34 times in [Clay's] sermon on *The Governor Among the Nations*, is similar to the closing phrase in the Declaration of Independence which declared reliance "on the protection of Divine Providence." . . . Clay also referred to "God as the Author of Nature," "God the Supreme ruler," "God the Fountain of All power," "the Supreme Governor of the World," "the Supreme Universal King and Lord," "the Governor among the Nations," and the "Great Governor of the World, the King of Nations." These terms were common to the sermons of the day, and to the common prayer books, and therefore if Jefferson used such language in his writings, it would not be accurate to assume that he derived it from enlightenment or deistic sources.[40]

Writers today regularly ignore the fact that the religious terms Jefferson used in his political writings were also commonly used by evangelical ministers, including not only the Reverend Charles Clay but many others.[41] They wrongly claim that Jefferson's use of such terms proves he was a deist,[42] but if such language proves Jefferson to be a deist, then it similarly proves many evangelical ministers of the day were also deists—clearly an unsustainable assertion. Such logic is a product of Modernism, which wrongly insists that since the words Jefferson used two centuries ago are not the words Evangelicals use today then Jefferson must not have been religious.

Another minister who strongly supported Jefferson was the Reverend Lorenzo Dow, one of the best known figures of the national revival known as the Second Great Awakening. Dow was originally associated with the Methodists; in 1794 he began traveling on horseback and preaching, often up to twenty times a week. Like the Reverend George Whitefield, he traversed the vast expanse of the nation preaching everywhere he went, including countries abroad.

On one occasion while speaking at a Baptist church near Jefferson's home, Dow praised Jefferson for disestablishing the Anglican church in Virginia. He also asserted that Jefferson's overall willingness to everywhere disestablish "law-religion" (or the state establishment of a particular denomination) was the real reason that Federalists so fiercely opposed Jefferson and called him an "infidel." (During the time that Jefferson was working for religious freedom, nearly every New England Federalist State had an official state established denomination.) Dow explained:

> Jefferson, seeing the evil of law religion, &c., had those barbarous laws . . . repealed. . . . These things procured the epithet "Infidel!" for a mark of distinguishment. . . . But religious venom of all things is the worst! From those circumstances arose the prejudice of the clergy of different societies who would be fond of a law religion as the ground of their animosity and ambition against him, because their hopes of gain are stagnated by it.[43]

Jefferson also believed this was the reason for most of the attacks against him. During the presidential election he had told his close friend Benjamin Rush:

[T]hey [the Federalist clergy] believe that any portion of power confided to me will be exerted in opposition to their schemes—and they believe rightly, for I have sworn upon the altar of God eternal hostility against every form of tyranny over the mind of man. But this is all they have to fear from me; and enough, too, in their opinion. And this is the cause of their printing lying pamphlets against me. . . . But enough of this. It is more than I have before committed to paper on the subject of all the lies which have been preached and printed against me.[44]

Years later Jefferson remained convinced that his position against state religious establishments had been the source of the religious attacks against him, explaining:

The priests indeed have heretofore thought proper to ascribe to me religious, or rather anti-religious sentiments of their own fabric, but such as soothed their resentments against the act of Virginia for establishing religious freedom. They wished him to be thought atheist, deist, or devil, who could advocate freedom from their [state-established] religious dictations.[45]

But numerous Bible-centered Evangelicals strongly supported Jefferson, including the Reverend Samuel Knox, a Presbyterian minister from Maryland and a vocal anti-Unitarian, who not only wrote *A Vindication of the Religion of Mr. Jefferson* in 1800 but who also worked for the Anti-Federalist (Republican) cause.[46] Others included the Reverend Samuel Miller, a Presbyterian minister from New York and New Jersey;[47] the Reverend Elias Smith, a Baptist minister in New Hampshire;[48] and many more. And the ministers who had worked hand in hand with Jefferson to introduce and pass religious liberty legislation in the Virginia legislature were also ardent Jefferson supporters, including the Reverends John Todd, William Irvin, Billy Wood, Jeremiah Moore, and others.

Another indication of Jefferson's strong overall support for churches and ministers is seen in his own financial records. He gave generously not only to churches he attended but also to many other churches, including the "German church," Gloria Dei Church, a local black church, the "Rev. Chambers church," a Methodist church, an Episcopal church at the Navy Yard in Washington, and others.[49] And he contributed to the construction of several new churches, including three Baptist, two Presbyterian, and two Episcopalian churches, a church in Louisiana, and so on.[50] He also financially supported missionaries[51] and contributed liberally to the support of many ministers, including the Reverends W. Coutts, Matthew Maury, John Leland, David Austin, Stephen Balch, Thomas Cavender, Jacob Eyerman, Andrew McCormick, John Bausman, and others.[52]

Clearly, Jefferson was very close to and supportive of many ministers. But if one reads only the instances in which he fired back with contempt against those ministers who either viciously attacked him or who supported state-established religion, then one could definitely (if wrongly) conclude that Jefferson was anti-clergy, at least toward "law religion" clergy. As Beliles affirmed:

> Some have mistakenly assumed . . . Jefferson's all-encompassing anti-clericalism. But . . . it is more accurately identified as a response against mainly Federalist clergy in the northern and middle states (Congregationalists, Presbyterian, and Unitarian) who were attacking him during the presidential campaign. These attacks have now become far too emphasized and generalized in modern representations of Jefferson without mentioning the facts that would provide a more accurate view of his relationship with ministers throughout his life. Although still being opposed to a state church with state-empowered clergy, Jefferson was certainly not against clergymen or Christianity in general.[53]

Critics have often wrongly interpreted an "all-encompassing anti-clericism" from reading many of Jefferson's letters denouncing the clergy of Period II (the "Age of Apostasy" or "Age of Corruption") and those in Period III who wanted to preserve state religious establishments.

This is one of the reasons that Jefferson connected so well with Anti-Federalist ministers such as the Reverend John Leland: they all had common goals in jointly opposing "priest-craft" and "law religion." The Reverend Leland took pains, however, to make clear that the term *priestcraft* (a term frequently used by Jefferson) did *not* encompass all clergy but only certain types:

> By *Priest-Craft*, no contempt is designed to be cast upon any of the Lord's priest's, from Melchizedeck to Zacharias, nor upon any of the ministers of Christ, either those who have been remarkably endowed with power from on high to work miracles, &c. or those of ordinary endowments who have been governed by supreme love to the Savior and benevolence to mankind. These, to the world, have been like the stars of night. But by priest-craft is intended the rushing into the sacred work for the sake of ease, wealth, honor, and ecclesiastical dignity. Whether they plead lineal succession or Divine impulse, their course is directed for self-advantage. By good words and fair speeches, they deceive the simple and [use] solemn threatening of fines, gibbets [the gallows], or the flames of Hell to those who do not adhere to their institutes.[54]

(Concerning the latter category, there were clergy during the American Revolution who actually threatened their parishioners with Hell if they helped the patriots.[55])

Those who generally fit the category of "priest-craft" as described by the Reverend Leland were largely based in New England. As

Jefferson affirmed to his friend and fellow-signer of the Declaration Elbridge Gerry, one of Jefferson's few supporters in Massachusetts:

> In your corner alone [i.e., in New England], priestcraft and law-craft are still able to throw dust into the eyes of the people.[56]

When Jefferson is speaking of these types of negative religious leaders, he regularly uses terms such as *priests, priest-ridden*, or refers to those practicing *priest-craft* rather than terms such as *ministers, pastors*, or *clergy*.[57] For example, in a letter to his friend Horatio Spafford, the father of the man who authored the classic Christian hymn "It Is Well with My Soul," Jefferson declared:

> I join in your reprobation [disapproval] of our merchants, priests, and lawyers for their adherence to England and monarchy in preference to their own country and its constitution. . . . In every country and in every age, the priest has been hostile to liberty; he is always in alliance with the despot, abetting his abuses in return for protection to his own. . . . [T]hey have perverted the purest religion ever preached to man into mystery and jargon unintelligible to all mankind.[58]

Jefferson's context is clear: he was referencing only those clergy who had an "adherence to . . . monarchy in preference to their own country and its constitution." Yet secularists lift a single line from this letter to claim that Jefferson was an opponent of all ministers. For example, Ferrill Till, atheist editor of the *Skeptical Review*, writes:

> Thomas Jefferson, in fact, was fiercely anti-cleric. In a letter to Horatio Spafford in 1814, Jefferson said, "In every country and every age, the priest has been hostile to liberty. He is always in

alliance with the despot, abetting his abuses in return for protection to his own."[59]

Clearly, that was not the context of Jefferson's letter. Note also that in describing the narrow category of clergy to whom he was opposed, Jefferson often conjoins the term *priests* with *kings*, or *priestcraft* with *kingcraft* as he did in the letter above with *priests* and *monarchy*. He means to exclude those ministers who did not affiliate themselves with the state so as to force their specific religious tenets upon the public. Jefferson was not opposed to all clergy but only those who joined with kings and government to practice "law religion" to the detriment of human rights and liberties. He saw that harmful alliance still exerting a negative influence in far too many countries in his day. For example, he wrote of Spanish America:

I fear the degrading ignorance into which their priests and kings have sunk them has disqualified them from the maintenance or even knowledge of their rights and that much blood may be shed for little improvement in their condition.[60]

In reviewing political conditions in South America, he similarly lamented:

Their people are immersed in the darkest ignorance and brutalized by bigotry and superstition. Their priests make of them what they please, and though they may have some capable leaders, yet nothing but intelligence in the people themselves can keep these faithful to their charge. Their efforts, I fear, therefore will end in establishing military despotisms in the several provinces.[61]

For today's critics to take Jefferson's comments about "law religion" clergy and impute them to all clergy is like saying that the

Founding Fathers who specifically condemned and denounced Benedict Arnold were actually condemning all military leaders. Yet this is what Deconstructionists and Minimalists regularly do with Jefferson's comments about the specific practices of a particular type of clergy.

A final proof that Jefferson was not opposed to all clergy can found in his work on the Virginia constitution. The original 1776 state constitution contained a prohibition against clergy serving in the legislature.[62] Jefferson had fully supported this provision at the time, explaining:

> The clergy are excluded because if admitted into the legislature at all, the probability is that they would form its majority, for they are dispersed through every county in the state; they have influence with the people and great opportunities of persuading them to elect them into the legislature. This body, though shattered, is still formidable, still forms a *corps*, and is still actuated by the *esprit de corps*. The nature of that spirit has been severely felt by mankind, and has filled the history of ten or twelve centuries with too many atrocities not to merit a proscription from meddling with government.[63]

Recall that this was the early constitution in a state that by law had protected an official state denomination established for the previous century and a half. Jefferson believed that what had occurred in the previous 150 years when Virginia had persecuted ministers from other denominations might still continue in the new independent state, and he wanted that possibility precluded.

Years later, however, Jefferson no longer supported that clause, explaining to the Reverend Jeremiah Moore:

I observe . . . an abridgment of the right of being elected, which after 17 years more of experience and reflection, I do not approve: it is the incapacitation of a clergyman from being elected. . . . Even in 1783, we doubted the stability of our recent measures for reducing them [the clergy] to the footing of other useful callings [but i]t now appears that our means were effectual. The clergy here seem to have relinquished all pretension to privilege and to stand on a footing with lawyers, physicians &c. They ought therefore to possess the same rights.[64]

In summary, many of Jefferson's writings praise clergymen and their important work, they were among his close friends, and he regularly opened his pocketbook and exerted his influence to help them. The modern claim that Jefferson was anticlerical is another one of the many Jefferson lies that has penetrated deeply into American thinking today; it is yet another Jefferson lie that must be shaken off.

Lie # 7

Thomas Jefferson Was an Atheist and Not a Christian

Jefferson's own words and actions have proven many of the allegations against him are lies. But each has tended to exhibit a subtle nuance of one overarching theme: Jefferson was not religious. Or more to the point, he was not a Christian. Is this true? For modern writers the answer is simple:

> Jefferson hated religion. . . . [Professor Joseph] Ellis claims that "like Voltaire, Jefferson longed for the day when the last king would be strangled with the entrails of the last priest."[1]

> Several of our founding fathers were deist and even hated Christianity . . . [including] Thomas Jefferson.[2]

> Jefferson hated organized religion.[3]

> Jefferson. . . . It's very likely he was an atheist.[4]

> [His] writings clearly prove that he was not a Christian, but a Freethinker.[5]

The term *Freethinker* may be unfamiliar to some, but it is the euphemism for atheist.[6] Atheists believe that this name improves the public's view of atheism. By definition, a Freethinker—an atheist—is:

- one who believes that there is no deity[7]

- anyone who does not believe in the existence of any gods[8]

- a person who denies or disbelieves the existence of a supreme being or beings[9]

As already demonstrated, Jefferson does not fit any of these definitions—not even remotely. To the contrary, his own writings make clear that many of his endeavors were inspired by a strong belief in God and in His first principles. Jefferson definitely was not an atheist, but was he a Christian?

While Jefferson truly was a complex person, he was not confusing, obfuscating, or disingenuous. He was straightforward and truthful on the topics he addressed. And as with other subjects, Jefferson also spoke honestly about his personal faith and views of Christianity. But because he was so forthright on this topic, it is the most complicated area for historians to analyze.

Across his long life Jefferson went through several phases regarding his own personal beliefs about specific doctrines of Christianity. There are times when he took a firm position on a particular Christian doctrine then perhaps twenty years later changed his view and then again two decades after that reverted back to his original view. For this reason, quotes can be selected to make Jefferson appear to be either a mainstream Christian or a pagan heretic, depending on the period of Jefferson's life from which the statements are taken. This chapter will present Jefferson's views on Christianity in each of those phases, identifying times that he slips into and out of traditional orthodoxy in regard to specific Christian doctrines.

While there definitely were periods when Jefferson did challenge some specific doctrines, there never was a time when he questioned the overall value of Christianity to individuals or to a nation. And there never was a time when he was anti-Jesus or when he rejected Christianity. It is only in the nuances of some particular doctrines of Christianity that Jefferson's personal faith becomes difficult to pin down or to draw a fixed and definite conclusion.

Jefferson penned at least nineteen thousand letters during his lifetime. Of the scores of his letters that address the subjects of God, Christianity, and religion, only a handful, primarily from late in his life, raise concerns for traditional Christians. These few letters cannot, however, be dismissed out of hand simply because they represent such a tiny fraction of Jefferson's otherwise positive declarations about Christianity. But neither can they be the only basis on which Jefferson's faith is judged as many secularists and Jefferson critics do today.

To illustrate what might cause a period of change in Jefferson's religious views, recall his earlier comments about David Hume. Hume had openly declared, "I expected in entering on my literary course, that all the Christians . . . should be my enemies."[10] Jefferson acknowledged that there was a time when he had voraciously studied and absorbed Hume's writings and philosophy before eventually rejecting them:

> I remember well the enthusiasm with which I devoured [Hume's work] when young, and the length of time, the research and reflection which were necessary to eradicate the poison it had instilled into my mind.[11]

It would, then, not be surprising that during the time of Jefferson's "enthusiasm" about Hume, one might find him making statements or writing letters on religion and government that would reflect Hume's philosophy before he was finally able "to eradicate the poison it had instilled into [my] mind."

A spiritual change is also apparent in the period of Jefferson's life surrounding his marriage to his wife, Martha. The twenty-nine-year old Jefferson married her in 1772, and those who knew her described her as "saintly."[12] At the time of their wedding, America was four decades deep into the national revival known as the Great Awakening. This revival dramatically impacted the nation, including both Martha and Thomas. In fact, throughout the time of the Great Revival and for well over a decade after it, Jefferson's writings and statements on religious faith can be considered as nothing less than orthodox.

For example, when elected as a vestryman in his Anglican Church in 1768, Jefferson promised "to conform to the Doctrine and Discipline of the Church of England."[13] Anglican theological doctrine at that time completely embodied orthodox Christian tenets to which Jefferson swore his allegiance. And in 1776 (four years after his marriage to Martha) he penned his *Notes on Religion* in which he affirmed that Jesus was the Savior, the Scriptures were inspired, and that the Apostles' Creed "contain[ed] all things necessary to salvation."[14]

Jefferson loved and adored Martha, and they had six children—five daughters and one son. Martha was his constant companion and closest friend, and they were devoted to each other. In fact, the children clearly recalled and spoke of the sweet and precious relationship between the two, including Martha's "passionate attachment to him, and her exalted opinion of him."[15] But the two also shared much loss and grief over their dear children. Of the six, only two lived to adulthood; Martha saw three of her children die, and Thomas saw five of them buried.

Martha's tragic death occurred after only ten years of blissful marriage. It was a stunning blow to Jefferson, and he was emotionally devastated. As presidential biographer William Stoddard affirms:

[H]e was utterly absorbed in sorrow and took no note of what was going on around him. His dream of life had been shattered, and it seemed as if life itself had lost its claim upon him, for no faith or hope of his reached onward and inward to any other.[16]

Jefferson's eldest daughter, Martha, named for her mother, was with him at the time of his wife's death, and she was her father's "constant companion" during "the first month of desolation which followed."[17] She recounted Jefferson's frame of mind during that tragic period, recalling:

> A moment before the closing scene, he was led from the room almost in a state of insensibility by his sister Mrs. Carr, who with great difficulty got him into his library where he fainted and remained so long insensible that they feared he never would revive. The scene that followed I did not witness; but the violence of his emotion when, almost by stealth, I entered his room at night, to this day I dare not trust myself to describe. He kept [never left] his room three weeks, and I was never a moment from his side. He walked almost incessantly night and day, only lying down occasionally, when nature was completely exhausted, on a pallet that had been brought in during his long fainting-fit. My aunts remained constantly with him for some weeks—I do not remember how many. When at last he left his room, he rode out, and from that time he was incessantly on horseback, rambling about the mountain in the least frequented roads, and just as often through the woods.[18]

Not long after Martha's death, Jefferson was sent by the Continental Congress as a diplomat to France. During those years, with the deep impact and clear remembrances and grief over Martha still so real to him, many questions remained, unanswered, and his faith was shaken. This is reflected in his writings. But by the time he became president, he had returned to a stronger and more orthodox position.

This was evident only four years into his presidency when he faced another personal tragedy. In 1804 his twenty-five-year-old daughter, Mary (Polly), was in poor health after giving birth to her third child. Her husband, a congressman, was away in Washington with her father, so Polly moved into Monticello where she could receive constant attention. As soon as the legislative session was over, Jefferson rushed home to help care for her, but only a few short weeks after he returned, his beloved Polly died. This left only his eldest daughter, Martha, and himself remaining from the family of eight. Martha's daughter (Jefferson's granddaughter) reported his reaction to the death of Polly:

> My mother [Martha] has told me that on the day of her sister's death, she left her father alone for some hours. He then sent for her, and she found him with the Bible in his hands. He who has been so often and so harshly accused of unbelief, he, in his hour of intense affliction, sought and found consolation in the Sacred Volume.[19]

While such events impacted Jefferson's faith, the greatest influence on his personal religious views was the religious disposition of the community around him. In many ways Jefferson was a mirror that accurately reflected the spiritual condition of his cherished central Virginia region around Charlottesville, the region in which he grew up and lived and to which he retired after his presidency.

Jefferson was born in 1743 during the early stages of the Great Awakening, which lasted approximately from 1730 to 1770, but in Virginia both the beginning and end of that revival occurred about a decade behind the rest of the nation. (Interestingly, it was just the opposite with the Second Great Awakening—it began and ended earlier in Virginia than the rest of the country.) The Great Awakening was characterized by an explosive growth of personal faith and piety as well as a period of unprecedented interdenominational cooperation.

Virginia had been heavily Anglican since its founding, but the revival caused the rapid growth of the Presbyterians, Baptists, Quakers, and Methodists in the state. Ministers in central Virginia during that time often moved easily between denominations (such as the Reverend Devereaux Jarratt who was trained as a Presbyterian, became an Anglican priest, and spoke regularly in Methodist churches). Similarly, the area's devout laymen were also often active in multiple denominations. Jefferson's good friend and neighbor Henry Fry served with Jefferson on the board of Anglican churches in the area but was converted to Methodism and worked in both denominations.

This type of interdenominational cooperation was possible primarily because leading ministers during the Great Awakening began emphasizing the vital areas of the Scriptures on which nearly all Christians agreed rather than the few areas about which they vigorously disagreed. Under the influence of this revival and its interdenominational cooperation even the Anglican Church in Virginia, softened its policy. As affirmed by Virginia historian William H. B. Thomas, "[t]he necessity of attending an Anglican church was relaxed—provided every man attend some church regularly."[20]

Most pastors in the Charlottesville region at this time can be described as evangelical, regardless of their denominations. They also preached a practical Christianity that specifically addressed daily personal behavior and provided relevant Biblical teaching and social applications. It touched issues such as interpersonal interactions, business dealings, and one's personal relationship with God as well as moral issues such as integrity, courage, drunkenness, profanity, and immorality. Many sermons also addressed legislative policies of the day, contrasting public policies with Biblical positions on those issues, including taxation, good government, gambling, and slavery. In fact, when Quaker leader John Woolman visited Virginia during this period and witnessed Southern slavery for the first time, he began advocating vigorously in behalf of emancipation. This eventually resulted in the Quakers becoming national leaders in the abolition movement.

Another characteristic of the First and Second Great Awakenings was that blacks were very active and involved. Many ministers, both black and white, would preach to mixed crowds. National leaders such as Harry Hoosier, the famous black evangelist, spent time in and preached to groups across central Virginia, as did black evangelist John Early. Of this period the Reverend John Leland observed:

> The poor slaves, under all their hardships, discover as great inclination for religion as the free-born do. When they engage in the service of God, they spare no pains. It is nothing strange for them to walk twenty miles on Sunday morning to meeting, and back again at night. . . . [T]hey are remarkably fond of meeting together to sing, pray, and exhort, and sometimes preach. . . . When they attempt to preach, they seldom fail of being very zealous.[21]

It was during this time of revival in Virginia that many of the Dissenting (that is, non-Anglican) churches and ministers became active in politics, working to separate the church from the state and to keep the government from interfering with their own religious expressions and activities. For example, the Separate Baptists refused to comply with the Anglican requirement in state law mandating that they obtain government permission before conducting religious services. They asserted that it was their right to do what God had told them, without need of government approval. The Great Awakening not only promoted the concepts of individualism and inalienable rights (personal liberty, religious expression, freedom of conscience, and so on), but also that such rights should be protected by government rather than regulated by it.

While these traits were common in Charlottesville and across most of the nation during the Great Awakening, there was one area in which Charlottesville differed from the rest of the country. It tended to be a bit more Armenian and less Calvinistic—a characteristic that greatly influenced Jefferson in the years following. And generally speaking, many of the spiritual practices apparent in Charlottesville during that time became established features of Jefferson's personal religious views.

For example, he developed a lifelong affinity for things such as interdenominational cooperation and emphasizing the doctrinal majors uniting Christians rather than the things dividing them. He also focused on identifying and protecting God-given inalienable rights; separating state from church and thereby preserving the freedom of conscience; emancipating slaves; leaning against Calvinism; etc.

The first Great Awakening had barely ended in Virginia before the Second Great Awakening began. But by 1810, while the revival was still going strong in other parts of the country, the spiritual condition of the Charlottesville area had turned in a very unsatisfactory direction. According to evangelical minister John Rice Holt, who had helped Jefferson found the University of Virginia:

> Presbyterian congregations are decreasing every year, and appear as if they would dwindle into nothing. The Baptists and Methodists are at a stand. A strange apathy has seized the people. . . . The people feel about nothing but money. As to religion, the very stillness of death reigns amongst us. I can find no resemblance to this part of the country but in Ezekiel's valley of dry bones [Ezekiel 37: 1–14].[22]

In fact, Holt said that the Methodists were not just "at a stand," but that "Mr. O'Kelly, the chief of the Christian Methodists, . . . is nearly deserted by his followers."[23]

During that time, many evangelical churches could find no replacements as their pastors died off or retired, and so they closed their doors. In other churches, the pulpit remained unfilled for more than a decade.[24]

Concurrent with these gloomy developments in Virginia, several ministers in other parts of the country began a parallel spiritual movement that was to take a deep root in Charlottesville. This new movement was characterized by what became a radical call for a return to the primitive form of Christianity practiced by the Apostles. It decried the corruption of the modern Christian church and wanted to revive an earlier and simpler version of Christianity. This movement became known as Christian Primitivism or the Restoration Movement, and it developed from four primary leaders.

One was Presbyterian minister Barton Stone of Kentucky, who led the famous Cane Ridge revival. He called for an end to denominations and advocated that Christians have no creed but the Bible. He therefore used only the simple descriptive title "Christian" for his congregations. (Stone had grown up Anglican but had also been a Baptist, Methodist, and Presbyterian.)

Another Restoration leader was Presbyterian minister Thomas Campbell of Pennsylvania. He held many of the same beliefs as Stone and Campbell's son, Alexander, advocated those positions in the western parts of Virginia. Their followers also embraced the unpretentious title of "Christian." Alexander explained that their purpose was to "espouse the cause of no religious sect, excepting that ancient sect called Christians first at Antioch" [Acts 11:26].[25]

A third leader was the Reverend Elias Smith of New Hampshire, who left the Baptist denomination and began a new group that "agreed to consider ourselves Christians, without the addition of any unscriptural name."[26]

A fourth leader was Jefferson's good friend, the Reverend James O'Kelly of Virginia, who had actually started this trend well before any of the other three changing the name of his group from "Republican Methodists" to simply "Christians."

The followers of Stone, Smith, and O'Kelly came together in 1810, calling themselves "Christian Connection" (sometimes "Christian Connexion"). Campbell's group, while philosophically aligned with the other three, did not combine with them until years later, but in 1811 it did take the name "Christian Association."

Ministers of these four groups became leaders in the Charlottesville area, having great spiritual influence, and their followers increased rapidly for the next decade. But regrettably, in their fervor to restore primitive Christianity and return to the Bible as the only model, they ended up rejecting several long-standing doctrines of ortho-dox Christianity, including the concept of the Trinity. As bluntly explained by the Reverend Barton Stone, "The word Trinity is not found in the Bible."[27]

The Reverend Elias Smith agreed:

In all the glorious things said of Christ, there is no mention of his Divinity, his being God-man, his incarnation, the human and the Divine nature, the human soul of Christ, his being God the Creator and yet the son of the Creator; these things are inven-tions of men and ought to be rejected.[28]

Of the four major leaders, only O'Kelly openly embraced Trinitarianism.[29] Smith and Stone did not embrace the doctrine, and since Thomas Campbell took no position on the doctrine,[30] his fol-lowers included those from both Trinitarian and Anti-Trinitarian posi-tions. It is interesting to note that none of the four groups rejected Jesus as the son of God, but only as a part of the Trinity. Sadly, this was the doctrinal position widely expounded by leading Christian minis-ters across Charlottesville for the last fifteen years of Jefferson's life.

Because Restorationists (Primitivists) claimed that the Bible was their only guidebook, they also rejected several other "traditions" of Christianity. For example, Smith thundered:

I am a Christian . . . holding as abominable in the sight of God, everything . . . such as Calvinism, Arminianism, Freewillism, Universalism, Reverends, Parsons, Chaplains, Doctors of Divinity, Clergy, Bands, Surplices, Notes, Creeds, Covenants, and Platforms.[31]

While the Primitivists rejected many church practices, there were many that they still continued to embrace. Holt recounted the Reverend O'Kelly's description of what was preserved by the movement.

He says, "That there has sprung up in the country a sect under the general name of 'Christians,' who administer adult baptism only to please the Baptists; who hold Arminian sentiments to catch the Methodists; and yet will not allow a man to be a Calvinist if he chooses; that they prove Socinian tenets [that Jesus was a man inspired by God but not Divine Himself] and make that profession the only bond of union. . . . He states too, that they are increasing rapidly.[32]

The distinct religious tenets, that characterized the Restoration Movement included:

- A rejection of denominationalism and all denominational titles except that of Christian

- A stress on Christian unity

- An emphasis on the Gospels rather than the Epistles—on getting back to the teachings of Jesus, and therefore a de-emphasis on the Epistles and the Old Testament

- A rejection of church hierarchal structure: each church was local, and locally controlled

- Anti-Trinitarianism, with an emphasis on using only Bible language and Bible terms

- Anti-Calvinic almost to the point of loathing it

Interestingly, the movement's hatred for Calvinism was so strong that part of the reason Restorationists rejected the Trinity was simply because Calvin had embraced it. For example, Alexander Campbell declared, "I object to the Calvinistic doctrine of the Trinity."[33] He thereafter attempted to defend his own concept of the Trinity, but his effort was so convoluted that the Reverend Stone rebuked him, claiming that by his attempt to defend Trinitarianism, he was actually embracing the Calvinism that they all claimed to deplore.[34]

Restorationist leaders reached the point that if *any* doctrine had been espoused by Calvin, then they believed it must be wrong. In fact, the Reverend Elias Smith even characterized Calvinism as part of ungodliness, declaring, "[M]y mind was delivered from Calvinism, universalism, and deism—three doctrines of men, which people love who do not love holiness."[35]

The Restoration and Christian Primitivist Movement came to be the dominant religious force in Charlottesville, and Jefferson openly embraced and promoted it. Not surprisingly, then, Jefferson's writings during his latter years reflect all the major tenets of Christian Primitivism and Restorationism, using almost the exact tenor and words as the Restoration minsters surrounding him. Consider some of Jefferson's declarations about each of the major beliefs of the Movement.

On Primitivism and Restoration

In his latter years Jefferson repeatedly wrote of the need to return to primitive Christianity and restore it to the time of Jesus and the Apostles.

[T]he genuine and simple religion of Jesus will one day be restored such as it was preached and practiced by Himself. . . . I hope that the day of restoration is to come.[36]

Happy in the prospect of a restoration of primitive Christianity, I must leave to younger athletes to encounter and lop off the false branches which have been engrafted into it by the mythologists of the middle and modern ages.[37]

I . . . express my gratification with your efforts for the revival of primitive Christianity in your quarter.[38]

[I]t is only by . . . getting back to the plain and unsophisticated precepts of Christ that we become real Christians.[39]

Had the doctrines of Jesus been preached always as pure as they came from His lips, the whole civilized world would now have been Christian.[40]

On Christian Unity and Cooperation

Jefferson had already adopted this precept during the Great Awakening, and it remained with him throughout his life, including during the Restoration Movement. This trait had been apparent in his 1779 Virginia Statute for Religious Freedom, which established denominational nonpreferentialism in the state. Again in 1800, when the church at the Capitol was started, Jefferson demonstrated a sense of unity by helping establish the policy whereby ministers from all denominations were invited to preach and yet again in 1819 when he invited all denominations to establish seminaries at his beloved University of Virginia. Recall, too, that Jefferson had regularly given financially to all types of Christian churches and helped build new ones for many differing denominations.

Jefferson also openly celebrated those parts of the country wherein the denominations "condescend to interchange with . . . the other sects the civilities of preaching freely and frequently in each other's meeting-houses,"[41] and he specifically praised the locations in Charlottesville (such as the "union building" and the county courthouse) where ministers from various denominations would rotate preaching. As he extolled to a friend during the height of the Restoration Movement:

> In our village of Charlottesville . . . [w]e have four sects, but without either church or meeting-house. The court house is the common temple, one Sunday in the month to each. Here, Episcopalian and Presbyterian, Methodist and Baptist meet together, join in hymning their Maker, listen with attention and devotion to each other's preachers, and all mix in society with perfect harmony.[42]

Jefferson believed strongly that the teachings of Jesus brought unity but that the teachings of denominations brought disunity and conflict. As he explained to John Adams in 1819:

> No doctrines of His lead to schism. It is the speculations of crazy theologists which have made a Babel of a religion the most moral and sublime ever preached to man, and calculated to heal and not to create differences. These religious animosities I impute to those who call themselves His ministers and who engraft their casuistries [personal interpretations] on the stock of His simple precepts. I am sometimes more angry with them than is authorized by the blessed charities which He preached.[43]

On Emphasizing the Gospels and De-emphasizing the Epistles and Old Testament

Jefferson had always drawn a clear distinction between the teachings found in the Gospels and those found in the rest of the Bible, but during the Restoration Movement that distinction took on a new fervor, leading almost to a wholesale rejection of those things not found in the Gospels. For example, he declared during the Movement:

> In the New Testament, there is internal evidence that parts of it [i.e., the Gospels] have proceeded from an extraordinary man, and that other parts [i.e., the Epistles] are of the fabric of very inferior minds. It is as easy to separate those parts as to pick out diamonds from dunghills.[44]

> Among the sayings and discourses imputed to Him [Jesus] by His biographers [in the Gospels], I find many passages of fine imagination, correct morality, and of the most lovely benevolence; and others [in the Epistles], again, of so much ignorance, so much absurdity, so much untruth, charlatanism and imposture as to pronounce it impossible that such contradictions should have proceeded from the same Being. I separate, therefore, the gold from the dross; restore to Him the former and leave the latter to the stupidity of some, and roguery of others of His disciples. Of this band of dupes and impostors, Paul was the great Coryphaeus [leader and spokesperson] and first corruptor of the doctrines of Jesus.[45]

Another non-Gospel book on which Jefferson held a clear opinion was the book of Revelation. In 1825 General Alexander Smyth, a military officer from the War of 1812 and a longtime Virginia legislator, sought Jefferson's opinion about a work he had prepared on the end times and the book of Revelation. Jefferson responded, telling Smith:

> [Y]ou must be so good as to excuse me, because I make it an invariable rule to decline ever giving opinions on new publications in any case whatever. No man on earth has less taste or

talent for criticism than myself, and least and last of all should I undertake to criticize works on the Apocalypse. It is between fifty and sixty years since I read it, and I then considered it as merely the ravings of a maniac, no more worthy nor capable of explanation than the incoherencies of our own nightly dreams.[46]

But this negative opinion about the book of Revelation did not mean that Jefferson had no opinion on the end times, for he did. Jesus had specifically addressed this subject in the Gospels, so Jefferson had reached a conclusion on it much earlier in life. He therefore instructed his daughter Martha:

I hope you will have good sense enough to disregard these foolish predictions that the world is to be at an end soon. The Almighty has never made known to anybody at what time He created it, nor will He tell anybody when he means to put an end to it—if ever He means to do it. As to preparations for that event, the best way is for you to be always prepared for it. The only way to be so is never to do nor say anything amiss or to do anything wrong. Consider beforehand; you will feel something within you which will tell you it is wrong and ought not to be said or done; this is your conscience, and be sure to obey it. Our Maker has given us all this faithful internal monitor, and if you always obey it you will always be prepared for the end of the world, or for a much more certain event which is death.[47]

Jefferson also wrote a lengthy letter to William Short, whom he considered an adopted son, extolling what Jesus taught in the Gospels but deriding what had been taught in the Old Testament:

That sect [the Jews] had presented for the object of their worship a Being of terrific character: cruel, vindictive, capricious, and unjust. Jesus, taking for His type the best qualities of the human head and heart (wisdom, justice, goodness) and adding to them power, ascribed all of these (but in infinite perfection) to the Supreme Being, and formed Him really worthy of their adoration.[48]

Jefferson also denounced the Old Testament tendency toward continual fighting between nations, contrasting that practice with what Jesus had taught:

The one [Moses] instilled into his people the most antisocial spirit towards other nations; the other [Jesus] preached philanthropy and universal charity and benevolence.[49]

Jefferson also noted that the Old Testament position of "an eye for an eye, a tooth for a tooth" was quite different from the system Jesus brought.[50] He also disagreed with Old Testament theology "which supposes the God of infinite justice to punish the sins of the fathers upon their children, unto the 3rd and 4th generations."[51] In short, in late life, Jefferson, just like the ministers in Christian Primitivism, focused almost solely on the Gospels, criticizing both the Epistles and the Old Testament.

Anti-Calvinistic

Throughout most of his life, Jefferson had viewed the Presbyterians as his allies, declaring that "the Presbyterian spirit is known to be so congenial with friendly liberty,"[52] but in the Restoration Movement he reversed course. With the Movement's strident rejection of Calvinism, Presbyterians—the denomination most closely affiliated with Calvinism—became the object of Jefferson's denunciation:

The Presbyterian clergy are loudest, the most intolerant of all sects, the most tyrannical and ambitious—ready at the word of the lawgiver (if such a word could be now obtained) to put the torch to the pile and to rekindle in this virgin hemisphere the flames in which their oracle Calvin consumed the poor Servetus [a leader in the Reformation whom Calvin permitted to be burned at the stake for heresy regarding Trinitarianism], because he could not find in his Euclid the proposition which has demonstrated that three are one and one is three, nor subscribe to that of Calvin that magistrates have a right to exterminate all heretics to Calvinistic creed. They want to re-establish by law that holy inquisition which they can now only infuse into public opinion.[53]

He further declared that "[m]y fundamental principle would be the reverse of Calvin's"[54] and that "Calvinism has introduced into the Christian religion more new absurdities than its leader had purged it of old ones [during the Reformation]."[55] Jefferson listed several specific teachings of Calvin with which he vehemently disagreed, including Calvin's claim "that God, from the beginning, elected certain individuals to be saved and certain others to be damned; and that no crimes of the former can damn them, no virtues of the latter save."[56] He also denounced Calvin's teaching "that good works, or the love of our neighbor, are nothing" and "that reason in religion is of unlawful use."[57]

Jefferson pointedly told John Adams:

I can never join Calvin in addressing his God. He was indeed an atheist (which I can never be), or rather his religion was daemonism [worship of an evil god]. If ever man worshipped a false god, he did. The being described in his five points is not the God Whom you and I acknowledge and adore—the Creator and Benevolent Governor of the world, but a demon of malignant spirit. It would be more pardonable to believe in no God at all than to blaspheme Him by the atrocious attributes of Calvin.[58]

Bible Specific Language and Anti-Trinitarianism

As noted earlier, Restorationists thought that if a term was not in the Bible then it should not be in Christianity. This is why the Reverend Stone said that because the word *Trinity* did not appear in the Bible, the doctrine should therefore be rejected. In the latter years of Jefferson's life, he embraced the same view, even though it was a view that he had not held in earlier years. So, like the Reverend Elias Smith before him, Jefferson delineated things that did not appear in actual language of the Scriptures and should therefore be rejected, including the "immaculate conception of Jesus, his deification, the creation of the world by him [instead of God], his miraculous powers, his resurrection and visible ascension, his corporeal presence in the Eucharist, the Trinity; original sin, atonement, regeneration, election, orders of Hierarchy, &c."[59]

In earlier years, however, Jefferson had openly embraced doctrinal beliefs he was now rejecting. But having fully embraced the Christian Primitivist position, he predicted, wrongly:

> [T]he day will come when the mystical generation [i.e., the conception] of Jesus by the Supreme Being as his father, in the womb of a virgin, will be classed with the fable of the generation of Minerva [the Roman virgin goddess] in the brain of Jupiter.[60]

Are such statements heretical by the standards of orthodox Christianity? Absolutely. But unfortunately, this is what was being preached and advocated by the major Christian leaders in central Virginia. Jefferson attended their churches and heard this message directly from them. In fact, it was during his affiliation with Christian Primitivism that he first expressed Anti-Trinitarian views in a letter to John Adams in 1813.[61] Of course, it should be remembered that the Restoration Movement also had many sound doctrines (that Jesus was the Savior, baptism and communion were important, the teachings of Jesus were to be diligently studied and followed, and so forth), but they also clearly had several errant ones. It is Jefferson's writings in the latter category that understandably cause so much consternation among traditional Christians.

Unitarianism

The Primitivist emphasis on Christian unity and Anti-Trinitarianism provided the seedbed in which Unitarianism flourished. However, it is important to note that Unitarianism in Jefferson's day was not at all what it is has become today.

Unitarianism appeared in America as early as 1785. Its doctrines were stated by William Ellery Channing in 1819, and the American Unitarian Association was formed in 1825.[62] Unitarianism had some definite theological problems at that time, but it was still universally considered a Christian denomination.[63] As observers in that day noted, "[S]everal of the ablest defenders of Christianity against the attacks of infidels have been Unitarians."[64] But in 1838 it underwent a radical change when Ralph Waldo Emerson began slowly reshaping Channing's 1819 teachings, which were still largely Christian, into

> a Transcendentalist version of the ethical theism of Plato, the Stoics and Kant, coordinated with the nascent evolutionist science of the day and the newly explored mysticism of the ancient East. This new religious philosophy, as construed and applied by the Boston preacher Theodore Parker and other disciples of Emerson, included the other great ethnic faiths with

Christianity in a universal religion of Humanity and through its intellectual hospitality operated to open Unitarian fellowship to evolutionists, monists, pragmatists, and humanists.[65]

Many of today's ultra-heretical Unitarian doctrines did not exist at the time of Jefferson. The primary heterodox doctrine at that time (which still was a genuine problem) was that Jesus was the son of God but not God Himself. But there were at least four reasons why Jefferson found himself comfortable with early Unitarians.

First, perhaps more than any other religious group in that day, the Unitarians placed a very strong emphasis on teaching morals. Recall Jefferson's keen interest in this subject with his personal and diligent study of the moral teachings of leaders from the previous three millennia. In fact, the Unitarians' emphasis on morality was so strong that it was the sole reason that President John Quincy Adams (an evangelical Christian) attended a Unitarian Church in Washington, DC. After acknowledging, "I did not subscribe to many of his [the minister's] doctrines, particularly not to the fundamental one of his Unitarian creed,"[66] Adams explained that he attended the church because the minister's "moral discourses were always good, and . . . I listened to them with pleasure and profit."[67] Jefferson likewise found Unitarian moral teachings to be very appealing, for Unitarian ministers at that time laid great stress on the practical day-to-day aspects of the moral teachings of Jesus and the Bible, as did Jefferson.

Second, Unitarians took a strong position against slavery and for emancipation. Abolition advocates reported that "the Unitarians, next to the Quakers, seem to have acted with more zeal in behalf of the negroes."[68] But some Unitarians disagreed, believing that they had done even more than the Quakers. As Unitarian minister Samuel May explained, "We Unitarians have given to the antislavery cause more preachers, writers, lecturers, agents, poets, than any other denomination."[69] Emancipation was obviously a position that Jefferson had advocated throughout his life, so it is understandable that he felt at home among Unitarians.

Third, Unitarians emphasized the interdenominational cooperation and acceptance that was a lifelong hallmark of Jefferson's personal beliefs, as has already been demonstrated.

Fourth, while other denominations confined their membership to only those Christians who embraced their specific doctrines, the Unitarians embraced all who called themselves Christian. This type of open Christian acceptance was particularly appealing to Jefferson, for he had been continually attacked and vilified by certain denominations of Christians, even when expressing completely orthodox Christian beliefs. But among Unitarians he found acceptance and a personal peace—relief from unrelenting attacks and controversies. He seemed, however, to forget that many of the Federalists who attacked him during his campaigns had been Unitarians; but at that time he was probably more cognizant of their Federalist political affiliation than their Unitarian religious one.

Perhaps as a result of the vicious attacks he had suffered, Jefferson became generally loath to talk about his personal faith with others unless they were among a handful of close personal friends.[70] And even with these, he would still ask them to return his letter after they had read it[71] or else burn, destroy, or keep it secret[72] so that its contents would not become fodder for his enemies.

In fact, two decades earlier, at a time when his Christian beliefs were still orthodox, Jefferson told his attorney general, Levi Lincoln, that if content from his private letters about religion should "get into print," the effect would be that he "would become the butt of every set of disquisitions which every priest would undertake to write on every tenet it expresses. Their object is not truth, but matter whereon to write against."[73]

Lengthy experience had taught Jefferson to let nothing about his religious views become public, except in general terms. He therefore largely adopted a live-and-let-live philosophy. As he explained to one inquirer:

> I take no part in controversies, religious or political. At the age of eighty, tranquility is the greatest good of life; and the strongest of our desires, that of dying in the good will of all mankind. And with the assurances of all my good will to Unitarian and Trinitarian, to Whig and Tory, accept for yourself that of my entire respect.[74]

Perhaps it was because Jefferson was so drawn to the cooperation and acceptance of early Restoration and Primitivism that he also accepted so many of their other Unitarian beliefs. Nevertheless, he found early Unitarianism to be personally satisfying and hoped it would sweep the country, optimistically declaring, "I confidently expect that the present generation will see Unitarianism become the general religion of the United States."[75] Jefferson so embraced the Unitarian emphasis on returning to primitive Christianity that in 1822 he hopefully expressed, "I trust that there is not a young man now living in the United States who will not die an Unitarian."[76]

But, in this, Jefferson was wrong. By the time he died four years later, the trend was swinging back; the effect of the Second Great Awakening was substantially slowing Unitarianism across the rest of the country. O'Kelly, one of the Founders of the Restoration Movement and the only clear Trinitarian among its four major leaders, wrote in 1824:

> The Arians [those who do not believe that the Godhead is equal], or Unitarians, in this state perhaps are fading fast; some of their preachers, I hope, may be convinced of their dangerous error and return to the Christian Church. To me it appears that

to deny Jesus Christ as being equal Deity is a destructive idea and in fact is, at least in effect, denying the Atonement.[77]

Regrettably, Jefferson did not live long enough to experience the reversal that eventually occurred in his central Virginia valley, and, given the pattern of his life, it is certainly possible that had time permitted, he well might have changed his position and come back to his previous and more traditional Christian beliefs on the Trinity. Happily, much of the Anti-Trinitarian element that took hold in Charlottesville did not survive elsewhere, and the Trinitarian branch of the Restoration Movement gradually developed into the denominations known as the Churches of Christ, the Christian Church, and the Disciples of Christ.

So what conclusions can be made about Jefferson's spiritual condition and whether or not he was a Christian? Well, Jefferson definitely called himself a Christian. For example, during the Restoration Movement he told his old friend Charles Thomson, "I am a real Christian, that is to say, a disciple of the doctrines of Jesus."[78]

Even well before the Restoration movement, he had similarly told Benjamin Rush:

To the corruptions of Christianity I am indeed opposed; but not to the genuine precepts of Jesus Himself. I am a Christian in the only sense in which He wished any one to be: sincerely attached to His doctrines in preference to all others.[79]

But such unequivocal declarations are not the end of the story, for many of the declarations made by Jefferson during the period of the Restoration Movement definitely do not comport with an orthodox understanding of what it means to be a Christian, although they are consistent with Christian Primitivism. Apparently, Jefferson himself recognized this, and in 1819 he acknowledged to the Reverend Ezra Stiles, a military chaplain during the Revolution and the president of Yale, "I am of a sect by myself, as far as I know."[80]

Dumas Malone, the Pulitzer Prize–winning biographer of Thomas Jefferson, understood the difficulty of analyzing the orthodoxy of Jefferson's faith. He acknowledged that on the one hand, "This apostle of spiritual freedom regarded himself as a Christian, and unquestionably he was one in his ethical standards."[81] But on the other hand, when one references the statements he made during his latter fifteen years, "Jefferson did not refer to the Messiah, the Savior, or the Christ," although he did continue to have "unbounded admiration for Jesus."[82]

Significantly, for nearly every Christian doctrine that Jefferson called into question in his last fifteen years, across his earlier sixty-eight years he had embraced that very same doctrine as orthodox. In fact, only a decade before Jefferson entered the Restoration Movement, he personally assured Dr. Benjamin Rush that "he believed in the Divine mission of the Savior of the World," "in the Divine institution of the Sabbath," and "likewise in the resurrection, and a future state of rewards and punishments." (Although Rush acknowledged that there still existed some theological differences between himself and Jefferson.[83]) After conversing with Jefferson on his personal religious views of Christianity, Rush confessed to Jefferson that "you are by no means so heterodox as you have been supposed to be by your enemies."[84]

Probably no human today can know for sure whether or not Jefferson finished his life as a Christian in good standing with God through Jesus Christ; only God knows for sure. Perhaps Jefferson, having once had a strong early Christian faith which later became contaminated and weak, fits into the category of 1 Corinthians 3:15 that "[i]f anyone's work is burned up, he will suffer loss, though he himself will be saved, but only as through fire."

Several things are certain, however, including the clear fact that Jefferson was *not* an atheist. As he affirmed to John Adams, "[A]n atheist . . . I can never be."[85]

Jefferson also was definitely not a deist. A deist believes in an impersonal God uninvolved with mankind and embraces the "clockmaker theory" that there was once a God Who made the universe and wound it up like a clock but that it now runs of its own volition; the clockmaker is gone. Prayer is therefore unavailing, for the clockmaker no longer intervenes in the affairs of men.[86] It is clear that none of Jefferson's religious writings from any period of his life reveal anything less than his strong conviction in a personal God[87] Who answers prayers and intervenes in the affairs of mankind[88] and before Whom every individual would stand to be judged.[89]

Not only was Jefferson definitely not an atheist or a deist, he clearly was not a secularist—nor was he irreligious. To the contrary, he strongly promoted religion in general and Christianity in particular. He regularly expressed his personal affinity for the teachings of Jesus[90] and frequently referenced the Bible in his own writings.[91] In fact, after Jefferson's death when his grandson was asked about Jefferson's religious opinions and beliefs, he reported:

> I never heard from him the expression of one thought, feeling, or sentiment inconsistent with the highest moral standard or the purest Christian charity in its most enlarged sense. His moral character was of the highest order, founded upon the purest and sternest models of antiquity, softened, chastened and developed by the influences of the all-pervading benevolence of the doctrines of Christ, which he had intensely and admiringly studied. . . . In his contemplative moments, his mind turned to religion, which he studied thoroughly. He had seen and read much of the abuses and perversions of Christianity; he abhorred those abuses and their authors and denounced them without

reserve. He was regular in his attendance on church, taking his prayer-book with him. He drew the plan of the Episcopal Church in Charlottesville, was one of the largest contributors to its erection, and contributed regularly to the support of its minister. I paid, after his death, his subscription of $200 to the erection of the Presbyterian Church in the same village. A gentleman of some distinction calling on him, and expressing his disbelief in the truths of the Bible, his reply was, "Then, sir, you have studied it to little purpose." He was guilty of no profanity himself, and did not tolerate it in others—he detested impiety, and his favorite quotation for his young friends as a basis for their morals was the XV Psalm of David.[92]

The condition of Jefferson's private personal theology and Christian faith in his last years might be questioned, but what cannot be questioned is the fact that throughout his life, Jefferson was pro-Christian and pro-Jesus in his beliefs, demeanor, and public endeavors.

CONCLUSION

Thomas Jefferson: An American Hero

O ur examination of historical primary-source documents has clearly demonstrated that the picture of Jefferson's faith and morals painted by modern critics is definitively wrong. Any point his critics make might initially seem to be irrefutable, but once the rest of the story is told, reality emerges and truth can prevail. Thus, let us review the modern Jefferson lies.

1. DNA evidence has *not* proved that Jefferson fathered any children outside of his marriage to Martha. His moral reputation was attacked two centuries ago by enemies attempting to besmirch him during a presidential election, but the charges were groundless, not based on any fact. Jefferson, knowing that God knew the truth, regularly appealed to Him as his judge on this issue. He actually longed for the time when the Great Judge would not only clear him of any moral wrongdoing but also prove the accusations false. There is absolutely no historical, factual, or scientific evidence to tarnish the sexual morality of Jefferson. He therefore deserves to be listed alongside John Adams, Benjamin Rush, Roger Sherman, and so many other Founding Fathers whose reputations of moral purity remain untainted to this day.

2. Jefferson enjoyed a thoroughly religious education and was not responsible for instituting secular, religion-free

education in *any* educational endeavor in which he was involved. Because he worked extensively to disestablish a state-approved denomination and to institute denominational nonpreferentialism, he therefore founded America's first trans- or nondenominational university. He ensured that multiple Christian denominations would be an active part of university life and that Christian instruction and activities would definitely occur on campus.

3. Jefferson did not write a Bible, not of any kind. He did create two religious works about Jesus that were exactly what he titled them. The first was an abridgment of the New Testament for the use of the Indians and the second was a compilation of the moral teachings of Jesus for his own personal study and meditation. In both he included multiple references to the supernatural and miraculous. Jefferson was a supporter of organizations that widely distributed the Bible. He owned a number of Bibles that he personally used and studied, was a member of the Virginia Bible Society, and financially supported the printing of Bibles. He gave Bibles to younger family members, and the Bible was openly used in institutions he helped start or direct, from Washington's public schools to the University of Virginia.

4. Jefferson was not a racist who opposed blacks and civil rights but rather was a lifelong unwavering advocate for emancipation. He was largely unsuccessful because of the state of Virginia in which he lived but it was not from a lack of effort or desire on his part. Had his efforts been undertaken in any state north of his own, he likely would be heralded today as one of America's leading early civil rights advocates. He was regularly praised by subsequent generations for his civil rights efforts and was favorably invoked by numerous civil rights leaders, both black and

white. Jefferson referenced religious beliefs and teachings as the basis of his views on emancipation and equality, repeatedly declaring that because God was just, He would eventually bring slavery to an end in America, one way or another.

5. Jefferson regularly incorporated religious activities into public settings and invoked the "separation of church and state" phrase only to affirm the historic understanding that the government had *no* authority to stop, inhibit, or regulate public religious expressions. He therefore called for days of prayer, introduced religious bills in the state legislature, signed numerous federal acts promoting religious groups and activities, and facilitated official churches in the US Capitol, Treasury Building, War Office, and Navy Yard. Were Jefferson alive today, he would undoubtedly be one of the loudest voices against a secularized public square.

6. Jefferson did not hate clergy, but he did repeatedly denounce the Period II clergy who participated in the unholy alliance of "kingcraft and priestcraft." He similarly reprobated American clergy who supported "law religion" that sought the establishment of a particular denomination in a state. Such clergy viewed Jefferson as their enemy (and he, they), but clergy who sought denominational nonpreferentialism were outspoken advocates and supporters of Jefferson. Jefferson praised many clergy, wrote letters of recommendation for them, gave generously to their churches, and recruited them to run for political office. Jefferson was the hero of countless clergy and remained close friends with many of them throughout his long life.

7. Jefferson was not a secularist, deist, or atheist. He never wavered from his belief that God actively intervened in the

affairs of men. He thus regularly prayed, believing that God would answer his prayers for his family, his country, the unity of the Christian church, and the end of slavery. And while he always called himself a Christian, he ended his life as a Christian Primitivist, being in personal disagreement with some orthodox theological tenets of Christianity that he had affirmed earlier in life, although still holding fast to many other traditionally sound theological tenets. But notwithstanding his own personal theological difficulties over specific doctrines, there never was a time in his life when Jefferson was not pro-Christian and pro-Christianity.

On none of these seven points was it difficult to establish truth. Each inquiry was answered by plentiful personal statements directly from Jefferson and those closest to him. Those multiple declarations resoundingly refute the modern lies about his faith and morals.

The reason that an investigation of Jefferson's faith and morals was even necessary is the deplorable slip in accurate historical knowledge over the past half-century. We briefly touched on the five modern tools of historical malpractice in an earlier chapter:

1. *Deconstructionism* pours out a steady flow of negatives about traditional heroes, values, and institutions through sniping remarks, belittling criticism, and inaccurate portrayals. It poses "a continuous critique" to "lay low what was once high."[1] Consequently, even though Jefferson was venerated and honored for generations, today he is regularly attacked, belittled, and dismissed with pejorative epithets such as "rapist," "deadbeat dad," "vindictive racist," "slave-owning, serial slave, sex addict," and more.

2. *Poststructuralism* rejects absolutes such as God or truth, instead asserting that each individual must interpret history for himself, basing its meanings on one's personal views rather than on objective standards. It encourages individual anarchy against traditional, national, unifying values and institutions, and citizens are made to be part of interest groups rather than allowed to stand individually. Hence, Jefferson is examined as an individual only in order to identify the group into which he should be placed, whether it is that of racists, Enlightenment writers, secularists, immoral slaveholders, Freethinkers, or any other.

3. *Modernism* examines historical incidents and persons as if they lived today rather than in the past, thereby separating history from its context and producing many flawed conclusions. Because it is certain that no state university today would include religious activities and classes for *all* its students, then it must have also been that way then, and so Jefferson's views on education were definitely antireligious. Because religious expressions today must be separated from the public square, it must have been that way two centuries ago, and so Jefferson was clearly a secularist. Because clergy today do not attack candidates from the pulpit as was done then, Jefferson's comments about the specific clergy who lied about him clearly indicate that he hated all clergy. Such are the suppositions of Modernism.

4. *Minimalism* unreasonably insists on oversimplicity and reducing everything to easy answers that don't require thinking or analysis, condensing complex situations into one-line characterizations and squeezing historical individuals into preconceived, preshaped molds they do not fit. Since

Jefferson made some comments late in life rejecting specific tenets of Christianity, he is therefore deemed a lifelong atheist, so there is no need to investigate any of the complicated spiritual cycles through which he traveled or even to take note of the adverse effects of Christian Primitivism and Restorationism upon him. These are simply dismissed out of hand because they are too complex for popular consideration.

5. *Academic Collectivism* relies on the claims of "experts" rather than original documents as the standard for truth. It advances an incestuous system of peer review as the measurement for whether a historical fact is accurate or errant. Thus, modern professors quote each other in their declarations that the University of Virginia was secular and had no chaplain, that Jefferson hired only Unitarians to be its instructional staff, that Jefferson penned the first Amendment, and so forth, when in reality Jefferson's own writings, documents of the university, and the testimony of original professors prove exactly the opposite.

The countless errors resulting from these five historical malpractices have so thoroughly infused modern textbooks, the Web, and popular knowledge that it has now become difficult for the average citizen to even discern when history is being misrepresented. But recognition is the first step to avoidance; that is, once one knows what the five tools are, it becomes much easier to spot them and avoid being caught in their errors.

Because early detection helps defeat an enemy, recognition training has always been a regular part of military preparation. For this reason, GIs in World War II were regularly grilled and tested on the identification of Axis tanks and planes so that they would be able to quickly spot and destroy enemy forces. Similarly, the reason animals are caught in traps is that they don't recognize the snare into which they have stepped; once a beaver, wild hog, or any other animal learns to recognize the device, it is no longer effective. This is why 2 Corinthians 2:11 reminds us that if we can identify Satan's traps, then he won't have an advantage over us.

This same principle should guide our approach to the study of history: recognize and avoid the traps of historical malpractice. But once you recognize a trap, there is more. It is not enough simply to personally avoid the trap; it must also be exposed and removed so that others will not be injured. Thus, when a soldier discovers an IED, minefield, RPG, or weapons cache, he takes steps to neutralize and remove the danger so that no one else will be harmed by inadvertently stumbling into it.

The best means for overcoming the five modern historical traps is given in Romans 12:21, which instructs us to defeat the evil with the good—that is, not just to avoid evil ourselves but also to apply its antithesis, or its antidote, to neutralize the effect of its poison. For example, praise prevails over criticism, light over darkness, gentleness over anger, humility over arrogance, and so on. So what is the antithesis for each of the five poisons so often injected into American history today?

The effects and influences of *Deconstructionism* can be avoided by training oneself to search out the rest of the story and discover if there is a second view or whether there are positive aspects of the account that were omitted from the original portrayal. Of course, the negatives will always be easy to find, just as they were in Numbers 13 and 14 when ten of twelve leaders went into a land filled with milk and honey but came back talking only about its giants and problems. Joshua and Caleb demonstrated in that story that while the negatives are indeed present and cannot be ignored, the positives must also be pointed out: it was a vast, abundant, verdant land of prosperity and plenty just waiting to be entered. Identifying the negatives comes naturally; acknowledging the positives takes deliberate effort.

Thomas Jefferson understood this and therefore refused to let negatives prevail in his conversations. His grandson recalled learning this lesson directly from Jefferson.

> He [my grandfather] spoke only of the good qualities of men, which induced the belief that he knew little of them; but no one knew them better. I had formed this opinion, and on hearing him speak very favorably of men with defects known to myself, [I] stated them to him; when he asked if I supposed he had not observed them (adding others not noted by me, and evincing [demonstrating] much more accurate knowledge of the individual character than I possessed), observing, "My habit is to speak only of men's good qualities."[2]

Especially in today's Deconstructionist-dominated environment, it will always be easy to find (or concoct) negatives about any historical figure, but it will require deliberate effort to identify the positives that have been omitted. And omission is one of the most egregious but most effective tools of revisionists.

This point was brilliantly made by Dr. Paul C. Vitz, a professor at New York University. He was contracted to review history textbooks through a grant from the Department of Education and after examining those texts, he concluded:

> Over and over, we have seen that liberal and secular bias is primarily accomplished by exclusion, by leaving out the opposing position. Such a bias is much harder to observe than a positive vilification or direct criticism, but it is the essence of censorship.[3]

In fact, he observed a strikingly aggressive secularist tendency among those texts:

> And the facts are clear: religion, especially Christianity, has played and continues to play a central role in American life. To neglect to report this is simply to fail to carry out the major duty of any textbook writer—the duty to tell the truth.[4]

It is indeed the duty of those who present history to tell the truth—to tell the whole truth, not just a part of it. As John Adams explained:

> [T]ruth and right are invariably the same in all times and in all places. . . . But passion, prejudice, interest, custom, and fancy are infinitely precarious [unstable]; if therefore we suffer our understandings to be blinded or perverted by any of these . . . we shall embrace errors.[5]

Very simply, when we don't tell the whole truth but are "blinded or perverted" by passion or bias, then "we shall embrace errors."

One of the best ways to find the complete story about an individual is not through a sterile academic study whereby one slice out of a complex historical life is extracted and analyzed under a modern microscope. Rather, the best means is by examining the full life, events, and writings of an individual.

In the case of Thomas Jefferson, one of the easiest ways to check his complete story is to read some of the earlier biographies about him, such as the 1858 three-volume set by Henry Stephens Randall. Even today, this work is still considered the most authoritative ever written on Jefferson, for Randall was the only biographer approved by the family and given full access to the family papers, records, family members, and family remembrances. Many other early biographies of Jefferson are also worth the read[6] and are usually available for reading online or downloading, as is Randall's work.[7]

In short, an antidote for Deconstructionism is to get the full story, especially the part that includes the good things. Lady Margaret Thatcher once wisely repeated the words of a great educator on this point.

> Teach them [children] everything that is *best* in life—teach them all the *good* things our country has done—and you will find we shall get a very much better education.[8] (emphasis added)

The remedy for the second device, *Poststructuralism*, is (1) to acknowledge individuality—to examine the person himself rather than the various groups and agents to which others are trying to attach him and (2) to recognize and acknowledge fixed and absolute overarching transcendent principles. For example, citizens are entitled to enjoy their God-given inalienable rights (as specified in the Bill of Rights) not because they belong to any particular group but rather because they are individual human beings. Someone does not receive the right of habeas corpus or religious expression or self-protection because he or she belongs to the majority or the minority, is black or Latino, is male or young. Rather, it is because those rights are bestowed on every individual by our Creator. Recognizing individuality is the approach that God takes: everyone is accountable to God individually rather than as part of some group; God provides salvation to individuals not groups. So, too, good history focuses on an examination of the individual and not just his group.

And because Poststructuralism also encourages personal interpretation of history based on how one "feels" about the person or event, individual feelings must be set aside in the quest for truth. It really doesn't matter how someone "feels" about Jefferson or whether or not they like him; what matters are facts and truth. As James Madison affirmed, "For what is the object of our discussion? Truth, sir—to draw a true and just conclusion."[9]

Personal feelings must be subjugated to objective truth. Either Jefferson did or did not promote emancipation, did or did not encourage public religious expressions, did or did not include religion in education, regardless of whether someone agrees or disagrees with him on those issues. Truth is transcendent and immutable, not individually constructed and interpreted. Therefore, in order to overcome Poststructuralism, make the quest for objective truth the highest goal. Realize, too, that achieving this goal will always require hard work and deliberate, even aggressive, effort rather than just sitting back and complacently accepting whatever is set before us.

Jefferson expressed this truth when he declared, "If a nation expects to be ignorant, and free, in a state of civilization, it expects what never was and never will be."[10] You can have truth and security; or you can have an unworried oblivious ease; but you cannot have both at the same time.

The antidote to *Modernism* is to learn about and understand the past, not just the present. Unfortunately, this is becoming difficult for two reasons. The first is a growing lack of knowledge about even the most basic facts of American history among those who have been educated in our governmental school system. For example, for citizens who have been trained with our current educational methods:

- 65 percent do not know what happened at the Constitutional Convention.

- 88 percent cannot name even one writer of the *Federalist Papers*.

- 40 percent cannot name an American enemy during World War II.

- 81 percent cannot name even one of the federal government's powers.

- 70 percent do not know that the US Constitution is the supreme law of the land.[11]

Because our educational system now graduates students lacking even minimal proficiency of the simplest facts, whatever extravagant charges Modernists may make about Jefferson or any other historical figure or event seem plausible. The general public is simply no longer knowledgeable enough about history to recognize the claims as false. Regrettably, much of this growing historical illiteracy is actually a direct result of current education laws.

For example, federal laws such as "No Child Left Behind" require student accountability testing in order for schools to secure federal funds, but that testing covers reading, math, and science, not history. Most schools instruct their teachers to focus on teaching students the subject matter covered in the testing, whether mandated by state or federal law. History is rarely a part of that focus, so it receives minimal attention.

The second impediment to historical literacy is evolution, which is not simply a science controversy but rather a philosophy-of-life debate. Even attorney Clarence Darrow, who argued the case for evolution in the famous 1925 *Scopes* trial,[12] acknowledged that he was arguing it as "a death struggle between two civilizations."[13]

When evolutionary belief is applied to law, it results in the "living Constitution," asserting that what was written two centuries ago is not applicable today and that judges must allow the Constitution to evolve to meet today's needs. Constitutional history, therefore, becomes irrelevant, and has largely been dropped from legal studies in most law schools.

When evolutionary belief is applied to education, it results in the constant seeking of new methodologies of instruction, even if the old ones still work well. Consequently, traditional "old" math instruction that involves memorizing the math tables is discarded and replaced with "new" math. Of this, a US senator correctly observed:

> This new-new mush-mush math will never produce quality engineers or mathematicians who can compete for jobs in the global market place. In Palo Alto, California, public school math students plummeted from the 86th percentile to the 56th in the first year of new math teaching. This awful textbook obviously fails to do in 812 pages what comparable Japanese textbooks do so well in 200. The average standardized math score in Japan is 80. In the United States it is 52.[14]

Similarly, on the grounds that old methods of teaching English are boring and need to be evolved, diagramming sentences and traditional grammar instruction was dropped several years ago. But now only one-fourth of students can write at a proficient level, and only 1 percent can write at an advanced level.[15]

Since evolution seeks to leave the past behind and move forward to something new, the academic study of history is the most severely impacted by this philosophy. After all, since evolution states that man is ever progressing, then what is in the past is of little relevance today. The study of history is therefore a complete waste of time.

Embracing this evolutionary approach to history, several states have adopted what is now termed the Twentieth-Century Model, requiring high school students to learn only that which happened from 1900 forward and sometimes back to 1877 (from Reconstruction forward).[16]

It would seem that high school students—young adults on the verge of entering active national citizenship—should study the Founding Fathers, Declaration of Independence, Constitution, and Bill of Rights along with responsible civics and participatory constitutional government. But in most states, these specific topics are covered in fifth-grade history; and what eleven-year-old really cares about habeas corpus, trial by jury, the rights of conscience, judicial tyranny, or taxation without representation? Fifth graders don't, but high schoolers should. Yet we teach this material to fifth graders and not high schoolers.

But early American history is not only de-emphasized in high school, but also among post-graduate institutions. According to the *US News and World Report, none*—not one—of the fifty-five elite colleges and universities they ranked requires *any* course in American history for graduation,[17] and none of the top fifty even requires a course in Western history.[18] Since all that matters today is who we are now rather than who we were then, history courses have been replaced with modern culture courses.

But for the more than 80 percent of Americans who believe that God made man,[19] there is still much that can be learned from history. In fact, God Himself insists that we study history, admonishing us to "remember the former things of old" (Isaiah 46:9) and "call to remembrance the former days" (Hebrews 10:32 KJV). As the Apostle Paul explained in 1 Corinthians 10, history provides lessons and illustrates principles that we can still apply today (see also Romans 15:4). But with so many Americans having been separated from even a rudimentary knowledge of their own history and its simplest facts, Modernism now has far too significant an influence.

One of the best ways to overcome Modernism is similar to the antidote for Deconstructionism: biographical history. Study history through the eyes of those who made it. For generations we examined the American Revolution by reading biographies of Paul Revere and George Washington; we studied the Civil War by reading the life and struggles of Abraham Lincoln and Harriet Tubman; we learned the progress of science by reading about the tireless efforts of George Washington Carver and Thomas Edison. This long-established custom of learning history by studying the lives of its heroes has fallen into disfavor over the past half-century, but it is this practice that best overcomes Modernism, for it helps us understand what it was like to walk in another's moccasins and thus understand their times and circumstances. Fortunately, many early biographies are still readily available today and can be downloaded, printed, or read online through sites such as Google Books, Gutenberg, PageByPageBooks, Monergism, ReadPrint, Archive, and others.[20]

In my personal experience, I have found that biographies written before 1900 tend to present the most honest and accurate view of the good, the bad, and the ugly about the individuals they cover. Older books generally have not been infected with our modern agendas and therefore more accurately acquaint us with the period, customs, facts, and circumstances of that particular time. I place about a 75 percent confidence in biographies printed from 1900 to 1920 since various historical agendas were beginning to emerge at that time. I place only about a 50 percent reliance on biographies from 1920 to 1950 and less than a 20 percent reliance on those from the 1960s forward. Generally, the newer the book, the more likely it has been infected with the five modern malpractices. Exceptions to this trend are books that have an abundance of primary source documentary citations, such as those by David McCullough, Dumas Malone, Daniel Dreisbach, James Hutson, and others.

In short, to overcome Modernism, develop a broader, macro knowledge of historical persons, events, customs, and beliefs rather than just the modern micro view.

The remedy for the fourth malpractice, *Minimalism,* is to establish context. Because human nature always has and always will prefer things to be simple, the tendency toward Minimalism is definitely not a new problem. In fact, it has been a trap to be avoided by Christians for the past two millennia. Its solution was long ago set forth by the Apostle Paul when he stated that he "did not shrink from declaring . . . the whole counsel of God" (Acts 20:27) rather than just picking and choosing items that interested him. He similarly admonished those following in his steps to "rightly divid[e] the word of truth" (2 Timothy 2:15 KJV)—that is, to look at the complete picture and then make an accurate analysis.

Those recommendations from Paul about how to avoid theological problems are exactly the same for avoiding historical ones. Get the entire context of what is being said; don't separate something from its historical setting. Thus, when a line is lifted from a letter—such as Jefferson's "separation of church and state" or "question with boldness even the existence of a god" phrase—go back and read the whole letter. And when a word or phrase that you don't understand appears in a quote, look it up so that you can grasp its meaning and thus understand its context.

The solution for *Academic Collectivism* is to personally investigate, study, and search out information rather than just accept what the "experts" claim. Become like a jury member of old; get all the evidence, listen to both sides, and reach an independent conclusion warranted by the facts.

The Apostle Paul especially endorsed this approach. He made three extended journeys that carried him from one end of the known world to the other. Having personally seen countless cultures and peoples, he identified those from Berea as being the most noble. He particularly praised them because they did not believe what he told them until they had personally investigated and confirmed it for themselves. Frankly, they were not impressed by the fact that he was an Apostle or that he had been commissioned by Jesus Himself on the road to Damascus. Instead they "examined the Scriptures every day to see if what Paul said was true" (Acts 17:11 NIV). It is truth that matters, not one's credentials. Therefore, insist on checking primary sources.

Consider the work *In Search of Christian America*.[21] Three academics purported to investigate whether the American Founding, defined as the period from 1760 to 1805, was Christian. They concluded that it was not. On what historical basis did they reach this conclusion? Strikingly, 88 percent of the "historical sources" on which they relied to reach their conclusion were published after 1900 and 80 percent were published after 1950. When a book examining the period from 1760 to 1805 does so by analyzing sources printed two centuries afterward, an errant conclusion is not surprising. But this is a common practice in Academic Collectivism: regurgitate what other modern "experts" have said rather than check the original sources. The solution for this problem is to investigate and check the sources for ourselves. As Thomas Paine long ago affirmed, "[I]nvestigation always serves to detect error and to bring forth truth."[22]

By practicing these remedies, the five traps of modern historical malpractice can be avoided. Learning accurate history should be our objective.

By the way, *history* was defined in America's original dictionary (1828) as "an account of facts" and "a narration of events in the order in which they happened, with their causes and effect."[23] All five modern historical devices fail to meet important parts of this definition.

Deconstructionists avoid telling about "events" in the way "they happened," preferring instead to selectively pick out a few things in order to construct a negative image. Poststructuralists avoid "an account of *facts*," believing instead that history is subjective and must therefore be individually interpreted based on the way one feels about what happened. Modernists and Minimalists both sidestep "causes and effects," one by avoiding context and the other by dismissing because examining them "causes and effects" would make things too complicated. And Academic Collectivists avoid "a narration of events," preferring instead to narrate only what other so-called "experts" have said about those events.

To ensure that justice is done in the portrayal of historical events and persons such as Thomas Jefferson, we must reestablish the traditional examination of history free from agendas. Since the practice of biographical history contributes so much to an accurate portrayal of historical fact, it is worth closing this work with some glimpses into the personal life of Jefferson, showing something of his heart, faith, and character.

Jefferson was one of the rare men who became a hero in his own lifetime, yet unlike many others who attained that distinction, he always remained humble and unpretentious, living and acting as the common person for whom he had sacrificed so much. As a result, people would often converse with him without recognizing who he was. Jefferson's granddaughter related such an account:

> On one occasion while traveling, he stopped at a country inn. A stranger who did not know who he was entered into conversation with this plainly-dressed and unassuming traveler. He [the stranger] introduced one subject after another into the conversation, and found him perfectly acquainted with each. Filled with wonder, he seized the first opportunity to inquire of the landlord who his guest was, saying that when he spoke of the law, he thought he was a lawyer; then turning

the conversation on medicine, felt sure he was a physician; but having touched on theology, he became convinced he was a clergyman. "Oh," replied the landlord, "why I thought you knew the Squire." The stranger was then astonished to hear that the traveler whom he had found so affable and simple in his manners was Jefferson.[24]

On another occasion Jefferson was going from Washington back home to Charlottesville, riding on horseback in company with others. As they approached a stream that had no bridge, they saw a traveler on foot standing and waiting at the edge of the stream, hoping to hitch a ride across. He silently watched the others pass and ford the stream, but upon seeing Jefferson (and not knowing who he was) he stopped him and asked if he could mount behind him and ride to the other side. Jefferson graciously agreed, and after putting the traveler down across the stream, he rode on to catch up with the rest of his party. A man who had witnessed the scene approached the traveler and asked why he had not asked any of the others to carry him across the stream. The traveler replied, "From their looks, I did not like to ask them; the old gentleman looked as if he would do it, and I asked him."[25] He was shocked to learn that the man who had carried him across the stream had been the president of the United States, but such was the character of Jefferson. Whenever he had the opportunity to help others or show kindness, he did so. This fact was further attested in his account books by the frequent charity he bestowed, often secretly, on those he saw in need, regardless of where or when he saw them.

Jefferson was not only unassuming and humble but he was also good-natured, and his manners never deserted him—even to those who opposed him. For example, on one occasion while returning on horseback to Washington, he greeted a passing pedestrian. The stranger did not recognize President Jefferson, but the two began a friendly conversation that soon turned to politics. The man began to attack and deride the president, even repeating several of the lies that had been spread about him. Jefferson was amused, and "he asked the man if he knew the President personally? 'No,' was the reply, 'nor do I wish to.' 'But do you think it fair,' asked Jefferson, 'to repeat such stories about a man and condemn one you dare not face?' 'I will never shrink from meeting Mr. Jefferson should he ever come in my way' replied the stranger."[26]

Jefferson then promised him that if he would come to the White House at a certain time the next day, that he would personally introduce him to the president. The next day the stranger appeared for the meeting and was taken to meet President Jefferson. The man was immediately embarrassed and began to apologize, but Jefferson, with a grin on his face, laughed off the apology and extended his hand in welcome greeting. The two then spent several hours in delightful conversation, and when the man rose to depart, Jefferson prevailed on him to stay for dinner.[27]

Jefferson was truly an amiable, polite, and pleasant individual. He also maintained a lifelong passion for accuracy and truth that was apparent on many occasions, including while serving America overseas in France. On one occasion he engaged in a discussion with the famous French naturalist Georges Comte de Buffon, who had penned a massive thirty-six-volume encyclopedia on natural history. Jefferson, himself a noted naturalist, had examined that enormous work and found inaccuracies relating to some American animals, specifically the American moose. He pointed these mistakes out to Buffon, who disagreed. Jefferson then secretly wrote his old friend General John Sullivan, then serving as the governor of New Hampshire, and asked him to send a moose skeleton. The general was surprised by the request but arranged a hunting party, bagged a moose, and sent its frame to Jefferson in Paris. Jefferson then arranged for a dinner with Buffon and during the meal produced the moose skeleton.

Buffon immediately acknowledged his error and expressed his great admiration for Mr. Jefferson's energetic determination to establish the truth. "I should have consulted you, monsieur," he said with usual French civility, "before publishing my book on natural history, and then I should have been sure of my facts."[28]

Although a famous public figure, Jefferson loved and cherished his private life, especially time with his family. He had lost so many of his own precious children, and according to his grandson Thomas, he loved his grandchildren as if they were "the younger members of his family."[29] Jefferson's granddaughter Ellen recalled of her grandfather:

> From him seemed to flow all the pleasures of my life. To him I owed all the small blessings and joyful surprises of my childish and girlish years. . . . When about fifteen years old, I began to think of a watch, but knew the state of my father's finances promised no such indulgence. . . . [But my grandfather gave me] an elegant lady's watch with chain and seals, [which] was in my hand, which trembled for very joy. My Bible came from him, my Shakespeare, my first writing-table, my first handsome writing-desk, my first Leghorn hat [a fancy hat adorned with ribbons], my first silk dress. What, in short, of all my small treasures did not come from him? . . . Our grandfather seemed to read our hearts, to see our invisible wishes, to be our good genie to wave the fairy wand to brighten our young lives by his goodness and his gifts.[30]

But Thomas did not spoil his grandchildren with his generous gifts; he also trained them and shaped their character, just as he had with his own children. Ellen recalled:

He reproved without wounding us, and commended without making us vain. He took pains to correct our errors and false ideas, checked the bold, encouraged the timid, and tried to teach us to reason soundly and feel rightly. Our smaller follies he treated with good-humored raillery [teasing], our graver ones with kind and serious admonition. He was watchful over our manners, and called our attention to every violation of propriety [politeness and decorum].[31]

Jefferson's grandson, Thomas, affirmed that his grandfather was "soft and feminine in his affections to his family; he entered into and sympathized with all their feelings, winning them to paths of virtue by the soothing gentleness of his manner."[32]

Jefferson also had a genuine sense of humor and would offer tongue-in-cheek comments that his grandchildren described as playful or "sportive."[33] Some targets for humor never seem to change, such as lawyers and doctors, and according to one of the original professors at the University of Virginia, Jefferson joked openly about doctors:

> [H]e would speak jocularly [jokingly], especially to the unprofessional, of medical practice; and on one occasion . . . [i]n the presence of Dr. Everett . . . he remarked that whenever he saw three physicians together, he looked up to discover whether there was not a turkey-buzzard in the neighborhood. The annoyance of the doctor, I am told, was manifest.[34]

Jefferson was truly a remarkable man. He had some faults, probably much fewer than many other great leaders, but he had numerous virtues worthy of study and emulation. He was unquestionably used as an instrument of God, and all races and generations of Americans—especially God-loving Americans—have benefited from the blessings he helped secure for this nation and its posterity.

CONCLUSION

What was once said about George Washington by President Calvin Coolidge can equally be said of Thomas Jefferson:

> We cannot yet estimate him. We can only indicate our reverence for him and thank the Divine Providence which sent him to serve and inspire his fellow men.[35]

Notes

INTRODUCTION

1. Robert G. Parkinson, "First from the Right: Massive Resistance and the Image of Thomas Jefferson in the 1950s," *Virginia Magazine of History and Biography* 112/1. Abstract available at http://www.vahistorical.org/publications/abstract_parkinson.htm (accessed February 11, 2011).

2. John Leland, "A Blow at the Root: Being a Fashionable Fast-Day Sermon, Delivered at Cheshire, April 9, 1801," in *The Writings of the Late Elder John Leland, Including Some Events in His Life, Written by Himself, with Additional Sketches,* ed. L. F. Greene (New York: G. W. Wood, 1845), 255.

3. Edwin A. Alderman, *Classics Old and New; A Series of School Readers; A Fifth Reader* (New York: American Book Company, 1907), 99.

4. Moses Jacob Ezekiel, "Thomas Jefferson," United States Senate, accessed January 31, 2011, http://www.senate.gov/artandhistory/art/artifact/Sculpture_22_00002.htm.

5. Leland, "A Blow at the Root," 55.

6. Dumas Malone, *Jefferson and His Time: The Sage of Monticell,* vol. 6 (Boston: Little, Brown and Company, 1981).

7. Thomas Marshall Green, *Historic Families of Kentucky* (Cincinnati: Robert Clarke Co., 1889), 73.

8. Thomas Jefferson, *The Papers of Thomas Jefferson,* ed. Julian P. Boyd, vol. 7 (Princeton: Princeton University Press, 1953), 585.

9. Benjamin Rush, *Letters of Benjamin Rush,* ed. L. H. Butterfield, vol. 2 (Philadelphia: American Philosophical Society, 1951), 779.

10. John Quincy Adams, *Diary of John Quincy Adams,* ed. David Grayson Allen, vol. 1 (Cambridge: Harvard University Press, 1981), 233.

11. Ezra Stiles, *The Literary Diary of Ezra Stiles,* ed. Franklin Bowditch Dexter, vol. 3 (New York: Charles Scribner's and Sons, 1901), 125.

12. George Washington, *The Papers of George Washington,* ed. W. W. Abbott, vol. 6 (Charlottesville: University Press of Virginia, 1997), 294.

13. Alexis De Tocqueville, *Democracy in America,* trans. Henry Reeve, vol. 2 (New York: George Adlard, 1838), 186.

14. John Kennedy, "Remarks at a Dinner Honoring Nobel Prize Winners of the Western Hemisphere," The American Presidency Project, accessed April 29, 1962, http://www.presidency.ucsb.edu/ws/index.php?pid=8623&st=&st1.

15. Leilani Corpus, "Tiananmen Square Massacre," The Forerunner, June, 1989, accessed October 24, 2011, http://www.forerunner.com/forerunner/X0092_Tiananmen.html.

16. Esther B. Fein, "Clamor in the East; Unshackled Czech Workers Declare Their Independence," *New York Times*, November 28, 1989, http://www.nytimes.com/1989/11/28/world/clamor-in-the-east-unshackled-czech-workers-declare-their-independence.html.

17. Thomas L. Friedman, "Upheaval in the East; Havel's 'Paradoxical' Plea: Help Soviets," *New York Times*, February 22, 1990, http://www.nytimes.com/1990/02/22/world/upheaval-in-the-east-havel-s-paradoxical-plea-help-soviets.html?scp=2&sq=Thomas+Jefferson&st=nyt&pagewanted=all.

18. Ethan Schwartz, "Kosinski's Literary Homecoming: 'Painted Bird' to Be Published in Poland," *Washington Post*, April 5, 1989, 1.

19. Mikhail Gorbachev, "Notable Comments on Jefferson (20th Century)," Monticello, April 13, 1993, accessed October 24, 2011, http://www.monticello.org/site/jefferson/notable-comments-jefferson-20th-century.

20. David Remnick, "Ukraine Split on Independence as Republic Awaits Bush Visit," *Washington Post*, August 1, 1991, 1.

21. Margaret Thatcher, "Lady Margaret Thatcher at Monticello, on the Occasion of the 253rd Anniversary of the Birth of Thomas Jefferson and the Presentation of the First Thomas Jefferson Medal for Statesmanship," Monticello, April 13, 1996, accessed October 24, 2011, http://www.monticello.org/site/jefferson/notable-comments-jefferson-20th-century.

22. Benson J. Lossing, *Biographical Sketches of the Signers of the Declaration of American Independence* (New York: George F. Cooledge & Brother, 1848), 174.

23. George Bancroft, *History of the United States of America, from the Discovery of the American Continent*, vol. 3 (Boston: Little, Brown, & Company, 1864), 462–463.

24. 24. Richard Frothingham, *The Rise of the Republic of the United States* (Boston: Little, Brown, & Company, 1872), 235.

25. Benson J. Lossing, *Harpers' Popular Cyclopedia of United States*, vol. 1 (New York: Harper & Brothers, 1889), 717.

26. John Fiske, *The American Revolution*, vol. 1 (Boston: Houghton, Mifflin and Company, 1897), 193.

27. Edward S. Ellis, *Great Americans of History: Thomas Jefferson a Character Sketch* (Chicago: Union School Furnishing Company, 1898), 38, 47.

28. William Eleroy Curtis, *The True Thomas Jefferson* (Philadelphia: J. B. Lippincott Company, 1901), 388.

29. Henry William Elson, *History of the United States of America* (New York: The Macmillan Company, 1914), 405.

30. Ken Burns, "Notable Comments on Jefferson (20th Century)," Monticello, June 7, 1996, accessed October 24, 2011, http://www.monticello.org/site/jefferson/notable-comments-jefferson-20th-century.

31. Jack M. Balkin, "Tradition, Betrayal, and the Politics of Deconstruction—Part II," Yale.edu, 1998, accessed October 24, 2011, http://www.yale.edu/lawweb/jbalkin/articles/trad2.htm.

32. Kyle-Anne Shiver, "Deconstructing Obama," AmericanThinker.com, July 28, 2008, accessed October 24, 2011, http://www.americanthinker.com/2008/07/deconstructing_obama.html.

33. *Encyclopædia Britannica Online*, s.v. "deconstruction," accessed November 08, 2011, http://www.britannica.com/EBchecked/topic/155306/deconstruction.

34. Of the 27, 14 women and 5 men were tired, found guilty and hung; 1 man was tortured to death by crushing because he refused to cooperate with the court by not answering their questions. To persuade him to talk they took him to a field and put a board on him with rocks. They increased the number of rocks until he would cooperate, but he continued to refuse and was crushed to death. He was therefore never convicted but is considered the 20th victim as he was on trial for being a wizard. And 7 individuals died in prison awaiting trial; one was a baby in prison with her mother, who was awaiting trial as a witch. "The Salem Witch Trials of 1692," *Salem Witch Museum*, January 13, 2011 (at: http://www.salemwitchmuseum.com/education/index.shtml) per the museum's Department of Education.

35. William Warren Sweet, *The Story of Religion in America* (New York: Harper & Brothers, 1950), 61.

36. Charles B. Galloway, *Christianity and the American Commonwealth* (Nashville: Publishing House Methodist Episcopal Church, 1898), 110

37. Ibid.

38. *Dictionary of American Biography*, ed. Allen Johnson, (New York: Charles Scribber's Sons, 1929), s.v. "John Wise," "Increase Mather," and "Thomas Brattle." *See also* Mark Gribbean, "Salem Witch Trials: Reason Returns," *Court TV: Crime Library*, accessed February 3, 2001, (http://www.crimelibrary.com/notorious_murders/not_guilty/salem_witches/12.html?sect=12.

39. 39. John Fiske, *Civil Government in the United States Considered with Some Reference to Its Origins* (Boston: Houghton, Mifflin, and Company, 1890), 147–148, 192.

40. Francis J. Bremer, *The Puritan Experiment* (Lebanon, NH: University Press of New England, 1995), 62; "The Massachusetts Body of Liberties," Hanover Historical Texts, 1641, accessed October 24, 2011, http://history.hanover.edu/texts/masslib.html.

41. Ann Vileisis, *Discovering the Unknown Landscape* (Washington, DC: Island Press, 1997), 30; William Bradford, *History of Plymouth Plantation*, ed. Charles Deane (Boston: Privately Printted, 1856), 135–136.

42. Charles H. Thurber, ed., *The School Review*, vol. 6 (Chicago: University of Chicago Press, 1898), 680; Royal Ralph Hinman, *A Catalog of the Names of the Early Puritan Settlers of the Colony of Connecticut* (Hartford: Press of Case, Tiffany and Company, 1852), 185; *The Code of 1650, Being a Compilation of the Earliest Laws and Orders of the General Court of Connecticut* (Hartford: Silus Andurs, 1822), 90–92, containing America's first common or public school law.

43. Dr. John Lye, "Some Post-Structural Assumptions," Brock University, 1997, accessed October 24, 2011, http://www.brocku.ca/english/courses/4F70/poststruct.php.

44. Ibid.

45. "Poststructuralist Approaches," cnr.edu, accessed October 13, 2009, http://www2.cnr.edu/home/bmcmanus/poststructuralism.html.

46. *Encyclopædia Britannica Online*, s.v. "**particularism**," accessed November 9, 2011, http://www.britannica.com/EBchecked/topic/445119/particularism; *Encyclopædia Britannica Online*, s.v. "anthropology," accessed November 09, 2011; "Stanford Encyclopedia of philosophy, Identity Politics," Stanford University accessed June, 16 2011, https://leibniz.stanford.edu/friends/preview/identity-politics/. *See also* "Identity Politics" or "Particularism," Merriam-Webster, accessed October 24, 2011,

http://www.merriam-webster.com/dictionary/particularism?show=0&t=130825
9578.

47. Isaac Kramnick and Laurence Moore, *The Godless Constitution* (New York: W. W. Norton & Company, 1996), 12, 22, 27 passim.

48. *See* Ross Anderson, "ACLU President Says Organization Is Not Anti-Religion." University Wire, 2006, HighBeam Research, accessed November 14, 2011, http://www.highbeam.com/doc/1P1-119656688.html; Jill Goetz, "Authors Argue the Religious Right Is Wrong about the Constitution," *Cornell Chronicle*, accessed February 3, 2011, http://www.news.cornell.edu/chronicle/96/2.1.96/godless.html; Ed Buckner, "It's a Free Country, Not a Christian Nation," Stephenjaygould.com, 1998, accessed October 24, 2011, http://www.stephenjaygould.org/ctrl/buckner_ncn.html; Matthew Dallek, "The Godless Constitution," *Washington Post*, February 18, 1996, accessed October 24, 2011, http://www.washingtonpost.com/wp-srv/style/longterm/books/reviews/matthewdallek.htm.

49. Kramnick and Moore, *The Godless Constitution*, 179.

LIE #1: THOMAS JEFFERSON FATHERED SALLY HEMINGS' CHILDREN

1. Eugene A. Foster et al., "Jefferson Fathered Slave's Last Child," *Nature* 396 (November 5, 1998), 27–28.

2. Eric Lander and Joseph Ellis, "Founding Father," *Nature* 396 (November 5, 1998), 1.

3. Christopher Hitchens, "What Do Jefferson and Clinton Have in Common (Besides Randiness)?" *Ivory Tower*, November 18, 1998, accessed October 24, 2011, http://www1.salon.com/it/feature/1998/11/cov_18featureb.html.

4. Dr. David N. Mayer, "The Thomas Jefferson-Sally Hemings Myth and the Politicization of American History," John M. Ashbrook Center for Public Affairs, April 9, 2001, accessed October 24, 2011, http://www.ashbrook.org/articles/mayer-hemings.html.

5. Henry Gee, "The Sex Life of President Thomas Jefferson," Nature News, November 12, 1998, accessed October 24, 2011, http://www.nature.com/news/1998/981112/full/news981112-1.html.

6. Mayer, "The Thomas Jefferson-Sally Hemings Myth and the Politicization of American History."

7. *See* Andrea Dworkin, *Woman Hating* (New York: E. P. Dutton & Co., Inc., 1974), 184; Gloria Steinem, *Revolution from Within: A Book of Self-Esteem* (Boston: Little, Brown and Company, 1992), 259–261; Marilyn French, *The War Against Women* (New York: Summit Books, 1992), 182; Robin Morgan, *The Word of a Woman* (New York: W. W. Norton & Company, 1992), 84; Catharine A. MacKinnon, *Feminism Unmodified* (Cambridge: Harvard University Press, 1987), 88; Naomi Wolf, *The Beauty Myth* (New York: William Morrow and Company, Inc., 1991), 138; Andrea Dworkin, *Our Blood* (New York: Harper & Row, 1976), 20; Andrea Dworkin, *Letters from a War Zone: Writings 1976–1989* (New York: E. P. Dutton, 1988), 14, 118–119; Christina Hoff Sommers, *Who Stole Feminism? How Women Have Betrayed Women* (New York: Simon & Schuster, 1994), 44–46, 220, 222.

8. Peter S. Onuf, "Every Generation Is an 'Independent Nation': Colonization, Miscegenation, and the Fate of Jefferson's Children," *The William and Mary Quarterly*, 3rd. ser., vol. 57, no. 1 (January 2000), 157.

9. Fawn M. Brodie, *Thomas Jefferson, An Intimate History* (New York: W. W. Norton & Co., 1974); Barbara Chase-Riboud, *Sally Hemings: A Novel* (New York: St. Martin's Press, 1979); Annette Gordon-Reed, *Thomas Jefferson and Sally Hemings: An American Controversy* (Charlottesville: The University Press of Virginia, 1997).

10. Several historical studies indicate that sexual relations between white masters and black slaves occurred only in a small minority of cases and that the overwhelming majority of white masters did not exercise a sexual prerogative over their female slaves. For example, by 1850, the American population had grown to a burgeoning 23.2 million; the slave population was 3.2 million, or 13.8 percent of the total population. Among the black population, over the sixty years since the first census in 1790, census numbers show a maximum of 11.2 percent of the 1850 population to be mulatto, which represents only 1.55 percent of the total America population. *See*, J. D. B. DeBow, *Statistical View of the United States, Embracing Its Territory, Population—White, Free Colored, and Slave—Moral and Social Condition, Industry, Property, and Revenue; the Detailed Statistics of Cities, Towns, and Counties; Being a Compendium of the Seventh Census* (Washington, DC: Beverley Tucker, 1854), 39, 63, 82; Department of Commerce Bureau of the Census, dir. William J. Harris, *Negroes in the United States* (Washington, DC: Government Printing Office, 1915), 129:15. *See also* Edward Byron Reuter, *The Mulatto in the United States* (Boston: The Gorham Press, 1918), 116.. Yet despite the clear statistical facts and numerous studies, writers such as Peter S. Onuf, "Every Generation Is an 'Independent Nation': Colonization, Miscegenation, and the Fate of Jefferson's Children," *The William and Mary Quarterly*, (January 2000), 3rd. ser., vol. 57, no. 1, wherein he uniformly stereotypes all Anglos by decrying the "whites' despotic power over their . . . female slaves' bodies" (157); "the despotic power of white masters over the bodies of black female slaves," (158); "white men exploited black women" (160); "White slave owners exploited their slave women" (160) passim.

11. Eugene A. Foster et al., "Reply: The Thomas Jefferson Paternity Case," *Nature* 396 (January 7, 1999), 32.

12. Thomas Jefferson, *The Papers of Thomas Jefferson*, ed. Barbara B. Oberg, vol. 31 (Princeton: Princeton University Press, 2004), 274.

13. *See* Jone Johnson Lewis, "Mistress of Thomas Jefferson?" About.com, accessed July 14, 2011, http://womenshistory.about.com/od/hemingssally/a/sally_hemings. htm; Gordon-Reed, *Thomas Jefferson and Sally Hemings*, 1, 72; Brodie, *Thomas Jefferson, An Intimate History*, 228–232.

14. The children generally agreed upon by most scholars include Thomas (born in 1790), Harriet I (apparently died in infancy), Beverly (son, born 1798), Harriet II (1801), Madison (1805), and Eston (1808). However, authorities from Monticello, where Hemings was a slave, indicate that she had six children. Other modern writers have placed the number of Hemings' children at anywhere from four to seven or more. For example: *four children*—"Sally Hemings," *New York Times*, accessed February 24, 2011, http://topics.nytimes.com/top/reference/timestopics/people/h/sally_hemings/ index. html; *five children*—McKenzie Wallenborn, "Dr. Wallenborn's Minority Report," Monticello, March 23, 2000, accessed October 24, 2011, http://www. monticello.org/site/plantation-and-slavery/minority-report-monticello-research-committee-thomas-jefferson-and-sally); *six children*—"Thomas Jefferson and Sally Hemings: A Brief Account," Monticello, accessed February 24, 2011, http://www.

monticello.org/plantation/hemingscontro/hemings-jefferson_contro.html; Lewis, "Sally
Hemings: Mistress of Thomas Jefferson?"; R. F. Holznagel and Paul Hehn, "Who2.
com profile of Sally Hemings," Who2.com, accessed February 24, 2011, http://www.
who2.com/sallyhemings.html; and *seven children*—Glenn Speark, "'The Hemingses
of Monticello' by Annette Gordon-Reed: A Look at the Third President, His Slave
Mistress and the Antebellum South," *Los Angeles Times*, November 14, 2008,
accessed October 24, 2011, http://articles.latimes.com/2008/nov/14/entertainment/
et-book14; and *other varying numbers*—Patrick Mullins, "Scholars Overturn
Case for Thomas Jefferson's Relationship with Slave Sally Hemings," Capitalism
Magazine, June 2, 2001, accessed November 17, 2011, http://www.tjheritage.org/
newscomfiles/CapitalismMagazine.pdf; "Thomas Jefferson and Sally Hemings: Case
Closed?" Claremont Institute, August 30, 2001, accessed October 24, 2011, http://
www.claremont.org/publications/crb/id.1015/article_detail.asp; Harry Hellenbrand,
review of "Thomas Jefferson and Sally Hemings: An American Controversy," by
Annette Gordon-Reed, H-Net Reviews, February, 1998, accessed October 24, 2011,
www.h-net.msu.edu/reviews/showpdf.cgi?path=8812887909950.

15. *See* Jan Lewis, Joseph J. Ellis, Lucia Stanton, Peter S. Onuf, Annette Gordon-Reed,
Andrew Burstein, and Fraser D. Neiman, comments in the forum published in *The
William and Mary Quarterly*, 2nd ser., vol. 7, no. 1, (January 2000) 121–210.

16. Eric Lander and Joseph Ellis, "Founding Father," *Nature* 396 (November 5, 1998), 1.

17. Joseph J. Ellis, "Jefferson: Post-DNA," *The William and Mary Quarterly*, 3rd ser.,
vol. 57, no. 1 (January 2000), 136, n14.

18. Barbra Murray and Brian Duffy, "Jefferson's Secret Life," U. S. News Online,
November 9, 1998, accessed October 24, 2011, http://www.usnews.com/usnews/
culture/articles/981109/archive_005152.htm.

19. Dinitia Smith and Nicholas Wade, "DNA Tests Offer Evidence that Jefferson
Fathers a Child with His Slave," *The New York Times "Science,"* November 1,
1998.

20. Dennis Cauchon, "Jefferson Affair No Longer Rumor," *USA Today*, November
2, 1998.

21. Donna Britt, "A Slaveholder's Hypocrisy Was Inevitable," *Washington Post*,
November 6, 1998, B01.

22. Clarence Page, "New Disclosures Show Two Thomas Jeffersons," *Chicago Tribune*,
November 5, 1998, 1.

23. Ibid., 2.

24. Hitchens, "What Do Jefferson and Clinton Have in Common," 3–4

25. Richard Cohen, "Grand Illusion," *Washington Post*, December 13, 1998, W10.

26. Page, "New Disclosures Show Two Thomas Jeffersons," 2.

27. Smith and Wade, "DNA Test Finds Evidence."

28. Annette Gordon-Reed, "The All Too Human Jefferson," *Wall Street Journal*,
November 24, 1998, in Dr. David N. Mayer, "The Thomas Jefferson-Sally Hemings
Myth and the Politicization of American History," John M. Ashbrook Center for
Public Affairs, April 9, 2001, accessed October 24, 2011, http://www.ashbrook.org/
articles/mayer-hemings.html.

29. Ellis, "Jefferson: Post-DNA," 130.

30. Eugene A. Foster et al., "Jefferson Fathered Slave's Last Child," *Nature* 396
(November 5, 1998), 27–28.

31. Foster et al. "Reply: The Thomas Jefferson Paternity Case," 32.

32. *The Jefferson-Hemings Controversy Report of the Scholars Commission*, ed. Robert F. Turner (Durham, NC: Carolina Academic Press, 2011), 11.

33. Ibid., 8.

34. Gene Edward Veith, "Founder's DNA Revisited," *World*, February 20, 1999, 24.

35. Mona Charen, "Was Jefferson Libeled by DNA?" *Jewish World Review*, January 19, 1999, accessed October 25, 2011, http://jewishworldreview.com/cols/charen 011999asp.

36. Herbert Barger, "The Jefferson-Hemings DNA Study," Angel Fire, last updated August 30, 2000, accessed October 24, 2011, http://www.angelfire.com/va/TJTruth/background.html.

37. For a list of the professors and the schools they're associated with, see this link: http://www.tjheritage.org/scholars.html.

38. *The Jefferson-Hemings Controversy Report of the Scholars Commission*, ed. Turner, 6.

39. Ibid., 16.

40. Foster et al., "Reply: The Thomas Jefferson Paternity Case," 32.

41. Herbert Barger, "Letters to the Editor: Rushing to Rescue TJ," *C-ville Weekly*, November, 2005, accessed October 24, 2011, http://www.c-ville.com/index. php?cat=121304064644348&z_Issue_ID=1892509061555962&ShowArchiveAr ticle_ID=1892509061586567. *See also* Herbert Barger, review of "Sally Hemings and Thomas Jefferson: History, Memory and Civic Culture," by Jan Ellen Lewis and Peter S. Onuf, Thomas Jefferson Heritage Society, accessed June 15, 2011, http://www.tjheritage.org/booksfiles/Barger-Hemings_and_Jefferson_by_Lewis. pdf.

42. Walter V. Robinson, "Professor's Past in Doubt Discrepancies Surface in Claim of Vietnam Duty," *Boston Globe*, June 18, 2001, A1. *See also* Dennis Loy Johnson, "The History Lesson of Joseph Ellis," Mobylives.com, June 20, 2001, accessed October 24, 2011, http://www.mobylives.com/Joseph_Ellis.html.

43. Johnson, "The History Lesson of Joseph Ellis."

44. "Review & Outlook: Founding Fatherhood," *Wall Street Journal*, February 26, 1999, W15.

45. Veith, "Founder's DNA Revisited," 24.

46. Charen, "Was Jefferson Libeled by DNA?"

47. "DNA Test Fails to Link Jefferson, Monticello Slave Descendant," *Washington Post*, March 23, 2000. Additionally, on March 20, 2000, our WallBuilders office personally spoke with Dr. Eugene Foster, who had conducted the testing, to affirm that his most recent testing had again proved that Thomas Jefferson was *not* the father of Thomas Woodson. Dr. Foster confirmed that such was the case.

48. Madison Hemings, "Life Among the Lowly," *Pike County (Ohio) Republican*, March 13, 1873, in Gordon-Reed, *Thomas Jefferson and Sally Hemings*, 246.

49. Hemings, "Life Among the Lowly," 247. *See also* Dumas Malone, *Jefferson and His Time: Jefferson the Virginian*, vol. 1 (Boston: Little, Brown and Company, 1948), 384; Malone, *Jefferson and His Time: The Sage of Monticello*, 6:xv, 146.

50. Gordon-Reed, *Thomas Jefferson and Sally Hemings*, 259.

51. Letter from Ellen Randolph Coolidge to Joseph Coolidge on October 26, 1858, original on file at the University of Virginia Library; David N. Myer, "The Thomas Jefferson-Sally Hemings Myth and the Politicization of American History," Ashbrook

Center, April 9, 2001, accessed October 24, 2011, http://www.ashbrook.org/articles/mayer-hemings.html.

52. Jan Lewis, "Introduction," *The William and Mary Quarterly*, 3rd ser., vol. 7, no. 1 (January 2000), 122.

53. Ellis, "Jefferson: Post-DNA," 136–137, n15.

54. Allen Johnson ed., *Dictionary of American Biography* (New York: Charles Scribner's Sons, 1929), s.v. "James Thomson Callender."

55. Jefferson, *The Papers of Thomas Jefferson*, ed. Oberg, 30:583.

56. James Madison, *The Papers of James Madison. Secretary of State Series*, ed. Robert J. Brugger, vol. 1 (Charlottesville: University Press of Virginia, 1986), 117; Jefferson, *The Papers of Thomas Jefferson*, ed. Oberg, vol. 33, 573–574.

57. Thomas Jefferson, *Memoir, Correspondence, and Miscellanies*, ed. Thomas Jefferson Randolph, vol. 4 (Charlottesville: F. Carr, and Co., 1829), 23.

58. James Madison, *Letters and Other Writings of James Madison*, vol. 2 (Philadelphia: J. P. Lippincott & Co., 1865), 172.

59. Thomas Jefferson, *The Works of Thomas Jefferson*, ed. Paul Leicester Ford, vol. 9 (New York: G. P. Putnam's Sons, 1900), 260.

60. Jefferson, *The Works of Thomas Jefferson*, ed. Ford, 9:262–263.

61. James Monroe, *The Writings of James Monroe*, ed. Stanislaus Murray Hamilton, vol. 3 (New York: G. P. Putnam's Sons, 1900), 289.

62. Madison, *Letters and Other Writings of James Madison*, 2:173.

63. Ibid.

64. Monroe, *The Writings of James Monroe*, ed. Hamilton, 3:290.

65. Madison, *The Papers of James Madison*, ed. Brugger, 1:117.

66. Ibid.

67. Allen Johnson, ed., *Dictionary of American Biography* (New York: Charles Scribner's Sons, 1929), s.v. "James Thomson Callender."

68. Malone, *Jefferson the President, First Term, 1801-1805*, 4:220, n43.

69. Malone, *Jefferson the President, First Term*, 4:208.

70. J. T. Callender, "The President Again," *The Recorder; Or, Lady's and Gentleman's Miscellany* (Richmond), September 1, 1802.

71. Ibid.

72. Ibid., December 8, 1802.

73. Thomas Jefferson Memorial Foundation, "Report of the Research Committee on Thomas Jefferson and Sally Hemings," Monticello, January 2000, accessed October 25, 2011, http://www.monticello.org/sites/default/files/inline-pdfs/jefferson-hemings_report.pdf.

74. J. T. Callender, "More about Sally and the President," *The Recorder; Or, Lady's and Gentleman's Miscellany* (Richmond), September 22, 1802.

75. Thomas Jefferson Memorial Foundation, "Report of the Research Committee on Thomas Jefferson and Sally Hemings."

76. Ibid.

77. J. T. Callender, "The President Again," *The Recorder; Or, Lady's and Gentleman's Miscellany* (Richmond), September 1, 1802.

78. J. T. Callender, *The Prospect Before Us*, vol. 1 (Richmond: 1800), 27, 34, passim.

79. Ibid., 4, 9, 18, 22, 24, 26–28, 32, 34, and passim.

80. Malone, *Jefferson the President, First Term, 1801–1805*, 4:207.

81. James Truslow Adams, *The Living Jefferson* (New York: Charles Scribner's Sons, 1936), 315.

82. Virginius Dabney, *The Jefferson Scandals: A Rebuttal* (New York: Dodd, Mead, & Company, 1981), 15.

83. Malone, *Jefferson the President, First Term*, 4:212.

84. John Chester Miller, *The Wolf by the Ears: Thomas Jefferson and Slavery* (New York: The Free Press, 1977), 153.

85. Ibid., 154.

86. Benjamin Ellis Martin, "Transition Period of the American Press," *Magazine of American History* 17 (January–June 1887), 285.

87. Ibid., 285–286.

88. Thomas Jefferson, *The Works of Thomas Jefferson*, ed. Paul Leicester Ford, vol. 10 (New York: G. P. Putnam's Sons, 1905), 368. *See also* Thomas Jefferson, *Memoir, Correspondence, and Miscellanies*, ed. Thomas Jefferson Randolph, vol. 4 (Boston: Gray and Bowen, 1830), 129.

89. Charles Warren, *Odd Byways in American History* (Cambridge: Harvard University Press, 1942), 127. *See also* Malone, *Jefferson and the Ordeal of Liberty*, 3:479.

90. Malone, *Jefferson the President, First Term, 1801–1805*, 4:206.

91. Jefferson, *The Works of Thomas Jefferson*, ed. Ford, 11:366.

92. Jefferson, *The Writings of Thomas Jefferson*, ed. Lipscomb, 11:155.

93. Jefferson, *Memoir, Correspondence, and Miscellanies*, ed. Randolph, 4:129.

94. Ibid., 3:439.

95. Kenneth Chang, "DNA Tests Sheds Light on Old Scandal: Jefferson Fathered Slave Son," ABC News, November 5, 1998.

96. Jefferson, *Memoir, Correspondence, and Miscellanies*, ed. Randolph, 3:494–495.

97. Ibid., 4:23.

98. Ibid., 4:129; Thomas Jefferson, *Thomas Jefferson Correspondence: Printed from the Originals in the Collections of William K. Bixby*, ed. Worthington Chauncey Ford (Boston: Plimpton Press, 1916), 115.

99. Brodie, *Thomas Jefferson: An Intimate History*, 229.

100. Ibid.

101. University of Texas/Texas State Historical Association, "Southwestern Historical Quarterly: A. W. Moore, A Reconnaissance in Texas in 1846," University of Texas, accessed March 10, 2011, http://texashistory.unt.edu/ark:/67531/metapth117142/m1/278; emphasis added.

102. Alfred Theodore Andreas, *A. T. Andreas Illustrated Historical Atlas of the State of Iowa* (Andreas Atlas Co., 1875), 468; emphasis added.

103. James V. Drake, *An Historical Sketch of Wilson County, Tennessee, from Its First Settlement to the Present Time* (Nashville: Tavel, Eastman & Howell, 1879), 10; emphasis added.

104. Alfred Theodore Andreas, *History of the State of Kansas*, ed. William C. Cutler (Chicago: A. T. Andreas, 1883), 486; emphasis added.

105. *Biographical and Historical Memoirs of Fulton County, Arkansas* (1889; repr. Higginsville, MO: Hearthstone Legacy Publications, 2004), 261; emphasis added..

106. Willard Sterne Randall, *Thomas Jefferson: A Life* (New York: Henry Holt and Co., 1994), 476.

107. Gary Wills, "Uncle Thomas's Cabin," *New York Review of Books*, April 18, 1974.

NOTES

Lɪᴇ # 2: Tʜᴏᴍᴀs Jᴇꜰꜰᴇʀsᴏɴ Fᴏᴜɴᴅᴇᴅ ᴀ Sᴇᴄᴜʟᴀʀ Uɴɪᴠᴇʀsɪᴛʏ

1. Dr. Daryl Cornett, David Barton, William Henard, and John Sassi, *Christian America? Perspectives on Our Religious Heritage* (Nashville: Broadman & Holman, 2011, 289–290.

2. Anita Vickers, *The New Nation* (Westport, CT: Greenwood Press, 2002), 74.

3. Leonard Levy, *Jefferson and Civil Liberties: The Darker Side* (Cambridge: The Belknap Press of Harvard University Press, 1989), 15.

4. John S. Brubacher and Willis Rudy, *Higher Education in Transition: A History of American Colleges and Universities* (New Brunswick, NJ: Transaction Books, 2004), 147–148.

5. Thomas Jefferson, *The Works of Thomas Jefferson*, ed. Henry A. Washington, vol. 1 (New York: Townsend Mac Coun., 1884, 2.

6. George Marsden, *The Soul of the American University* (Oxford University Press, Oxford, 1994), 59.

7. Gaillard Hunt, *The Life of James Madison* (New York: Doubleday, Page and Co., 1902), 13.

8. *Case of Fries*, 9 Fed. Cas. 826, no. 5, 126 (C.C.D. Pa. 1799).

9. Thomas Jefferson, *The Writings of Thomas Jefferson*, ed. Andrew A. Lipscomb, vol. 12 (Washington, DC: The Thomas Jefferson Memorial Association, 1904), 392.

10. Sir William Blackstone, *Commentaries on the Laws of England*, vol. 1 (Philadelphia: Robert Bell, Union Library, 1771), 39–43.

11. Henry Sage, "The Enlightenment in America," Academic American, 2007, accessed October 24, 2011, http://www.academicamerican.com/colonial/topics/enlighten.htm.

12. "Product of the Enlightenment," The Academy of Natural Sciences, accessed February 23, 2011, http://www.ansp.org/museum/jefferson/otherPages/enlightenment. php.

13. "Enlightenment Ideas and Philosophers," historycorner.net, accessed November 9, 2011.

14. Thomas Jefferson, *The Writings of Thomas Jefferson*, ed. Henry A. Washington, vol 7 (Washington, DC: Taylor & Maury, 1854), 305.

15. Ibid., 407.

16. Thomas Jefferson, *Memoir, Correspondence, and Miscellanies*, ed.Thomas Jefferson Randolph, vol. 2 (Boston: Gray and Bowen, 1830) 221.

17. Donald S. Lutz, *The Origins of American Constitutionalism* (Baton Rouge: Louisiana State University Press, 1988), 143.

18. Benjamin Franklin, *The Works of Benjamin Franklin*, ed. John Bigelow, vol. 5 (New York: G. P. Putnam's Son, 1904), 325–326.

19. John Adams, *Diary and Autobiography of John Adams*, ed. L. H. Butterfield, vol. 2 (Cambridge: Belknap Press, 1962), 391.

20. James Madison, *The Letters and Other Writings of James Madison*, vol. 4 (New York: R. Worthington, 1884), 58.

21. John Quincy Adams, *An Oration Addressed to the Citizens of the Town of Quincy, on the Fourth of July, 1831* (Boston: Richardson, Lord & Holbrook, 1831), 15.

22. John Witherspoon, "The Absolute Necessity of Salvation Through Christ, January 2, 1758," in *The Works of John Witherspoon*, vol. 5 (Edinburgh: J. Ogle, 1815), 242.

23. Benjamin Rush, *Letters of Benjamin Rush*, ed. L. H. Butterfield, vol. 2 (New Jersey: Princeton University Press, 1951), 748.

24. William Wirt, *Sketches of the Life and Character of Patrick Henry* (Philadelphia: James Webster, 1817), 386–387.

25. Thomas Jefferson, *Memoir, Correspondence, and Miscellanies*, ed.Thomas Jefferson Randolph, vol. 4 (Charlottesville: F. Carr, 1829), 80.

26. Jefferson, *The Writings of Thomas Jefferson*, ed. Lipscomb, 12:405.

27. Thomas Jefferson, *The Works of Thomas Jefferson*, ed. Paul Leicester Ford, vol. 5 (New York: G. P. Putnam's Sons, 1904), 181.

28. Ibid., 171.

29. Ibid., 12:111.

30. Ibid., 11:168.

31. *The Works of Francis Bacon*, ed. James Spedding, vol. 3 (London: Spottiswoode & Co., 1857), 509, "Preface to the *De Interpretatione Naturae Prooemium*"; and John Timbs, *Stories of Inventors and Discoverers in Science and the Useful Arts* (London: Kent and Co., 1860), 91, "Lord Bacon's 'New Philosophy.'"
"Father of the Scientific Method," Dr. Peter Hammond, "How the Reformation Changed the World," Frontline Fellowship, accessed November 14, 2011, http://www.frontline.org.za/articles/howreformation_changedworld.htm; "Father of Modern Science," David C. Innes, "The Novelty and Genius of Francis Bacon," Piety and Humanity, accessed February 11, 2010, http://pietyandhumanity.blogspot.com/2010/02/novelty-and-genius-of-francis-bacon.html.

32. John William Cousin, *A Short Biographical Dictionary of English Literature* (New York: E. P. Dutton & Co., 1910), s.v. "Sir Francis Bacon," accessed April 27, 2011, http://www.luminarium.org/sevenlit/bacon/bio.php.

33. Sir Francis Bacon, "Essays of Francis Bacon: Of Atheism," Public Domain Books, accessed March 7, 2011, http://www.authorama.com/essays-of-francis-bacon-17.html.

34. Charles E. Hummell, "The Faith Behind the Famous: Isaac Newton," Christian History, April 1, 1991, accessed October 24, 2011, http://www.ctlibrary.com/ch/1991/issue30/3038.html. *See also* Mitch Stokes, *Isaac Newton* (Nashville: Thomas Nelson, 2010), 82–84.

35. "Sir Isaac Newton," University of St. Andrews, January 2000, accessed October 24, 2011, http://www-history.mcs.st-andrews.ac.uk/Biographies/Newton.html.

36. Sir Isaac Newton, *Newton's Principia, the Mathematical Principles of Natural Philosophy* (1687; repr. New York: Daniel Adee, 1848), 504.

37. John Locke, "The Fundamental Constitutions of Carolina, 1669," in *The Works of John Locke*, vol. 10 (London: T. Davison, 1801), 175.

38. *See*, John Bowker, ed., *Concise Oxford Dictionary of World Religions* (Oxford: Oxford University Press, 2000), 151; James A. Herrick, *The Radical Rhetoric of the English Deists: The Discourse of Skepticism, 1680–1750* (Columbia: University of South Carolina Press, 1997), 15; Kerry S. Walters, *Rational Infidels: The American Deists* (Durango, CO: Longwood Academic, 1992), 24, 210; Kerry S. Walters, *The American Deists: Voices of Reason and Dissent in the Early Republic* (Lawrence: University Press of Kansas, 1992), 6–7; John W. Yolton, *John Locke and the Way of Ideas* (Oxford: Oxford University Press, 1956), 25, 115.

39. *See* Richard Watson, *Theological Institutes: Or a View of the Evidences, Doctrines, Morals, and Institutions of Christianity* (New York: Carlton and Porter, 1857), 32.

40. John Locke, *The Works of John Locke*, vol. 7 (London: Awnsham & Churchill,

1722), "A Paraphrase and Notes on St. Paul's Epistle to the Galatians" (originally published in 1705), 25–75; "A Paraphrase and Notes on St. Paul's First Epistle to the Corinthians" (originally published in 1706), 77–202; "A Paraphrase and Notes on St. Paul's Second Epistle to the Corinthians" (originally published in 1706), 203–270; "A Paraphrase and Notes on St. Paul's Epistle to the Romans" (originally published in 1707), 271–427; "A Paraphrase and Notes on St. Paul's Epistle to the Ephesians" (originally published in 1707), 429–495.

41. John Locke, *A Common Place-Book to the Holy Bible: or, the Scripture's Sufficiency Practically Demonstrated* (London: Awnsham & Churchill, 1697).

42. John Locke, *The Reasonableness of Christianity, as Delivered in the Scriptures* (London: Awnsham & Churchill, 1695).

43. John Locke, *A Vindication of the Reasonableness of Christianity, from Mr. Edward's Reflections* (London: Awnsham & Churchill, 1695), repr. in *The Works of John Locke*, vol. 6 (London: C. Baldwin, 1824), 159–190.

44. John Locke, *A Second Vindication of the Reasonableness of Christianity* (London: Awnsham & Churchill, 1697), repr. in *The Works of John Locke*, vol. 6 (London: C. Baldwin, 1824), 191–424.

45. John Adams, *The Works of John Adams*, ed. Charles Francis Adams (Boston: Little, Brown and Company, 1856), 10:311, 4:82–83, 1:53–54; Benjamin Franklin, *The Papers of Benjamin Franklin*, ed. William B. Willcox (New Haven: Yale University Press, 1973), 17:6, 4:107,; Thomas Jefferson, *The Writings of Thomas Jefferson*, ed. Paul Leicester Ford (New York: G. P. Putnam's Sons, 1895), 5:173, 11:222; Thomas Jefferson, *The Works of Thomas Jefferson*, ed. Paul Leicester Ford (New York: G. P. Putnam's sons, 1905), 12:307; Benjamin Rush, *The Selected Writings of Benjamin Rush*, ed. Dagobert D. Runes (New York: The Philosophical Library, Inc., 1947), 78; Benjamin Rush, *Medical Inquiries and Observations*, vol. 1, (Philadelphia: T. & G. Palmer, 1805), 402; Ibid., 2:19; John Quincy Adams, *The Jubilee of the Constitution* (New York: Samuel Colman, 1839), 40–41; James Wilson, *The Works of the Honourable James Wilson*, ed. Bird Wilson, vol. 1 (Philadelphia: Lorenzo Press, 1804), 67–68.

46. John Locke, *Two Treatises of Government* (London: Awnsham & Churchill, 1689), passim.

47. Thomas Jefferson, *The Writings of Thomas Jefferson*, ed. Paul Leicester Ford, vol.2 (New York: G. P. Putnam's Sons, 1893), 93–94; emphasis added.

48. Ibid., 11:115.

49. Thomas Jefferson, *The Papers of Thomas Jefferson*, ed. Julian P. Boyd, vol. 6 (Princeton: Princeton University Press, 1952), 432.

50. Thomas Jefferson, *The Papers of Thomas Jefferson*, ed. Charles T. Cullen, vol. 23 (Princeton: Princeton University Press, 1990), 271.

51. John Witherspoon, *The Works of John Witherspoon*, vol. 3 (Philadelphia: William W. Woodward, 1800), 42.

52. Williston Walker, *John Calvin: The Organiser of Reformed Protestantism: 1509–1564* (New York: G. P. Putnam's Sons, 1906), 363.

53. Walker, *John Calvin*, 367.

54. *Dictionary of American Biography* (New York: Charles Scibner's Sons, 1929), s.v. "Gideon Blackburn." See also *Debates and Proceedings in the Congress of the United States* (Washington, DC: Gales and Seaton, 1851), 7th Cong., 1602; Dorothy

C. Bass, "Gideon Blackburn's Mission to the Cherokees: Christianization and Civilization," *Journal of Presbyterian History* (Fall 1974), 209–210.

55. "Thomas Jefferson to the Nuns of the Order of St. Ursula on May 15, 1804," original on file with the New Orleans Parish, accessed October 24, 2011, http://dauthazbeechphagein.blogspot.com/2010/08/thomas-jeffersons-letter-to-sister.html.

56. Thomas Jefferson, "The Thomas Jefferson Papers," Library of Congress, accessed October 24, 2011, http://hdl.loc.gov/loc.mss/mtj.mtjbib015028. This link includes a "transcription" like that has a typed and easy to read version of this letter: http://memory.loc.gov/cgi-bin/query/r?ammem/mtj:@field%28DOCID+@lit%28nc000296%29%29.

57. Thomas Jefferson, "The Thomas Jefferson Papers," Library of Congress, accessed October 24, 2011, http://hdl.loc.gov/loc.mss/mtj.mtjbib015028.

58. *Records of the Columbia Historical Society*, vol. 1 (Washington, DC: Columbia Historical Society, 1895), 122–123.

59. Ibid., 127.

60. Samuel Yorke, *History of the Public Schools of Washington City, D.C.* (Washington, DC: Gill & Witherow, 1876), 1–6; William Benning Webb, John Wooldrige, and Harvey W. Crew, *Centennial History of the City of Washington, D.C.* (Dayton, OH: United Brethren Publishing House, 1892), 484–486.

61. *Records of the Columbia Historical Society*, vol. 8 (Washington, DC: Columbia Historical Society, 1905), 62.

62. Samuel Knox, *Essay on the Best System of Liberal Education* (Baltimore: Warner and Hanna, 1799), 78–79.

63. Jefferson, *The Writings of Thomas Jefferson*, ed. Lipscomb, 19:365–366.

64. Ibid., 367.

65. Leonard Levy, *Jefferson and Civil Liberties: The Darker Side* (Cambridge: The Belknap Press of Harvard University Press, 1989), 8.

66. Thomas Jefferson, *The Writings of Thomas Jefferson*, ed. Paul Leicester Ford, vol. 1 (Washington, DC: Taylor & Maury, 1853), 69–70.

67. Jefferson, *The Writings of Thomas Jefferson*, ed. Lipscomb, 1:71.

68. Thomas Jefferson, *The Works of Thomas Jefferson*, ed. Paul Leicester Ford, vol. 2 (New York: G. P. Putnam's Sons, 1904), 434.

69. Jefferson, *Writings of Thomas Jefferson*, ed. Lipscomb, 15: 405–406.

70. Ibid., 19:415.

71. Thomas Jefferson, "Report of the Commissioners for the University of Virginia," *The University of Virginia*, August 4, 1818, accessed October 24, 2011, http://etext.virginia.edu/etcbin/toccer-new2?id=JefRock.sgm&images=images/modeng&data=/texts/english/modeng/parsed&tag=public&part=1&division=div1.

72. Jefferson, *The Writings of Thomas Jefferson*, ed. Lipscomb, 19:415–416.

73. Ibid., 449–450; emphasis added.

74. Thomas Jefferson, "Report of the Commissioners for the University of Virginia," *The University of Virginia*, August 4, 1818, accessed October 25, 2011, http://etext.virginia.edu/etcbin/toccer-new2?id=JefRock.sgm&images=images/modeng&data=/texts/english/modeng/parsed&tag=public&part=1&division=div1.

75. Thomas Jefferson, *The Works of Thomas Jefferson*, ed. Paul Leicester Ford, vol. 12 (New York: G. P. Putnam's Sons, 1905), 272.

76. Thomas Jefferson, "Report of the Commissioners for the University of Virginia,"

The University of Virginia, August 4, 1818, accessed October 25, 2011, http://etext.
virginia.edu/etcbin/toccer-new2?id=JefRock.sgm&images=images/modeng&data=/
texts/english/modeng/parsed&tag=public&part=1&division=div1.

77. Jefferson, *The Writings of Thomas Jefferson*, ed. Lipscomb, 19:414.

78. Ibid.

79. William Henry Foote, *Sketches of Virginia, Historical and Biographical* (Philadelphia: J. B. Lippincott & Co., 1855), 325.

80. *See* Jefferson's articles expressing his strong support in his own *Virginia Evangelical and Literary Magazine*, such as that in (January 1818) vol. 1, 548; Philip Alexander Bruce, *History of the University of Virginia, 1819–1919* vol. 1 (New York: The MacMillian Company, 1920), 204; *See also* Robert P. Davis et al., *Virginia Presbyterians in American Life: Hanover Presbytery 1755–1980* (Richmond: Hanover Presbytery, 1892), 66, 72.

81. John Holt Rice, ed., *The Virginia Evangelical and Literary Magazine*, vol. 1 (Richmond: William W. Gray, 1818), 548.

82. Alexander Garrett, "Outline of Cornerstone Ceremonies," *The University of Virginia*, October 6, 1817, accessed October 25, 2011, http://etext.virginia.edu/etcbin/toccer-new2?id=Jef1Gri.sgm&images=images/modeng&data=/texts/english/modeng/parsed&tag=public&part=47&division=div1.

83. Thomas Jefferson, "Report of the Commissioners for the University of Virginia," *The University of Virginia*, August 4, 1818, accessed October 25, 2011, http://etext.virginia.edu/etcbin/toccer-new2?id=JefRock.sgm&images=images/modeng&data=/texts/english/modeng/parsed&tag=public&part=1&division=div1.

84. Henry S. Randall, *The Life of Thomas Jefferson*, vol. 3 (New York: Derby & Jackson, 1858), 467–468.

85. Ibid., 467.

86. Jefferson, *The Writings of Thomas Jefferson*, ed. Lipscomb, 11:413.

87. Ibid., 19:367.

88. Ibid., 19:389.

89. Roy Honeywell, *The Educational Work of Thomas Jefferson*, vol. 16 (Cambridge: Harvard University Press, 1931), 92.

90. Thomas Jefferson, "Report to the President and Directors of the Literary Fund," The Avalon Project, October 7, 1822, accessed October 25, 2011, http://avalon.law.yale.edu/19th_century/jeffrep3.asp.

91. Thomas Jefferson, "The Papers of Thomas Jefferson," Library of Congress, accessed October 25, 2011, http://memory.loc.gov/cgi-bin/ampage?collId=mtj1&fileName=mtj1page054.db&recNum=725&itemLink=/ammem/collections/jefferson_papers/mtjser1.html&linkText=7&tempFile=./temp/~ammem_kF9i&filecode=mtj&itemnum=1&ndocs=1.

92. James Madison, *The Writings of James Madison*, ed. Gaillard Hunt, vol. 9 (New York: G. P. Putnam's Sons, 1910), 203–207.

93. Jefferson, *The Writings of Thomas Jefferson*, ed. Lipscomb, 16:19.

94. Thomas Jefferson, "Report of the Commissioners for the University of Virginia," *The University of Virginia*, August 4, 1818, accessed October 25, 2011, http://etext.virginia.edu/etcbin/toccer-new2?id=JefRock.sgm&images=images/modeng&data=/texts/english/modeng/parsed&tag=public&part=1&division=div1. *See also* Jefferson, *The Writings of Thomas Jefferson*, ed. Lipscomb, 19:394, 411–412, 449–450.

95. Jefferson, *The Writings of Thomas Jefferson*, ed. Lipscomb, 19:449–450.

96. Ibid., 449–450.

97. Advertisement for the University of Virginia, printing a copy of a letter from the Rev. Mr. Tuston, the chaplain of the University of Virginia to Richard Duffield, Esq, originally printed in the *Charlestown Free Press*, repr. in *The Globe*, vol. 7 (Washington, DC: September 8, 1837), 2.

98. University of Virginia Advertisement *The Globe*, vol. 13 (Washington, DC: August 2, 1843.), no. 42, 2.

99. James Madison, "The Papers of James Madison," Library of Congress, May 1, 1828, accessed October 25, 2011, http://memory.loc.gov/cgi-bin/ampage?collId= mjm&fileName=22/mjm22.db&recNum=379&itemLink=D?mjm:13:./ temp/~ammem_LjNU.

100. Thomas Jefferson, *The Life and Selected Writings of Thomas Jefferson*, eds. Adrienne Koch and Williams Peden (New York: Random House, Inc., 1944), 697.

101. Frank Mead, ed., *Encyclopedia of Religious Quotations* (New Jersey: Fleming H. Revell Company, 1965), 50.

102. Thomas Jefferson, *Memoir, Correspondence, and Miscellanies*, ed. Thomas Jefferson Randolph, vol. 2 (Boston: Gray and Bowen, 1830), 216.

103. Ibid., 1:286.

104. Ibid., 1:287.

105. Steve Sheppard, ed., *The History of Legal Education in the United States: Commentaries and Primary Sources* (Pasadena: Salem Press Inc., 1999), Part I, Section A, 156.

106. Jefferson, *Memoir, Correspondence, and Miscellanies*, ed. Randolph, 2:215.

107. Ibid, 216.

108. *See* Rufus K. Noyes, *Views of Religion* (Boston: L. K. Washburn, 1906), 197; Jim Walker, "Thomas Jefferson," No Beliefs, accessed July 15, 2011, http://nobeliefs. com/jefferson.htm; Robin Morigan, "Fighting Words for a Secular America," Ms. Magazine, accessed July 18, 2011, http://www.msmagazine.com/fall2004/ fightingwords.asp; Gary Leupp, "On Jefferson, Diderot and the Political Use of God," The China Rose, accessed July 18, 2011, http://chinarose.wordpress.com/2010/01/09/ denis-diderot-humanist-avant-lettrist-philosopher-polymath/; and many others.

109. "Apologetics," Apologetics Index, accessed March 2, 2011, http://www. apologeticsindex.org/a13.html; "Apologetics," Merriam Webster, accessed March 2, 2011, http://www.merriam-webster.com/dictionary/apologetics.

110. Elias Boudinot, *The Age of Revelation, or the Age of Reason Shewn to Be an Age of Infidelity* (Philadelphia: Asbury Dickins, 1801), iii–iv.

111. Ibid., vi.

112. John Witherspoon, *Lectures on Moral Philosophy* (Philadelphia: Williams W. Woodward, 1822), 5, 38.

113. Ezra Stiles, *The United States Elevated to Glory and Honor; A Sermon, at the Anniversary Election, May 8th, 1783* (New Haven: Thomas & Samuel Green, 1783), 56.

114. Thomas Jefferson, *Memoirs, Correspondence, and Miscellanies*, ed. Thomas Jefferson Randolph, vol. 4 (Charlottesville: F. Carr & Co., 1829), 363–365.

115. Jefferson, *Memoirs, Correspondence, and Miscellanies*, ed. Randolph, vol. 4, 363–365.

116. Thomas Jefferson, *Memoir, Correspondence, and Miscellanies*, ed. Thomas Jefferson Randolph, vol. 2 (Boston: Gray and Bowen, 1830) 216–218.

117. *See Worcester v. Georgia*, 31 U.S. 515 (1832); *City of Charleston v Benjamin*, 2 Strob. 508 (Sup. Ct. S.C. 1846); etc.

118. Noah Webster, *An American Dictionary of the English Language*, vol. 1 (New York: S. Converse, 1828), s.v. "Evangelist."

119. *The Encyclopedia Britannica. A Dictionary of Arts, Sciences, Literature, and General Information*, vol. 3 (New York: Encyclopedia Britannica, Inc., 1910), 878, s.v. "Bible"; Brooke Foss Westcott, *A General Survey of the History of the Canon of the New Testament* (London: Macmillan and Co., 1866), 390–391; and Edward Reuss, *History of the Canon of the Holy Scriptures in the Christian Church*, trans. David Hunter (Edinburgh: James Gemmell, 1884), 205–206.

120. Mark A. Beliles, "*Religion and Republicanism in Jefferson's Virginia*" (PhD diss., Whitefield Theological Seminary, 1993), 102–103.

121. Robert M. Healey, *Jefferson on Religion in Public Education* (Hamden, CT: Archon Books, 1970), 27.

122. Thomas Jefferson, *Memoir, Correspondence, and Miscellanies*, ed. Thomas Jefferson Randolph, vol. 2 (Boston: Gray and Bowen, 1830), 216.

LIE # 3: THOMAS JEFFERSON WROTE HIS OWN BIBLE AND
EDITED OUT THE THINGS HE DIDN'T AGREE WITH

1. Craig Cabaniss, Bob Kauflin, Dave Harvey, and Jeff Purswell, *Worldliness: Resisting the Seduction of a Fallen World*, ed. C. J. Mahaney (Wheaton: Crossway Books, 2008), 15.

2. Robert S. Alley, "The *Real* Jefferson on Religion," secularhumanism.org, accessed February 8, 2011, http://www.secularhumanism.org/library/fi/alley_18_4.html.

3. Jim Walker, "Thomas Jefferson on Christianity & Religion," nobeliefs.com, accessed May 23, 2011, http://www.nobeliefs.com/jefferson.htm.

4. Don Landis, "Jonah and the Great Fish," Answers in Genesis, September 5, 2006, http://www.answersingenesis.org/articles/am/v1/n1/great-fish.

5. *See* Steve Waldman, *Founding Faith: Providence, Politics, and the Birth of Religious Freedom in America* (New York: Random House, 2008), 72; Stephen J. Nichols, *Jesus; Made in America: A Cultural History from the Puritans to the Passion of the Christ* (Downers Grove: IVP Academic, 2008), 55; Rev. Peter Edward Lanzillotta, "Insights from Jefferson's Bible," interfaithservicesofthelowcountry.com, June 28, 2010, accessed October 25, 2011, http://interfaithservicesofthelowcountry.com/for-july-4th-insights-into-jeffersons-bible/; George H. Shriver and Bill J. Leonard, eds, *Encyclopedia of Religious Controversies in the United States* (Westport: Greenwood Press, 1997), 238; Daniel G. Reid, ed., *Dictionary of Christianity in America*, (Downers Grove: InterVarsity Press, 1990), 590, sv "Thomas Jefferson"; Winford Claiborne, "Revised Version of Christianity," gosepelhour.net, accessed February 8, 2011, http://www.gospelhour.net/2211.html; Mark A. Noll, George M. Marsden, and Nathan O. Hatch, *The Search for Christian America* (Colorado Springs: Helmers & Howard, 1989), 75; "An Interview with Mikey Weinstein of Military Religious Freedom Foundation," Pagan + Politics, February 26, 2010, accessed

October 25, 2011, http://www.facebook.com/note.php?note_id=360240177811; and more.

6. Thomas Jefferson, *Memoir, Correspondence, and Miscellanies*, ed. Thomas Jefferson Randolph, vol. 4 (Charlottesville: F. Carr, and Co., 1829), 4:23, 4:228, 2: 48–50; Thomas Jefferson, *The Works of Thomas Jefferson*, ed. Paul Leicester Ford, vol. 2 (New York: G. P. Putnam's Sons, 1904), 253–254; Thomas Jefferson, *The Writings of Thomas Jefferson*, ed. Andrew A. Lipscomb, vol. 14 (Washington, DC: The Thomas Jefferson Memorial Association, 1904), 71–73.

7. William Maxwell, *A Memoir of the Rev. John H. Rice* (Philadelphia: J. Whetham, 1835), 127.

8. Ellen Coolidge, *The Domestic Life of Thomas Jefferson*, ed. Sarah N. Randolph (New York: Harper & Brothers, 1871), 345.

9. Dumas Malone, *Jefferson and His Time: The Sage of Monticello*, vol. 6 (Boston: Little, Brown and Company 1981), 122.

10. Thomas Jefferson, *The Writings of Thomas Jefferson*, ed. Paul Leicester Ford, vol. 9 (New York: G. P. Putnam's Sons, 1904), 485–488. *See also* Malone, *Jefferson and His Time: The Sage of Monticello*, 6:123.

11. Thomas Jefferson, *The Writings of Thomas Jefferson*, ed. Andrew A. Lipscomb, vol. 14 (Washington, DC: The Thomas Jefferson Memorial Association, 1904), 81.

12. "Subscribers' Names." in *The Holy Bible, Containing the Old and New Testaments: Together with the Apocrypha; Translated out of the Original Tongues and with the Former Translations, Diligently Compared and Revised*, vol. 1 (Philadelphia: John Thomason & Abraham Small, 1798).

13. *See* "Framed Bible Pages," Houston Baptist University, accessed December 2, 2010, http://www.hbu.edu/hbu/Framed_Bible_pages_.asp?SnID=2; "Thomas Jefferson and the Bible: Publications He Owned," Thomas Jefferson Foundation, January 2007, accessed October 25, 2011, http://www.monticello.org/library/exhibits/images/biblepublications.pdf.

14. "Subscribers' Names" in *The Holy Bible, Containing the Old and New Testaments: Together with the Apocrypha; Translated out of the Original Tongues and with the Former Translations, Diligently Compared and Revised*, vol. 1 (Philadelphia: John Thomason & Abraham Small, 1798). This lists President John Adams, Vice President Thomas Jefferson, Declaration signers John Hancock and Samuel Chase, Constitution signers Gunning Bedford, George Read, James Wilson, John Dickinson, Jared Ingersoll, Thomas Mifflin, and Alexander Hamilton, Constitutional Convention delegate John Lansing, Chief Justice and author of the *Federalist Papers* John Jay, and Revolutionary General and Secretary of State Timothy Pickering.

15. "Thomas Jefferson and the Bible: Publications He Owned," Thomas Jefferson Foundation, January 2007, October 25, 2011, http://www.monticello.org/library/exhibits/images/biblepublications.pdf.

16. Thomas Jefferson, *The Works of Thomas Jefferson*, ed. Paul Leicester Ford, vol. 11 (New York: G. P. Putman and Sons, 1905), 6.

17. Ibid., 84.

18. Henry S. Randall, *The Life of Thomas Jefferson*, vol. 3 (New York: Derby & Jackson, 1858), 654.

19. *See* Thomas Jefferson, *The Papers of Thomas Jefferson*, ed. Barbara B. Oberg (Princeton: Princeton University Press, 2003), 30:238, 31:394.

20. Richard Peters, ed., "An Act in Addition to an Act Entitled 'An Act, in Addition to an Act Regulating the Grants of Land Appropriated for Military Services, and for the Society of the United Brethren, for Propagating the Gospel Among the Heathen,'" *The Public Statutes at Large of the United States of America* (Boston: Charles C. Little and James Brown, 1845), 155.

21. The Reverend William Bennet, "The Excellence of Christian Morality, A Sermon Preached before the Society in Scotland for Propagating Christian Knowledge, at their Anniversary Meeting, Thursday, 6th June 1799" (Edinburgh: J. Ritchie, 1800).

22. *Thomas Jefferson's Abridgement of The Words of Jesus of Nazareth* (Charlottesville: Mark Beliles, 1993), 13–14.

23. Jefferson, *The Writings of Thomas Jefferson*, ed. Lipscomb, 10:376–377.

24. *Thomas Jefferson's Abridgement of the Words of Jesus of Nazareth* (Charlottesville: Mark Beliles, 1993), 14.

25. Walter Lowrie and Matthew St. Claire Clarke, eds., "The Kaskaskia and Other Tribes," *American State Papers: Documents, Legislative and Executive of the Congress of the United States*, vol. 4 (Washington, DC: Gales and Seaton, 1832), 687.

26. *Wallace v. Jaffree*, 472 U.S. 38, 103, n. 5 (1983) (Rehnquist, J. dissenting).

27. Richard Peters, ed., "An Act Granting Further Time for Locating Military Land Warrants, and for Other Purposes," *The Public Statutes at Large of the United States of America* (Boston: Charles C. Little and James Brown, 1845), 271–272.

28. *See* Michael Hinton, *The 100 Minute Bible* (Canterbury: The 100-Minute Press, 2007); Lee Cantelon, *The Words: Jesus of Nazareth* (Grand Rapids: Credo House Publishers, 2007); Phillip Law, *The Abridged Bible—from Adam to Apocalypse* (London: Continuum, 2006); and many others. Such works have been part of the American religious landscape for generations, including, J. Talboys Wheeler, *A Popular Abridgement of New Testament History, for Schools, Families, and General Reading* (London: Arthur Hall, Virtue & Co., 1854); and Henricus Oort, Isaac Hooykaas, Abraham Kuenen, and Philip Henry Wicksted, *The Bible for Learners* (Boston: Roberts Brothers, 1898); Caroline Maxwell, *The History of the Holy Bible; an Abridgment of the Old and New Testament* (London: Harvey and Darton, 1827); Roy B. Chamberlain, *The Dartmouth Bible* (Houghton Mifflin,1965); Paul Roche, *The Bible's Greatest Stories* (New York: Signet Classic, 2001); and others.

29. Thomas Jefferson, *Memoir, Correspondence, and Miscellanies*, ed. Thomas Jefferson Randolph, vol. 4 (Boston: Gray and Bowen, 1830), 14.

30. Dickinson W. Adams, *Jefferson's Extracts from the Gospels* (Princeton: Princeton University Press, 1983), 28.

31. Charles B. Sanford, *The Religious Life of Thomas Jefferson* (Charlottesville: University Press of Virginia, 1984).

32. Mark Beliles, *Thomas Jefferson's Abridgement of the Words of Jesus of Nazareth* (Charlottesville: Mark Beliles, 1993).

33. *Jefferson's "Bible" The Life and Morals of Jesus of Nazareth*, ed. Judd Patton (Grove City: American Book Distributors, 1996), xiv, summarizing the 1983 Dickinson W. Adams, *Jefferson's Extracts from the Gospels*, which was a reconstruction of Jefferson's *Philosophy of Jesus*.

34. Charles B. Sanford, *The Religious Life of Thomas Jefferson* (Charlottesville: University Press of Virginia, 1984), 189.

35. Jefferson, *The Writings of Thomas Jefferson*, ed. Lipscomb, 15:2.

36. Malone, *Jefferson the President, First Term 1801–1805*, 4:205.

37. John Maclean, *History of the College of New Jersey, from Its Origin in 1746 to the Commencement of 1854*, vol. 1 (Philadelphia: J. B. Lippincott & Co., 1877), 364–365.

38. John Witherspoon, "Lectures on Moral Philosophy," in *The Works of John Witherspoon*, vol. 3 (Philadelphia: William W. Woodward, 1802), 367–475.

39. "Officers of Government and Instruction: Instructors," in *Quinquennial Catalogue of the Officers and Graduates of Harvard University, 1636–1895* (Cambridge: Harvard University, 1895), 41.

40. Herbert Baxter Adams, *Thomas Jefferson and the University of Virginia*, issues 1–3, (Washington, DC: Government Printing Office, 1888), 158; Randall, *The Life of Thomas Jefferson*, 3:467–468.

41. *See* "Extracts from the Laws of the College of William and Mary," *The History of the College of William and Mary from Its Foundation, 1660 to 1874* (Richmond: J. W. Randolph & English, 1874), 153–162; *The Laws of Yale College, in New Haven, in Connecticut, Enacted by the President and Fellows, The Sixth Day of October, A.D. 1795* (New Haven: T & S Green, 1795), 13–14.

42. Adam Smith, *The Theory of Moral Sentiments* (London: A. Millar, 1759).

43. Richard Price, *A Review of the Principal Questions and Difficulties in Morals* (London: T. Cadall, 1757).

44. *See* Benjamin Rush, "An Address to the Ministers of the Gospel of Every Denomination in the United States upon Subjects Interesting to Morals," in *Essays: Literary, Moral, and Philosophical* (Philadelphia: Thomas & Samuel Bradford, 1798), 114–124; Benjamin Rush, *An Inquiry into the Effects of Ardent Spirits Upon the Human Body and Mind, with an Account of the Means of Preventing, and of the Remedies for Curing Them* (New York: 1811); Benjamin Rush, an illustration titled "A Moral and Physical Thermometer: Or, a Scale of the Progress of Temperance and Intemperance," http://ihm.nlm.nih.gov/luna/servlet/detail/NLMNLM~1~1~101449214~157641:A-Moral-and-Physical-Thermometer?printerFriendly=1; Benjamin Rush, "Observations upon the Influence of the Habitual Use of Tobacco upon Health, Morals, and Property," in *Essays: Literary, Moral, and Philosophical* (Philadelphia: Thomas & Samuel Bradford, 1798), 263–274; Benjamin Rush, *An Inquiry into the Physical Causes upon the Moral Faculty Delivered Before a Meeting of the American Philosophical Society, Held at Philadelphia, on the Twenty-Seventh of February, 1796* (Philadelphia: Haswell, Barrington, and Haswell, 1839); John Witherspoon, "Lectures on Moral Philosophy" in *The Works of the Rev. John Witherspoon*, vol. 3 (Philadelphia: William W. Woodward, 1802), 367–475; Noah Webster, *A Collection of Papers on Political, Literary, and Moral Subjects* (New York: Webster & Clark, 1843).

45. See, for example, Gouverneur Morris, *A Diary of the French Revolution*, vol. 2 (Boston: Houghton Mifflin Co., 1939), 172, 452; David Ramsay, *The History of the American Revolution*, vol. 2 (Dublin: William Jones, 1795), 452; Judge William Paterson, *United States Oracle* (New Hampshire), May 24, 1800, quoted in Maeva Marcus, ed., *The Documentary History of the Supreme Court of the United States, 1789-1800* (New York: Columbia University Press, 1988), 436; Richard Henry Lee, *The Letters of Richard Henry Lee*, ed. James Curtis Ballagh,

vol. 2 (New York: The MacMillan Company, 1914), 411; John Adams, *The Works of John Adams*, ed. Charles Francis Adams, vol. 9 (Boston: Little, Brown, and Company, 1854), 636; Joseph Story, *Vidal v. Girard's Executors*, 43 U.S. 127, 200 (1844); *Independent Chronicle* (Boston), February 22, 1787; Fisher Ames writing as Camillus, Fisher Ames, *The Works of Fisher Ames*, ed. Seth Ames, vol. 1 (Boston: Little, Brown and Company, 1854), 67; *The Speeches of the Different Governors of the Legislature of the State of New York, Commencing with Those of George Clinton and Continued Down to the Present Time* (Albany: J. B. Van Steenbergh, 1825), 108; John Adams, John Hancock, Samuel Adams et al., "Declaration of Rights, Part the First, Article III *A Constitution or Frame of Government Agreed Upon by the Delegates of the People for the State of Massachusetts* (Boston: Benjamin Edes & Sons, 1780), 7; John Sanderson, *Biography of the Signers to the Declaration of Independence,*vol. 4 (Philadelphia; R. W. Pomeroy, 1824), 333, James McHenry in Bernard C. Steiner, *One Hundred and Ten Years of Bible Society Work in Maryland, 1810-1920* (Baltimore: The Maryland Bible Society, 1921), 14; Daniel Webster, "Remarks to the Ladies of Richmond" in *The Works of Daniel Webster,* vol. 2 (Boston: Little, Brown and Company, 1853), 107–108; and many similar quotes.

46. See *The Civil and Executive Officers Assistant* (New Haven: Abel Morse, 1793), 254–255; Zephaniah Swift, *A System of the Laws of the State of Connecticut* (Windham, CT: John Byrne, 1795), 185; *The Code of 1650, Being a Compilation of the General Court of Connecticut: Also, the Constitution or Civil Compact, Entered into and Adopted by the Towns of Winsdor, Hartford and Wethersfield in 1638-9. To Which Is Added Some Extracts from the Laws and Judicial Proceedings of New Haven Colony Commonly Called Blue Laws* (Hartford: Silas Andrus, 1825), 28–29; *The Public Statute Laws of the State of Connecticut*, book 1 (Hartford: Hudson & Goodwin, 1808), 295, 304, 480; Oliver H. Prince, *Digest of the Laws of the State of Georgia* (Milledgeville: Grantland & Orme, 1822), 180–186, 349–350, 365–366, 380, 510–512; *Laws of the State of Maine* (Haldwell: Goodale, Glazier & Co., 1822), 58, 66–68, 71–72; *The Charters and General Laws of the Colony and Province of Massachusetts Bay* (Boston: T. B. Wait & Co., 1814), 58–61; *The Laws of the State of New Hampshire, the Constitution of the State of New Hampshire and the Constitution of the United States with its Proposed Amendments* (Portsmouth: John Melcher, 1797), 279, 285; *Constitution and Laws of the State of New Hampshire; Together with the Constitution of the United States* (Dover: Samuel Bragg, 1805), 267, 275, 278–279, 286, 374; *Laws of the State of New York, Comprising the Constitution and Acts of the Legislature Since the Revolution from the First to the Twentieth Session, Inclusive*, vol. 1 (New York: Thomas Greenleaf, 1798), 57–60, 336-338, 428; John Haywood, *A Manual of the Laws of North Carolina, Arranger Under Distinct Heads in Alphabetical Order* (Raleigh: J. Gales, 1814), 65, 264–265, 267; Collinson Read, *An Abridgment of the Laws of Pennsylvania, Being a Complete Digest of All Such Acts of Assembly, as Concern the Commonwealth at Large* (Philadelphia: Printed for the Author, 1801), 31, 175, 379, 286, 382; *Laws of the Commonwealth of Pennsylvania*, vol. 1 (Philadelphia: John Bioren, 1810), 26–27, 29, 113; *The Public Laws of the State of Rhode Island and Providence Plantations, as Revised by a Committee and Finally Enacted by the Honourable General Assembly*

at their Session in January, 1798 (Providence: Carter and Wilkinson, 1798), 585–586, 594–595; Joseph Brevard, *An Alphabetical Digest of the Public Statute Law of South Carolina* (Charleston: John Hoff, 1814), 1:99, 2:119, 2;179; James Coffield Mitchell, *The Tennessee Justice's Manual and Civil Officer's Guide* (Nashville: J. C. Mitchell and C. C. Norvell, 1834), 174–186; *Statutes of the State of Vermont* (Bennington: Anthony Haswell, 1791), 17–18, 50, 155, 265; *The Revised Code of the Laws of Virginia; Being a Collection of All Such Acts of the General Assembly, of a Public and Permanent nature, as Are Now in Force*, vol. 1 (Richmond: Thomas Ritchie, 1819), 585–586; William Waller Hening, *The Virginia Justice, Comprising the Office and Authority of a Justice of the Peace, in the Commonwealth of Virginia. Together with a Variety of Useful Precedents, Adapted to the Laws Now in Force* (Richmond: Shephard & Pollard, 1825), 155, 548–553; *Private and Local Laws Passed by the Legislature of Wisconsin in the Year Eighteen Hundred and Fifty-Nine* (Madison: James Ross, 1859), 226–227, 334–335.

47. Thomas Jefferson, *Memoir, Correspondence, and Miscellanies*, ed. Thomas Jefferson Randolph, (Boston: Gray and Bowen, 1830), 509, from his "Syllabus of an Estimate of the Merits of the Doctrines of Jesus, Compared with Those of Others," sent with a letter to Benjamin Rush on April 21, 1803.

48. Jefferson, *The Writings of Thomas Jefferson*, ed. Lipscomb, 15:219–220; emphasis added.

49. Ibid., 10:374–375.

50. Thomas Jefferson, *Memoir, Correspondence, and Miscellanies*, ed. Thomas Jefferson Randolph, vol. 4 (Boston: Gray and Bowen, 1830), 223; emphasis added. The Christian movements mentioned in this excerpt had each been studied by Jefferson. The *Platonists* were Christian theologians and ministers who used the philosophy of Plato to prove the existence of God and the immortality of the soul. *Plotinists* were those who combined the Christian mystical elements of Plotinus (a third-century philosopher) with Plato's philosophy. *Stagyrites* were Christians who followed the teachings of Aristotle. *Gamaelielites* were those Christians who adopted the philosophy of Gamaliel set forth in Acts 5:34-39. *Eclectics* were the Christians who mixed many elements together—often elements that contradicted each other. *Gnostics* were those on a never ending search for truth and wisdom. *Scholastics* were those who followed the teachings of St. Augustine in an effort to resolve ancient philosophical problems with new solutions. This website link has a good summary of Gnosticism: http://www.gnosis.org/gnintro.htm.

51. Thomas Jefferson, *Memoir, Correspondence, and Miscellanies*, ed. Thomas Jefferson Randolph, vol. 4 (Boston: Gray and Bowen, 1830), 242.

52. Jefferson, *The Writings of Thomas Jefferson*, ed. Lipscomb, 10:376–377, 12:315, 13:377–378, 14:232–233; Thomas Jefferson, *Memoir, Correspondence, and Miscellanies*, ed. Thomas Jefferson Randolph (Boston: Gray and Bowen, 1830), 3:506–507, 4:222–226; Thomas Jefferson, *The Works of Thomas Jefferson*, ed. Paul Leicester Ford, vol. 12 (New York: G. P. Putnam's Sons, 1905), 241.

53. Thomas Jefferson, *Memoir, Correspondence, and Miscellanies*, ed. Thomas Jefferson Randolph (Boston: Gray and Bowen, 1830), 4:13–14, 3:509.

54. Ibid., 4:223–224.

55. Jefferson, *The Writings of Thomas Jefferson*, ed. Lipscomb, 14:232–233.

56. Ibid., 14:385.

57. Ibid., 14:386.

58. Ibid., 14:246. *See also* Marie Kimball, *Jefferson: The Road to Glory, 1743 to 1776* (New York: Coward-McCann, 1943), 106–109.

59. Randall, *The Life of Thomas Jefferson,* 3: 671–672.

60. *See Congressional Record: Containing the Proceedings and Debates of the Fifty-Seventh Congress, First Session; Also Special Session of the Senate,* vol. 35 (Washington, DC: Government Printing Office, 1902), 5272–5273, 5783–5784.

61. Ibid., 5272.

62. Ibid., 5273.

63. Thomas Jefferson, ed., *The Life and Morals of Jesus of Nazareth, Extracted Textually from the Gospels in Greek, Latin, French, and English* (Washington, DC: Government Printing Office, 1904), 19.

64. Thomas Jefferson, *Jefferson's "Bible"; The Life and Morals of Jesus of Nazareth XV–XVI,* ed. Judd Patton (Grove City: American Book Distributors, 1996), xv.

65. Ibid.

66. Thomas Jefferson, *Memoir, Correspondence, and Miscellanies,* ed. Thomas Jefferson Randolph, vol. 3 (Boston: Gray and Bowen, 1830), 506.

LIE # 4: THOMAS JEFFERSON WAS A RACIST
WHO OPPOSED EQUALITY FOR BLACK AMERICANS

1. Conor Cruise O'Brien, "Thomas Jefferson: Radical and Racist," *Atlantic Monthly,* October 1997, accessed October 25, 2011, http://www.theatlantic.com/past/docs/issues/96oct/obrien/obrien.htm.

2. Stephen E. Ambrose, *To America: Personal Reflections of an Historian* (New York: Simon & Schuster, 2002), 2.

3. "Thomas Jefferson's Dark Side," *The Abolitionist,* February 12, 1997, accessed October 25, 2011, http://afgen.com/jeffersn.html.

4. Stephen J. Lyons. "Thomas Jefferson, Shameless Slavemaster," review of Negro President by Garry Wills, *Chicago Sun-Times,* November 16, 2003.

5. James Madison, "Journal of the Constitutional Convention of 1787," in *The Works of James Madison,* ed. Gaillard Hunt, vol. 3 (New York: G. P. Putnam's Sons, 1900), July 11–13, 1787, accessed October 25, 2011, http://oll.libertyfund.org/index.php?option=com_staticxt&staticfile=show.php%3Ftitle=1935&Itemid=99999999); John Elliot, ed., *The Debates in the Several State Conventions on the Adoption of the Federal Constitution,* vol. 2 (Washington, DC: Printed for the Editor, 1836), 226, June 17, 1788, accessed October 25, 2011, http://memory.loc.gov/ammem/amlaw/lwed.html; James Madison, *Debates on the Adoption of the Federal Constitution. In the Convention Held at Philadelphia in 1787,* ed. Jonathan Elliot, vol. 5 (Washington, DC: Printed for the Editor, 1845), 181, 295–305, 307–308, June 11, 1787, July 11–13, 1787, accessed October 25, 2011, http://memory.loc.gov/ammem/amlaw/lwed.html.

6. "The Constitution of the United States: A Transcription, Article 1, Section 2," *The U. S. National Archives and Records Administration,* September 17, 1787, accessed October 25, 2011, http://www.archives.gov/exhibits/charters/constitution_transcript.html.

NOTES

7. "Historical Census Browser," *University of Virginia Library*, Census Results for 1790, accessed June 10, 2011, http://mapserver.lib.virginia.edu/php/state.php.

8. James Madison, *Debates on the Adoption of the Federal Constitution. In the Convention Held at Philadelphia in 1787*, ed. Jonathan Elliot, vol. 5 (Washington, DC: Printed for the Editor, 1845), 392–393.

9. Jonathan Elliot, *The Debates of the Several State Conventions on the Adoption of the Federal Constitution*, vol. 1 (Washington, DC: Printed for the Editor, 1836), 363.

10. "The Constitution of the United States: A Transcription, Article 1, Section 2," *The U. S. National Archives and Records Administration*, September 17, 1787, accessed October 25, 2011, http://www.archives.gov/exhibits/charters/constitution_transcript.html; James Madison, *Debates on the Adoption of the Federal Constitution. In the Convention Held at Philadelphia in 1787*, ed. Jonathan Elliot, vol. 5 (Washington, DC: Printed for the Editor, 1845), 300–301.

11. *Dred Scott v. Sandford*, 60 U.S. 393, 572-573 (1856) (Curtis, J., dissenting); John Hancock, *Essays on the Elective Franchise; or, Who Has the Right to Vote?* (Philadelphia: Merrihew & Son, 1865), 22–23.

12. *The Records of the Federal Convention of 1787*, Max Farrand, ed., vol. 3 (New Haven: Yale University Press, 1966), 35.

13. Fredrick Douglass, *My Bondage and My Freedom* (New York: Miller, Orton & Mulligan, 1855), 395–398; Frederick Douglass, *Life and Times of Frederick Douglass* (Hartford: Park Publishing Company, 1882), 469–470.

14. *Dred Scott v. Sanford*, 60 U.S. 393, 572-573 (1856) (Curtis, J., dissenting); John Hancock, *Essays on the Elective Franchise; or, Who Has the Right to Vote?* (Philadelphia: Merrihew & Son, 1865), 22–23.

15. Thomas Jefferson, *The Papers of Thomas Jefferson*, ed. Julian P. Boyd, vol. 8 (Princeton: Princeton University Press, 1953), 258–259.

16. Thomas Jefferson, *Memoir, Correspondence, and Miscellanies*, ed. Thomas Jefferson Randolph, vol. 1 (New York: G. & C. & H. Carvill, 1830), 268.

17. Ibid., 268.

18. Ibid., 268–269.

19. Ibid., 269.

20. Thomas Jefferson, *The Works of Thomas Jefferson*, ed. Paul Leicester Ford, vol. 11 (New York: G. P. Putnam's Sons, 1905), 264.

21. W. O. Blake, *The History of Slavery and the Slave Trade; Ancient and Modern* (Ohio: J. & H. Miller, 1857), 374.

22. Ibid., 386.

23. George M. Stroud, *A Sketch of the Laws Relating to Slavery in the Several States of the United States of America* (Philadelphia: Henry Longstreth, 1856), 150.

24. "Virginia, ACT XXI. An act to authorize the manumission of slaves," University of Virginia, May 1782, accessed October 25, 2011, http://www2.vcdh.virginia.edu/xslt/servlet/XSLTServlet?xsl=/xml_docs/slavery/documents/display_laws2.xsl&xml=/xml_docs/slavery/documents/laws.xml&lawid=1782-05-02.

25. Dumas Malone, *Jefferson and His Time: The Sage of Monticello*, vol. 6 (Boston: Little, Brown and Company, 1981), 319.

26. *The Revised Code of the Laws of Virginia*, vol. 1 (Richmond: Thomas Ritcher, 1819), 434.

27. Ibid. 435.

28. Ibid., 436. *See also* George M. Stroud, *A Sketch of the Laws*, 150–151.

29. Thomas Jefferson, *The Works of Thomas Jefferson*, ed. Paul Leicester Ford, vol. 11 (New York: G. P. Putnam's Sons, 1905), 238.

30. William Cohen, "Thomas Jefferson and the Problem of Slavery," Institute of Advanced Studies, accessed July 1, 2011, http://www.iea.usp.br/iea/english/journal/38/cohen jefferson.pdf.

31. Thomas Jefferson, *The Works of Thomas Jefferson*, ed. Paul Leicester Ford, vol. 11 (New York: G. P. Putnam's Sons, 1898), 197.

32. Edward Ellis, *Thomas Jefferson, A Character Sketch* (Chicago: The University Association, 1898), 45–46.

33. Henry S. Randall, *The Life of Thomas Jefferson,* vol. 3 (New York: Derby & Jackson, 1858), 676.

34. "Jefferson and Slavery," Monticello, accessed May 31, 2011, http://www.monticello. org/site/jefferson/jefferson-and-slavery.

35. Thomas Jefferson, *The Papers of Thomas Jefferson*, ed. Charles T. Cullen, vol. 22 (Princeton: Princeton University Press, 1986), 49.

36. Ibid., 49–51.

37. Ibid., 51–52.

38. Ibid., 97–98.

39. Ibid., 98–99.

40. Franziska Massner, *Thomas Jefferson and Slavery—Was He Really an Opponent of the Institution?* (Norderstedt: Druck and Bindung, 2005), 7.

41. Oscar Reiss, *Blacks in Colonial America* (Jefferson, NC: McFarland & Company, 1997), 173.

42. Garry Wills, *Augustine's Confessions* (Princeton: Princeton University Press, 2011), 7.

43. Joseph M. Hentz, *The Real Thomas Paine* (Bloomington: iUniverse, 2010), 67.

44. Thomas Jefferson, *Notes on the State of Virginia* (Philadelphia: Matthew Carey, 1794), 232, 239.

45. Ibid., 239.

46. Ibid., 232.

47. Thomas Jefferson, *The Papers of Thomas Jefferson*, ed. Charles T. Cullen, vol. 22 (Princeton: Princeton University Press, 1986), 97–98, to Benjamin Banneker on August 30, 1791.

48. Ibid., 98–99, emphasis added.

49. Thomas Jefferson, *The Works of Thomas Jefferson*, ed. Paul Leicester Ford, vol. 11 (New York: G. P. Putnam's Sons, 1905), 99–100.

50. Ibid., 121.

51. Thomas Jefferson, *The Writings of Thomas Jefferson*, ed. Andrew A. Lipscomb, vol. 1 (Washington, DC: The Thomas Jefferson Memorial Association, 1903), 4.

52. Thomas Jefferson, *The Works of Thomas Jefferson*, ed. Paul Leicester Ford, vol. 11 (New York: G. P. Putnam's Sons, 1905), 417.

53. Jefferson, *The Writings of Thomas Jefferson*, ed. Lipscomb, 1:4.

54. Jefferson, *The Works of Thomas Jefferson*, ed. Ford, 1:474.

55. Thomas Jefferson, *The Thomas Jefferson Papers: Jefferson's Memorandum Books*, eds. James Bear and Lucia Stanton, vol. 1 (Princeton: Princeton University Press, 1997), 271.

56. Benjamin Franklin, *The Works of Benjamin Franklin*, ed. Jared Sparks, vol. 8 (Boston: Tappan, Whittemore, and Mason, 1839), 42.

57. Jefferson, *The Papers of Thomas Jefferson*, ed. Boyd, 1:130.

58. Ibid., 1:353.

59. Thomas Jefferson, "Rough Draft of the Declaration of Independence," ushistory. org, accessed May 31, 2011, http://www.ushistory.org/declaration/document/rough. htm.

60. Thomas Jefferson, *Memoir, Correspondence, and Miscellanies*, ed. Thomas Jefferson Randolph, vol. 1 (New York: G & C. & H. Carville, 1830), 16.

61. "Declaration of Rights,"*A Constitution or Form of Government Agreed Upon by the Delegates of the People of the State of Massachusetts-Bay* (Boston: Benjamin Edes and Sons, 1780), 7; Collinson Read, ed., *An Abridgment of the Laws of Pennsylvania*, (Philadelphia: 1801), 264–266; *The Public Statute Laws of the State of Connecticut*, book 1 (Hartford: Hudson and Goodwin, 1808), 623–62; *Rhode Island Session Laws* (Providence: Wheeler, 1784), 7–8; "Declaration of Rights," *The Constitutions of the Sixteen States* (Boston: Manning and Loring, 1797), 279; "New Hampshire Constitution, Bill of Rights," *The Constitutions of the Sixteen States* (Boston: Manning and Loring, 1797), 50 ; *Laws of the State of New York, Passed at the Twenty-Second Session, Second Meeting of the Legislature* (Albany: Loring Andrew, 1799), 721–723; *Laws of the State of New Jersey, Compiled and Published Under the Authority of the Legislature*, ed. Joseph Bloomfield (Trenton: James J. Wilson, 1811), 103–105. *See also* the *Dictionary of African American Slavery*, eds. Randall Miller and John Smith (Westport: Praeger Publishers, 1997), 394, 820–821.

62. Thomas Jefferson, *The Writings of Thomas Jefferson*, ed. Henry A. Washington, vol. 1 (Washington, DC: Taylor & Maury, 1853), 38.

63. Thomas Jefferson, "Query XIV The Administration of Justice and Description of the Laws?" in *Notes on the State of Virginia* (Philadelphia: Matthew Carey, 1794), 228.

64. Thomas Jefferson, *Memoir, Correspondence, and Miscellanies*, ed. Thomas Jefferson Randolph, vol. 1 (New York: G. & C. & H. Carvill, 1830), 41–42.

65. Ibid.

66. Jefferson, *Notes on the State of Virginia*, 270–272.

67. *Journals of the Continental Congress*, ed. Gaillard Hunt, vol. 26 (Washington, DC: Government Printing Office, 1928), 118–119; Jefferson, *The Papers of Thomas Jefferson*, ed. Boyd, 6:604.

68. Jefferson, *The Works of Thomas Jefferson*, ed. Ford, 3:65.

69. Jefferson, *The Works of Thomas Jefferson*, ed. Ford, 5:71–72.

70. Jefferson, *The Works of Thomas Jefferson*, ed. Ford, 5:388.

71. Ibid., 5:388.

72. Ibid., 10:126.

73. Jefferson, *The Writings of Thomas Jefferson*, ed. Lipscomb, 16:290.

74. Willard Carey MacNaul, *The Jefferson-Lemen Compact* (Chicago: The University of Chicago Press, 1915), 10. Lemen's records on December 11, 1782 and May, 1784, show Jefferson's encouragement to Lemen to go to Illinois and Lemen's decision to go.

75. Ibid., 30.

76. Jefferson, *The Works of Thomas Jefferson*, ed. Ford, 416–418.

77. Ibid., 11:418–419.

78. Ibid., 11:419–420.

79. Edward Coles, *Governor Edward Coles*, ed. Clarence Walworth Alvord (Springfield: Illinois State Historical Library, 1920), 28.

80. W. T. Norton, *Edward Coles, Second Governor of Illinois* (Philadelphia: J. B. Lippincott Co., 1911), 12, 24.

81. Jefferson, *The Works of Thomas Jefferson*, ed. Ford, 470–471.

82. "Missouri Compromise," Teaching American History, March 6, 1820, accessed October 25, 2011, http://teachingamericanhistory.org/library/index.asp?document=841.

83. George Adams Boyd, *Elias Boudinot* (Princeton: Princeton University Press, 1952), 290.

84. John Adams, *The Works of John Adams*, ed. Charles Francis Adams, vol. 10 (Boston: Little, Brown and Company, 1856), 386.

85. James Madison, *The Writings of James Madison*, ed. Gaillard Hunt, vol. 9 (New York: G. P. Putnam's Sons, 1910), 12.

86. Jefferson, *The Works of Thomas Jefferson*, ed. Ford, 12:157.

87. Jefferson, *Memoir, Correspondence, and Miscellanies*, ed. Randolph 4:323–324.

88. Ibid., 324.

89. Jefferson, *The Writings of Thomas Jefferson*, ed. Lipscomb, 16:119–120.

90. Ibid., 16:162–163.

91. John Quincy Adams, *An Oration Delivered Before the Inhabitants of the Town Of Newburyport at Their Request on the Sixty-First Anniversary of the Declaration of Independence, July 4, 1837* (Newburyport: Charles Whipple, 1837), 50.

92. Daniel Webster, *The Writings and Speeches of Daniel Webster*, ed. Edward Everett, vol. 15 (Boston: Little, Brown and Company, 1903), 205.

93. Abraham Lincoln, *The Collected Works of Abraham Lincoln*, ed. Roy P. Basler, vol. 2 (New Brunswick, NJ: Rutgers University Press, 1953), 249–250.

94. Fredrick Douglass, *My Bondage and My Freedom* (New York: Miller, Orton & Mulligan, 1855), 440.

95. Frederick Douglas, *The Frederick Douglass Papers, Series One, Speeches, Debates, and Interviews*, eds. John W. Blassingame and John McKivigan, vol. 4 (New Haven: Yale University Press, 1992), 307.

96. Frederick Douglass, *Frederick Douglass: A Critical Reader*, eds. Bill Lawson and Frank Kirkland (Malden, MA: Blackwell Publishers, 1999), 237.

97. Frederick Douglass, "Letter to Horace Greeley," The Gilder Lehrman Center for the Study of Slavery, Resistance, & Abolition, April 15, 1846, accessed October 25, 2011, http://www.yale.edu/glc/archive/1096.htm; Douglas, in *The Frederick Douglass Papers*, ed. Blassingame3:180.

98. Henry Highland Garnet, *Memorial Discourse* (Philadelphia: Joseph M. Wilson, 1865), 80–81.

99. Martin Luther King, Jr., "Letter from a Birmingham Jail," *Bates College*, April 16, 1963 (http://abacus.bates.edu/admin/offices/dos/mlk/letter.html), accessed June 2, 2011.

100. Colin Powell, "Acceptance Speech," *National Constitution Center*, July 4, 2002, accessed October 25, 2011, http://constitutioncenter.org/libertymedal/recipient_2002_speech.html.

NOTES

LIE # 5: THOMAS JEFFERSON ADVOCATED A SECULAR PUBLIC SQUARE THROUGH THE SEPARATION
OF CHURCH AND STATE

1. John E. Remsburg, *Six Historic Americans* (New York: The Truth Seeker Company, 1906), 81.
2. "Secularism," Dictionary.com, accessed April 13, 2011, http://dictionary.reference. com/browse/secularism.
3. "Secularism," Merriam-Webster, accessed April 12, 2011, http://www.merriam-webster.com/dictionary/secularism.
4. "Secularism," The Free Dictionary, accessed April 13, 2011, http://www.thefree dictionary.com/secularist.
5. Deuce, "Our Religious Forefathers II," Modern Ghana, November 15, 2007, accessed October 25, 2011, http://www.modernghana.com/blogs/147715/31/our-religious-forefathers-ii.html.
6. Sembj, "Humanism, Thomas Jefferson and the Constitution," Hub Pages, accessed April 18, 2011, http://hubpages.com/hub/Humanism-Thomas-Jefferson-and-The-Constitution.
7. Tom Head, "The First Amendment: Text, Origins, and Meaning," About.com, accessed May 10, 2011, http://civilliberty.about.com/od/firstamendment/tp/First-Amendment.htm.
8. *Proposed Restriction of Immigration: Hearing before the Committee on Immigration and Naturalization. House of Representatives, Sixty-Sixth Congress Second Session on H.R. 12320* (Washington, DC: Government Printing Office, 1921), 57. *See also* "A Few Words from the Father of the First Amendment," KintaLake Blog, accessed June 13, 2011, http://kintlalake.blogspot.com/2010/03/few-words-from-author-of-first.html.
9. B. A. Robinson, "The First Amendment to the U. S. Constitution: Religious Aspects," Religious Tolerance.org, accessed May 10, 2011, http://www.religioustolerance. org/amend_1.htm; "O'Reilly Ignored First Amendment, Misrepresented Jefferson's Position," Media Matters for America, December 15, 2006, accessed October 25, 2011, http://mediamatters.org/research/200612150010; Charles C. Haynes, "Farewell, Justice Souter, Defender of Mr. Jefferson's Wall," First Amendment Center, June 21, 2009, accessed October 25, 2011, http://www.firstamendmentcenter.org/farewell-justice-souter-defender-of-mr-jefferson%E2%80%99s-wall.
10. *Everson v. Bd. of Educ.* 330 U.S. 1, 13 (1947).
11. *See Abington Sch. Dist. v. Schempp*, 374 U.S. 203, 214, 234–235 (1963) and *McDaniel v. Paty*, 435 U.S. 618, 629, n9 (1978).
12. Forty-three major decisions on religion have been delivered since 1947, and Jefferson was cited authoritatively in sixteen: *Everson v. Bd. of Educ.* 330 U.S. 1, 13, 16 (1947); *McCollum v. Bd. of Educ.* 333 U.S. 203, 211 (1948); *McGowan v. Maryland*, 366 U.S. 420, 443 (1961); *Torcaso v. Watkins*, 367 U.S. 488, 493 (1961); *Engel v. Vitale*, 370 U.S. 421, 425 (1962); *Sch. Dist. of Abington TP. v. Schempp*, 374 U.S. 203, 234–235 (1963); *Bd. of Educ. v. Allen*, 392 U.S. 236, 251 (1968); *Epperson v. Arkansas*, 393 U.S. 97, 106 (1968); *Comm. for Pub. Educ. v. Nyquist*, 413 U.S. 756, 760–761, 771 (1973); *Larkin v. Grende's Den, Inc.*, 459 U.S. 116, 122–123 (1982); *Marsh v. Chambers*, 463 U.S. 783, 802 (1983); *Lynch v. Donnelly*, 465 U.S. 668, 673 (1984); *Lee v. Weisman*, 505 U.S. 577,

600–601 (1992); *Capitol Square Rev. & Advisory Bd. v. Pinette*, 515 U.S. 753 (1995); *Mitchell v. Helms*, 530 U.S. 793, 873 (2000); and *Zelman v. Simmons-Harris*, 536 U.S. 639, 711 122 S. Ct. 2460, 2485 (2002). Jefferson's "wall of separation between Church and State" metaphor (or some slight modification thereof) was cited in an additional ten: *Zorach v. Clauson*, 343 U.S. 306, 317 (1952); *Lemon v. Kurtzman*, 403 U.S. 602, 614 (1971); *Roemer v. Maryland Pub. Works Bd.* 426 U.S. 736, 768 (1976); *Wolman v. Walter*, 433 U.S. 229, 236, 257 (1977); *Comm. for Pub. Educ. v. Regan*, 444 U.S. 646, 671 (1980); *Aguilar v. Felton*, 473 U.S. 402, 420 (1985); *Bowen v. Kendrick*, 487 U.S. 589, 617–618, 638 (1988); *Texas Monthly, Inc. v. Bullock*, 489 U.S. 1, 1, 43 (1989); *Allegheny County v. Greater Pittsburgh ACLU*, 492 U.S. 573, 650–651, 657–658 (1989); and *Santa Fe Indep. Sch. Dist. v. Doe*, 530 U.S. 290, 323 (2000). Of the remaining seventeen cases, *all* of them relied on a case in which Jefferson had already been invoked by the Court as a primary authority in reaching its decision to restrict or remove religious expressions: *Walz v. Tax Comm'n*, 397 U.S. 664 (1970); *Tilton v. Richardson*, 403 U.S. 672 (1971); *Lemon v. Kurtzman*, 411 U.S. 192 (1973); *Levitt v. Comm. for Pub. Educ.*, 413 U.S. 472 (1973); *Sloan v. Lemon*, 413 U.S. 825 (1973); *Norwood v. Harrison*, 413 U.S. 455 (1973); *Wheeler v. Barrera*, 417 U.S. 402 (1974); *Meek v. Pittenger*, 421 U.S. 349 (1975); *Stone v. Graham*, 449 U.S. 39 (1980); *Larson v. Valente*, 456 U.S. 228 (1982); *Wallace v. Jaffree*, 472 U.S. 38 (1985); *Sch. Dist. of the City of Grand Rapids v. Ball*, 473 U.S. 373 (1985); *Estate of Thornton v. Caldor, Inc.* 472 U.S. 703 (1985); *Edwards v. Aguillard*, 482 U.S. 578 (1987); *Zobrest v. Catalina Foothills Sch. Dist.*, 509 U.S. 1 (1993); *Bd. of Educ. Kiryas Joel v. Grumet*, 512 U. . 687 (1994); and *Agostini v. Felton*, 521 U.S. 203 (1997). Therefore, Jefferson has been evoked either directly or indirectly as the constitutional authority in all forty-three major Supreme Court cases on religion.

13. See the documentation of this trend by Professor Mark David Hall, "Jeffersonian Wall and Madisonian Lines: The Supreme Court's Use of History and Religion Clauses Cases," *Oregon Law Review* 85, no. 2 (2006), 563–614.

14. Thomas Jefferson, *The Writings of Thomas Jefferson*, ed. Andrew A. Lipscomb, vol. 10 (Washington, DC: The Thomas Jefferson Memorial Association, 1904), 325.

15. Ibid., 10:325.

16. Ibid., 10:325.

17. "The Veto Power. To the Editor of *The Nation*: Notes," *The Nation* 46, no. 1196 (1888), 450; Thomas Jefferson, "The Thomas Jefferson Papers: to Martha Jefferson Randolph on April 25, 1803," Library of Congress, accessed October 25, 2011, http://hdl.loc.gov/loc.mss/mtj.mtjbib012345; Thomas Jefferson, *The Domestic Life of Thomas Jefferson*, ed. Sarah N. Randolph (New York: Harper & Brothers, 1871), 292.

18. Charles B. Galloway, *Christianity and the American Commonwealth* (Nashville: Publishing House Methodist Episcopal Church, 1898), 144.

19. "The Legitimization of Authority," Shelton Hall University, accessed May 16, 2011, http://pirate.shu.edu/~wisterro/coronation.htm.

20. See *An Ordinance of the Lords and Commons Assembled in Parliament. Together with Rules and Directions concerning Suspension from the Sacrament of the Lords Supper in Cases of Ignorance and Scandal. Also the Names of Such Ministers and Others That are Appointed Triers and Judges of the Ability of Elders in the Twelve*

Classes Within the Province of London (London: John Wright, October 21, 1645); *A Declaration of the Commons Assembled in Parliament Against all Such Persons as Shall Take Upon Them to Preach or Expound the Scriptures in any Church or Chapel, or any other Public Place, Except They be Ordained Either Here or in Some Other Reformed Church* (London: Edward Husband, January 2, 1646); etc.

21. Richard Hooker, *The Works of the Learned and Judicious Divine, Mr. Richard Hooker*, vol. 2 (Oxford: University Press, 1845), 484.

22. "Anglicanism," Catholic Encyclopedia, accessed May 19, 2011, http://www.newadvent.org/cathen/01498a.htm.

23. Frederick Greenwood, "The Execution of John Greenwood," in *Greenwood Genealogies, 1154–1914* (New York: The Lyons Genealogical Company, 1914), 30.

24. Ibid., 34.

25. Ibid., 35.

26. Claude H. Van Tyne, *The Causes of the War of Independence* (Boston: Houghton Mifflin Company, 1922), 3.

27. Roger Williams, *The Bloudy Tenent of Persecution for Cause of Conscience Discussed: and Mr. Cotton's Letter Examined and Answered* (London: 1644, repr. London: J. Haddon, 1848), 1–2, 171.

28. John Wise, *A Vindication of the Government of New-England Churches. And the Churches Quarrel Espoused, or a Reply to Certain Proposals* (Boston: John Boyles, 1772), 35.

29. Thomas Clarkson, *Memoirs of the Private and Public Life of William Penn* (London: Richard Taylor and Co., 1813), 240–244.

30. *See* John Wise, *A Vindication of the Government of New-England Churches. And the Churches Quarrel Espoused, or a Reply to Certain Proposals* (Boston: John Boyles, 1772), 47–48; Reverend Isaac Backus, *An Appeal to the Public for Religious Liberty Against the Oppressions of the Present Day* (Boston: John Boyle, 1773), 19, 26; Frederick Converse Beach, ed., "Pennsylvania," in *The Americana, A Universal Reference Library*, vol. 12 (New York: Scientific American Compiling Department, 1908), 312 Bishop Charles Galloway, *Christianity and the American Commonwealth* (Nashville: Publishing House Methodist Episcopal Church, 1898), 179; John Leland, *The Writings of the Late Elder John Leland, Including Some Events in His Life, Written by Himself, with Additional Sketches*, L. F. Greene, ed. (New York: G. W. Wood, 1845), 579–580; Roger Williams, *The Bloudy Tenent of Persecution for Cause of Conscience Discussed: and Mr. Cotton's Letter Examined and Answered* (London: 1644; repr. London: J. Haddon, 1848), 1–2, 171; etc.

31. Will C. Wood, *Five Problems of State and Religion* (Boston: Henry Hoyt, 1877), 92.

32. Galloway, *Christianity and the American Commonwealth*, 143.

33. William Cathcart, *Baptist Patriots in the American Revolution* (Philadelphia: S. A. George & Co., 1876), 12–18; Isaac Backus, *A History of New England, with Particular Reference to the Denomination of Christians Called Baptists*, vol. 2 (Newton, MA: Backus Historical Society, 1871), 97–98; George Bancroft, *A History of the United States of America*, vol. 1 (Boston: Little, Brown, and Company, 1858), 449–450; Sanford Hoadley Cobb, *The Rise of Religious Liberty in America Republicanism in Jefferson's Virginia* (New York: MacMillan, 1902), 112; etc.

34. *See* James Madison, *Debates on the Adoption of the Federal Constitution. In the Convention Held at Philadelphia in 1787*, ed. Jonathan Elliot, vol. 5 (Washington,

DC: Printed for the Editor, 1845), 564–565; Benson J. Lossing, "Constitutional Convention: The Names of the Delegates to the Convention Which Met at Philadelphia in May, 1787 to Frame a New Constitution," in *Biographical Sketches of the Signers of the Declaration of American Independence* (New York: J. C. Derby, 1854), 383–384; "Delegates to the Constitutional Convention," National Archives, accessed July 11, 2011, http://www.archives.gov/exhibits/charters/constitution_founding_fathers.html.

35. *See* John Eidsmoe, *Christianity and the Constitution* (Michigan: Baker Book House, 1987), 353. Eidsmoe compiled the figures from a dissertation by James Hutchinson Smylie, *American Clergyman and the Constitution of the United States of America* (Princeton: 1954).

36. B. L. Rayner, *Life of Thomas Jefferson* (Boston: Lilly, Wait, Colman, & Holden, 1834), 113–119; Henry S. Randall, *The Life of Thomas Jefferson*, vol. 1 (New York: Derby & Jackson, 1858), 203; John T. Morse, Jr., *Thomas Jefferson* (Boston: Houghton, Mifflin and Company, 1898), 41; Samuel M. Schmucker, *The Life of Thomas Jefferson* (New York: A. L. Burt Company, 1903), 67–71. *See also* Thomas Jefferson, "A Declaration by the Representatives of the United States of America, in General Congress Assembled," in *The Works of Thomas Jefferson*, ed. Paul Leicester Ford, vol. 1 (New York: G. P. Putnam's Sons, 1904), 61–64.

37. See, for example, Thomas Jefferson, "Thomas Jefferson Papers," Library of Congress, accessed October 25, 2011, http://hdl.loc.gov/loc.mss/mtj.mtjbib018945; Thomas Jefferson, "Thomas Jefferson Papers," Library of Congress, accessed October 25, 2011, http://hdl.loc.gov/loc.mss/mtj.mtjbib019174; Thomas Jefferson, *The Papers of Thomas Jefferson Retirement Series*, ed. J. Jefferson Looney, vol. 1 (Princeton: Princeton University Press, 2004), 63; etc.

38. Thomas Jefferson, *The Papers of Thomas Jefferson*, ed. Barbara B. Oberg, vol. 35 (Princeton: Princeton University Press, 2008), 407–408.

39. Ibid., 408.

40. Jonathan Elliot, ed., "Kentucky Resolutions of 1798 and 1799 [The Original Draft Prepared by Thomas Jefferson]," *Debate in the Several State Conventions, on the Adoption of the Federal Constitution, as Recommended by the General Convention at Philadelphia in 1787*, vol. 4 (Washington, DC: Printed for the Editor, 1836), 540.

41. James D. Richardson, "Second Inaugural Address," in *A Compilation of the Messages and Papers of the Presidents, 1789–1897*, vol. 1 (Washington, DC: Published by the Authority of Congress, 1899), 379.

42. Jefferson, *The Writings of Thomas Jefferson*, ed. Lipscomb, 16:325.

43. Ibid., 16:281–282

44. James L. Adams, *Yankee Doodle Went to Church: The Righteous Revolution of 1776* (Old Tappan, NJ: Fleming H. Revell Company, 1989), 12–13.

45. *Reynolds v. U.S.*, 98 U.S. 145, 162–164 (1878).

46. *Reynolds v. U.S.*, 98 U.S. 145, 164 (1878).

47. *Reynolds v. U.S.*, 98 U.S. 145, 163 (1878).

48. *See Commonwealth v. Nesbit*, 84 Pa. 398 (Pa. Sup. Ct. 1859); *Lindenmuller v. People*, 33 Barb 548 (Sup. Ct. N.Y. 1861); and others.

49. *Everson v. Bd. of Educ.* 330 U.S. 1, 18 (1947).

50. *McCollum v. Bd. of Educ.* 333 U.S. 203, 212 (1948).

51. *McCollum v. Bd. of Educ.* 333 U.S. 203, 207–209 (1948).

52. *Doe v. Santa Fe Indep. Sch.*, 530 U.S. 290 (1999).

53. *Graham v. C. Cmty. Sch. Dis.t of Decatur County*, 608 F. Supp. 531 (D. Iowa 1985); Kay v. Douglas Sch. Dist., 719 P.2d 875 (Or. App. 1986); *Lee v. Weisman*, 505 U.S. 577 (1992); *Gearon v. Loudon County Sch. Bd.*, 844 F. Supp. 1097 (E.D. Va. 1993); *Deveney v. Bd. of Educ.*, Kanawha County, 231 F. Supp. 2d 483 (S.D. W. Va. 2002).

54. *Chandler v. James*, 180 F.3d 1254 (11th Cir. 1999); *Doe v. Santa Fe Indep. Sch.*, 530 U.S. 290 (1999).

55. Patrick Buchanan, "The de-Christianization of VMI," World Net Daily, January 29, 2002, accessed October 25, 2011, http://www.wnd.com/index.php?pageId=12556.

56. Doug Huntington, "Graduation Choir Wants to Sing 'Lord's Prayer' in Honor of Deceased," Christian Post, May 28, 2007, accessed October 25, 2011, http://www.christianpost.com/news/graduation-choir-wants-to-sing-lords-prayer-in-honor-of-deceased-27653/.

57. *Roberts v. Madigan*, 921 F.2d 1047, 59 USLW 2415, 19 Fed.R.Serv.3d 530, 64 Ed. Law Rep. 1038 (1989).

58. *Brittney Kaye Settle v. Dickson County Sch. Bd.*, 53 F. 3d 152 (6th Cir. 1995).

59. Cicely Gosier, "Student Penalized Over Religious Artwork," Christian Broadcast Network, April 6, 2008, accessed October 25, 2011, http://www.cbn.com/cbnnews/us/2008/April/Student-Penalized-Over-Religious-Artwork-/.

60. "Student Files Suit to Defend His Right to Bring Bible to School," Standard News Wire, accessed June 29, 2011, http://www.standardnewswire.com/news/224236110.html; Harvey Rice, "Suit Claims Students Not Allowed to Carry Bibles," *Houston Chronicle*, May 23, 2000, accessed October 25, 2011, http://www.chron.com/CDA/archives/archive.mpl?id=2000_3216815.

61. Conrad deFiebre, "Suit Claims Man's Religious Freedom Is Being Thwarted; A Revenue Employee Says He's Not Allowed to Display Signs on His Car or Cubicle," *Star Tribune* [Minneapolis], July 2, 2004.

62. *Broadus v. Saratoga Springs City Sch. Dist.*, 02-cv-0136 (N.D.N.Y. 2002); Ellen Sorokin, "Deal Reached on Praying Toddler," *Washington Times*, June 12, 2002.

63. Diane Lynne, "Petition Posted to Defend 'God Bless America!'" World Net Daily, January 31, 2003, accessed October 25, 2011, http://www.wnd.com/?pageId=16879; "'God Bless' Spells Trouble for Guardsman," *World Net Daily*, August 22, 2003, accessed October 25, 2011, http://www.wnd.com/news/article.asp?ARTICLE_ID=34213.

64. "Seniors Sue After City Stifles Sermons at Community Center," Associated Press, October 31, 2003, accessed October 25, 2011, http://www.firstamendmentcenter.org/seniors-sue-after-city-stifles-sermons-at-community-center; Terry Eastland, "Understanding the First Amendment," *Weekly Standard*, January 15, 2004, accessed October 25, 2011, http://www.weeklystandard.com/Content/Public/Articles/000/000/003/599kpgpv.asp; "Dallas Suburb, Senior Citizens Settle Religious-Rights Case," Associated Press, January 9, 2004, accessed October 25, 2011, http://www.firstamendmentcenter.org/dallas-suburb-senior-citizens-settle-religious-rights-case; Robert Longley, "Texas Seniors Win Religious Speech Battle," About.com, accessed May 16, 2011, http://usgovinfo.about.com/cs/usconstitution/a/seniorswin.htm; issue decided in *J. B. Barton et al. v. City of Balch Springs* et al., No. 3:03-CV-2258-G (N.D. Tex. 2004).

65. *Draper v. Logan County Pub. Lib.*, 403 F. Supp. 2d 608 (W.D. Ky. Aug. 29, 2003).

66. Carrie Antlfinger, "UW-Eau Claire Is Reviewing Legalities of Bible Study Ban," Associated Press, November 3, 2005, accessed October 25, 2011, http://thefire.org/article/6399.html; Michael Gendall, "Campus Dorm Policy Under Review," *Badger Herald*, November 10, 2005, accessed October 25, 2011, http://badgerherald.com/news/2005/11/10/campus_dorm_policy_u.php; settled in *Steiger v. Lord-Larson*, No. 05-C-0700-S (W.D. Wis. Mar. 2006).

67. Susan Jones, "'Jesus Christ' Sweatshirt Ends Up Offending Everyone," Cybercast News Service, March 6, 2001, accessed October 25, 2011, http://www.christianity.com/news/religiontoday/525160/.

68. Laurie Goodstein, "Disciplining of Student Is Defended; Gingrich Said Prayer Brought Punishment," *Washington Post*, December 6, 1994.

69. The following cases and articles detail the facts surrounding the refusal of officials to permit handing out religious literature or preaching on public sidewalks: *Colston v. Crowley Indep. Sch. Dist.*, No. 4:06-CV-00097 (N.D. Tex. June 20, 2006); *Hodges v. City of Lebanon*, No. 1:03-cv-00596 (S.D. Ind. 2003); *Parks v. Finan*, 385 F.3d 694 (6th Cir. 2004); *Baumann v. City of Cumming*, 2:07-CV-0095 (N.D. Ga. Feb. 27, 2008); and *Pulver v. City of Hastings*, 4:07-cv-03006 (D. Neb. Feb. 4, 2008); "Blind Justice: Free Speech Prohibited on Sidewalk Outside Calif. Courthouse," Alliance Defense Fund, February 9, 2010, accessed October 25, 2011, http://www.adfmedia.org/News/PRDetail/3731; "Christian Arrested for Reading the Bible in Public," *Christian Newswire*, February 2, 2011, accessed October 25, 2011, http://www.christiannewswire.com/news/8717116846.html; "Black Preacher Arrested for Preaching on Public Right of Way," *Christian Newswire*, July 17, 2011, accessed October 25, 2011, http://www.christiannewswire.com/news/2704114444.html; Andrea Phillips, "Religious Freedom Sought in Public School," Worldwide Religious News, August 27, 2011, accessed October 25, 2011, http://wwrn.org/articles/4074/?&section=church-state; "One Man Is Not a Parade," Alliance Defense Fund, accessed May 26, 2011, http://www.alliancedefensefund.org/Home/ADFContent?cid=4213; Bob Unruh, "Mall to Christians: God Talk Banned," World Net Daily, January 30, 2010, accessed October 25, 2011, http://www.wnd.com/?pageId=123535; "Men Jailed for Being on the Public Sidewalk," World Net Daily, February 8, 2007, accessed October 25, 2011, http://www.wnd.com/?pageId=40073; "Pennsylvania Christians Face 47 Years in Prison for Reading Bible in Public," About.com, January 2005, accessed October 25, 2011, http://urbanlegends.about.com/library/bl_christians_arrested.htm; Elizabeth O'Brien, "Christian Minister Arrested for Praying Near Gay Fest," Life Site News, July 10, 2007, accessed October 25, 2011, http://www.lifesitenews.com/news/archive/ldn/2007/jul/07071001; Jack Minor, "Kansas Pastor Arrested for Gospel Tracts at Mosque," *Greeley Gazette*, November 30, 2010, accessed October 25, 2011, http://www.greeleygazette.com/press/?p=6893; Bob Unruh, "Praying in Park Puts Man in Jail for 9 Days," *World Net Daily*, March 24, 2010, accessed October 25, 2011, http://www.wnd.com/?pageId=131521; Lori Arnold, "Calif. Pastor Arrested for Reading Bible in Public," Christian Examiner Online, May 2011, accessed October 25, 2011, http://www.christianexaminer.com/Articles/Articles%20May11/Art_May11_23.html; Jack Minor, "Kansas Pastor Arrested for Gospel Tracts at Mosque," *Greeley Gazette*, November 30, 2010, accessed October 25, 2011, http://

www.greeleygazette.com/press/?p=6893; "Four Christians Arrested Outside Arab Festival," Christian Examiner Online, June 2010, accessed October 25, 2011, http://www.christianexaminer.com/Articles/Articles%20Jul10/Art_Jul10_01.html; etc.

70. For more examples, see the author's book *Original Intent: The Courts, the Constitution, and Religion* (Aledo: WallBuilder Press, 2011), 13–21. *See also* "Get Resources," Alliance Defense Fund, accessed October 25, 2011, http://www.alliancedefensefund.org/About/Detail/4236); "Press Releases," American Center for Law and Justice, accessed October 25, 2011, http://aclj.org/press-releases; "Newsletter Archive," Christian Law Associates, accessed October 25, 2011, http://www.christianlaw.org/cla/index.php/articles/; "Press Release Archives," Liberty Counsel, accessed October 25, 2011, http://www.lc.org/index.cfm?pid=14099; "Issues," Liberty Legal Institute, accessed October 25, 2011, http://www.libertylegal.org/issues_main.php; "Resources," The National Legal Foundation, accessed October 25, 2011, http://www.nlf.net/Resources/literature/Literature.htm; "Legal Battles," Pacific Justice Institute, accessed October 25, 2011, http://www.pacificjustice.org/news; "Legal Landmines," Religious Organization Legal Defense Association, accessed October 25, 2011, http://www.sharpefirm.com/rolda/landmines.html; "Press Room," Thomas More Law Center, accessed October 25, 2011, http://www.thomasmore.org/qry/page.taf?id=20; etc.

71. Thomas Jefferson, "Notice of Fast to the Inhabitants of the Parish of Saint Anne," in *The Works of Thomas Jefferson*, ed. Paul Ford, vol. 2 (New York: G. P. Putnam's Sons, 1904), 42.

72. Jefferson, "Resolution of the House of Burgesses Designating a Day of Fasting and Prayer," in *The Papers of Thomas Jefferson*, ed. Boyd, 1:105–106.

73. Jefferson, *The Papers of Thomas Jefferson*, ed. Boyd, 1:116.

74. Ibid., 1:117n.

75. Jefferson, "Report on a Seal for the United States, with Related Papers," in *The Papers of Thomas Jefferson*, ed. Boyd, vol. 1. *See also* John Adams, *Letters of John Adams*, ed. Charles Francis Adams, vol. 1 (Boston: Charles C. Little and James Brown, 1841), 152.

76. Jefferson, "A Bill for Punishing Disturbers of Religious Worship and Sabbath Breakers," in *The Papers of Thomas Jefferson*, ed. Boyd, 2:555.

77. Jefferson, "A Bill for Appointing Days of Public Fasting and Thanksgiving," in *The Papers of Thomas Jefferson*, ed. Boyd, 2:555.

78. Jefferson, "A Bill Annulling the Marriages Prohibited by the Levitical Law, and Appointing the Mode of Solemnizing Lawful Marriage," in *The Papers of Thomas Jefferson*, ed. Boyd, 1:556.

79. Jefferson, "A Bill for Saving the Property of the Church Heretofore by Law Established," in *The Papers of Thomas Jefferson*, ed. Boyd, 1:553.

80. Jefferson, "A Bill for Punishing Disturbers of Religious Worship and Sabbath Breakers," in *The Papers of Thomas Jefferson*, ed. Boyd, 1:555.

81. Jefferson, "A Bill for Appointing Days of Public Fasting and Thanksgiving," in *The Papers of Thomas Jefferson*, ed. Boyd, 2:556.

82. Jefferson, "A Bill Annulling the Marriages Prohibited by the Levitical Law, and Appointing the Mode of Solemnizing Lawful Marriage," in *The Papers of Thomas Jefferson*, ed. Boyd, 2:557.

83. Jefferson, "A Bill for Establishing a General Court," in *The Papers of Thomas Jefferson*, ed. Boyd, 1:621.

84. Jefferson, "Robert Scot's Invoice for Executing Indian Medal, with Jefferson's Memoranda," in *The Papers of Thomas Jefferson*, ed. Boyd, 4:35–36.

85. Jefferson, "Report on a Seal for the United States, with Related Papers," in *The Papers of Thomas Jefferson*, ed. Boyd, vol. 1:495. *See also* John Adams, *Letters of John Adams*, ed. Charles Francis Adams, vol. 1 (Boston: Charles C. Little and James Brown, 1841), 152.

86. Dumas Malone, *Jefferson the Virginian*, vol. 1 (Boston: Little, Brown and Co., 1948), 226.

87. Originally, the federal government met in New York City for its first year, then spent the next ten in Philadelphia before moving to the newly constructed Washington as its permanent home.

88. *Federal Orrery* (Boston), July 2, 1795, 2, "Domestic Intelligence."

89. *Debates and Proceedings in the Congress of the United States* (Washington, DC: Gales and Seaton, 1851), 6th Cong., 797, December 4, 1800.

90. Bishop Claggett's letter of February 18, 1801, attests that while vice president, Jefferson attended church services in the House. Available in the Maryland Diocesan Archives.

91. Margaret Smith, *The First Forty Years of Washington Society* (New York: Charles Scribner's Sons, 1906), 13; James Hutson, *Religion and the Founding of the American Republic* (Washington, DC: Library of Congress, 1998), 84.

92. Rev. Manasseh Cutler, *Life, Journal, and Correspondence of Rev. Manasseh Cutler*, eds. William Parker Cutler and Julia Perkins Cutler, vol. 2 (Cincinnati: Colin Robert Clarke & Co., 1888), 119.

93. Margaret Smith, *The First Forty Years of Washington Society* (New York: Charles Scribner's Sons, 1906), 13.

94. Ibid.

95. *See* Rev. Manasseh Cutler, *Life, Journal, and Correspondence*, eds. William Parker Cutler and Julia Perkins Cutler, vol. 2 (Cincinnati: Colin Robert Clarke & Co., 1888), 119.

96. Ibid.

97. Ibid., 2:114.

98. James Hutson, *Religion and the Founding of the American Republic* (Washington, DC: Library of Congress, 1998), 89.

99. Margaret Smith, *The First Forty Years of Washington Society* (New York: Charles Scribner's Sons, 1906), 14.

100. Ibid., 16.

101. John Quincy Adams, *Memoirs of John Quincy Adams*, ed. Charles Francis Adams, vol. 1 (Philadelphia: J. B. Lippincott & Co., 1874), 265, 268; *National Intelligencer*, December 9, 1820, 3; *National Intelligencer*, December 30, 1820, 3. *See also* James Hutson, *Religion and the Founding of the American Republic* (Washington, DC: Library of Congress, 1998), 89.

102. Rev. Ethan Allen, "Washington Parish, Washington City," Handwritten history in possession of the Library of Congress, quoted in James Hutson, *Religion and the Founding of the American Republic* (Washington, DC: Library of Congress, 1998), 96.

NOTES

103. James Hutson, *Religion and the Founding of the American Republic* (Washington, DC: Library of Congress, 1998), 91.

104. Jefferson, *The Papers of Thomas Jefferson*, ed. Oberg, 35:202.

105. Ibid., 30:545.

106. *Debates and Proceedings in the Congress of the United States* (Washington, DC: The Government Printing Office, 1851), 7th Cong., 1st Sess., 1332, "An Act in Addition to an Act, Entitled, 'An Act in Addition to an Act Regulating the Grants of Land Appropriated for Military Services, and for the Society of the United Brethren for Propagating the Gospel Among the Heathen,'" April 26, 1802; *Debates and Proceedings in the Congress of the United States*, 7th Cong., 2nd Sess., 1602, "An Act to Revive and Continue in Force An Act in Addition to an Act, Entitled, 'An Act in Addition to an Act Regulating the Grants of Land Appropriated for Military Services, and for the Society of the United Brethren for Propagating the Gospel Among the Heathen,' and for Other Purposes," March 3, 1803; *Debates and Proceedings in the Congress of the United States*, 8th Cong., 2nd Sess., 1279, "An Act Granting Further Time for Locating Military Land Warrants, and for Other Purposes," March 19, 1804.

107. Dorothy C. Bass, "Gideon Blackburn's Mission to the Cherokees," *Journal of Presbyterian History* (Fall 1974), 52.

108. Walter Lowrie, ed., "The Kaskaskia and Other Tribes," in *American State Papers: Documents, Legislative and Executive of the Congress of the United States*, vol. 4 (Washington, DC: Gales and Seaton, 1832), 687.

109. "Thomas Jefferson to the Nuns of the Order of St. Ursula on May 15, 1804," original on file with the New Orleans Parish.

110. Jonathan Elliot, ed., "Treaty of Peace and Amity Between the United States of America and the Bashaw, Bey, and Subjects of Tripoli in Barbary," *The American Diplomatic Code, Embracing a Collection of Treaties and Conventions Between the United States and Foreign Powers: From 1778 to 1834. With an Abstract of Important Judicial Decisions, on Points Connected with Our Foreign Relations*, vol. 1 (Washington, DC: Jonathan Elliot, 1834), 501; Ibid., 1: 498, "Treaty of Peace and Friendship Between the United States of America and the Bey and Subjects of Tripoli of Barbary."

111. Ibid., 1:499, "Treaty of Peace and Friendship Between the United States of America and the Bey and Subjects of Tripoli of Barbary."

112. *The Debates and Proceedings in the Congress of the United States* (Washington, DC: Gales and Seaton, 1852), 9th Cong., 1st Sess. 1238, "An Act for Establishing Rules and Articles for the Government of the Armies of the United States."

113. Jefferson, *The Writings of Thomas Jefferson*, ed. Lipscomb, 16:291.

114. See, for example, his signature on the presidential act of October 18, 1804 (from an original document in our possession), Four Language Ship's Papers on January 16, 1804, and Ship's Papers on September 24, 1807 (from originals in our possession); etc.

115. *Marsh v. Chambers*, 463 U.S. 783, 807 (1983) (Brennan, J. and Marshall, J., dissenting).

116. *Allegheny County v. Greater Pittsburgh ACLU*, 492 U.S. 573, 679, n. 8 (1989) (Kennedy, J., concurring and dissenting).

117. Thomas Jefferson, *Memoir, Correspondence, and Miscellanies*, ed. Thomas Jefferson Randolph, vol. 4 (Boston: Gray and Bowen, 1830), 104.

118. Thomas Jefferson, *The Works of Thomas Jefferson*, ed. Paul Lancaster Ford, vol. 1 (New York: G. P. Putnam's Sons, 1904), 11.

119. Thomas Jefferson, "Proclamation," in R. McIlwaine, ed., *Official Letters of the Governors of the State of Virginia*, vol. 2 (Richmond: Virginia State Library, 1928), 65; Thomas Jefferson, "Proclamation Appointing a Day of Thanksgiving and Prayer," in *The Papers of Thomas Jefferson*, ed. Boyd, 3:178.

120. Thomas Jefferson, "Proclamation," in H. R. McIlwaine, ed., *Official Letters of the Governors of the State of Virginia*, vol. 2 (Richmond: Virginia State Library, 1928), 65. Thomas Jefferson, "Proclamation Appointing a Day of Thanksgiving and Prayer," in *The Papers of Thomas Jefferson*, ed. Boyd, 3:178

121. Joseph J. Ellis, *American Sphinx: The Character of Thomas Jefferson* (New York: Vintage Books, 1998), 310.

LIE # 6: THOMAS JEFFERSON DETESTED THE CLERGY

1. John E. Remsburg, *Six Historic Americans* (New York: The Truth Seeker Project Company, 1906), 78.

2. Farrell Till, "The Christian Nation Myth," the Secular Web, accessed June 7, 2011, http://www.infidels.org/library/modern/farrell_till/myth.html.

3. Bill Fairchild, "Thomas Jefferson and the 'Clergy;'" the Painful Truth, accessed June 7, 2011, http://www.hwarmstrong.com/thomas_jefferson_clergy.htm.

4. Austin Cline, "What Is Anti-Clericalism?" About.com, accessed June 6, 2011, http://atheism.about.com/od/Criticism-Religious-Critique/f/Anti-Clericalism.htm.

5. Thomas Jefferson, *The Papers of Thomas Jefferson*, ed. Julian P. Boyd, vol. 8 (Princeton: Princeton University Press, 1953), 468.

6. Ibid.

7. John Adams, *The Works of John Adams*, ed. Charles Francis Adams, vol. 9 (Boston: Little, Brown and Company, 1854), 637.

8. *See* Charles Warren, *Odd Byways in American History* (Cambridge: Harvard University Press, 1942), 127–128; Dumas Malone, *Jefferson and the Ordeal of Liberty*, vol. 3 (Boston: Little, Brown and Company, 1962), 481; Charles O. Lerche, Jr., "Jefferson and the Election of 1800: A Case Study in the Political Smear," *The William and Mary Quarterly*, 3rd ser., vol. 5, no. 4 (October 1948), 466–491.

9. Wilburn E. MacClenny, *The Life of Rev. James O'Kelly and the Early History of the Christian Church in the South* (Suffolk: Edwards & Broughton Printing Company, 1910), 171–173.

10. John Adams, *The Works of John Adams*, ed. Charles Francis Adams, vol. 9 (Boston: Little, Brown and Company, 1854), 636.

11. *Appleton's Cyclopedia* (New York: D. Appleton and Company, 1887), s.v. "Cotton Mather Smith."

12. Thomas Jefferson, *The Papers of Thomas Jefferson*, ed. Barbara B. Oberg, vol. 32 (Princeton: Princeton University Press, 2005), 58–59.

13. Thomas Jefferson, *Memoir, Correspondence, and Miscellanies*, ed. Thomas Jefferson Randolph, vol. 3 (New York: G. & C. & H. Carvill, 1830), 438–440.

14. William Linn, *Serious Considerations on the Election of a President: Addressed to the Citizens of the United States* (New York: John Furman, 1800), 24, Evans no. 37835.

15. William Linn, *Serious Considerations on the Election of a President: Addressed to the Citizens of the United States* (New York: John Furman, 1800), 30.

16. John Mitchell Mason, *A Voice of Warning to Christians, on the Ensuing Election of a President of the United States* (New York: G. F. Hopkins, 1800), 22–23.

17. Ibid., 37–38.

18. Nathanael Emmons, "Jeroboam. Annual Fast, April 9, 1801," in *The Works of Nathanael Emmons, D. D., Late Pastor of the Church in Franklin, Mass., with a Memoir of His Life*, ed. Jacob Ide, vol. 2 (Boston: Crocker & Brewster, 1842), 194.

19. Nathanael Emmons, "Rights of the People. National Thanksgiving, November 25, 1813," *The Works of Nathanael Emmons, D. D., Late Pastor of the Church in Franklin, Mass. with a Memoir of His Life*, ed. Jacob Ide, vol. 2 (Boston: Crocker & Brewster, 1842), 284–285.

20. Thomas Jefferson, *Memoir, Correspondence, and Miscellanies*, ed. Thomas Jefferson Randolph, vol. 3 (New York: G. & C. & H. Carvill, 1830), 478.

21. Claude G. Bowers, *Jefferson in Power—the Death Struggle of the Federalists* (Cambridge: The Riverside Press, 1936), 145.

22. Saul K. Padover, *Jefferson* (1942, repr. New York: Penguin Books, 1970), 119.

23. Allen Johnson, ed., *Dictionary of American Biography* (New York: Charles Scribber's Sons, 1929), s.v. "Rev. John Leland."

24. John Leland, "A Blow at the Root, Being a Fashionable Fast-Day Sermon, Delivered at Cheshire, April 9, 1801," in *The Writings of the Late Elder John Leland, Including Some Events in His Life, Written by Himself, with Additional Sketches*, ed. L. F. Greene (New York: G. W. Wood, 1845), 255.

25. Rev. Manasseh Cutler, *Life, Journals and Correspondence of Rev. Manasseh Cutler*, eds. William Parker Cutler and Julia P. Cutler, vol. 2 (Cincinnati: Robert Clarke & Co., 1888), 54, editor's note in journal entry for January 1, 1802.

26. Charles Cist, *Cincinnati in 1841: Its Early Annals and Future Prospects* (Cincinnati: Published for the Author, 1841), 187; Dumas Malone, *Jefferson the Virginian*, vol. 1 (Boston: Little, Brown and Co., 1948), 226.

27. Ellen M. Raynor and Emma L. Petitclerc, *History of the Town of Cheshire* (Holyoke, MA: Clark W. Bryan & Company, 1885), 87.

28. Rev. Manasseh Parker, *Life, Journals and Correspondence of Rev. Manasseh Cutler*, eds. William Parker Cutler and Julia P. Cutler, vol. 2 (Cincinnati: Robert Clarke and Co., 1888), 66–67.

29. Ibid.

30. Thomas Jefferson, *The Papers of Thomas Jefferson; Jefferson's Memorandum Books*, eds. James Bear and Lucia Stanton, vol. 2 (Princeton: Princeton University Press, 1997), 1062.

31. Wilbur E. MacClenny, "James O'Kelly: A Champion of Christian Freedom," in *The Centennial of Religious Journalism*, ed. John Pressley Barrett (Dayton: Christian Publishing Association, 1908), 265.

32. Dr. J. P. Barrett, editor of the *Herald of Gospel Liberty*, Dayton, Ohio, quoted in Wilburn E. MacClenny, *The Life of Rev. James O'Kelly and the Early History of the Christian Church in the South* (Suffolk: Edwards & Broughton Printing Company, 1910), 171–173.

33. Thomas Jefferson, *The Works of Thomas Jefferson*, ed. Paul Leicester Ford, vol. 1 (New York: G. P. Putnam's Sons, 1904–1905), 13.

34. Thomas Jefferson, *The Papers of Thomas Jefferson*, ed. Boyd, vol. 1 (Princeton: Princeton University Press, 1950), 116.

35. Ibid., 2:6–7.

36. Ibid.

37. Ibid., 3:67.

38. Ibid., 1:23.

39. Thomas Jefferson, *The Papers of Thomas Jefferson*, ed. Barbara B. Osberg, vol. 35 (Princeton: Princeton University Press, 2008), 350–351.

40. Mark A. Beliles, "Religion and Republicanism in Jefferson's Virginia" (PhD diss., Whitfield Theological Seminary, 1993), 69–70.

41. Samuel Stanhope Smith, *The Divine Goodness to the United States of America—A Discourse on the Subjects of National Gratitude* (Philadelphia: William Young, 1795); Jonathan French, *A Sermon Delivered on the Anniversary of Thanksgiving, November 29, 1798* (Andover: Ames and Parker, 1799); Rev. Joseph Willard, *A Thanksgiving Sermon Delivered at Boston December 11, 1783* (Boston: T. and J. Fleet, 1784); William Hazlitt, *A Thanksgiving Sermon Preached at Hallowell, December 15, 1785* (Boston: Samuel Hall, 1786); John Evans, *The Happiness of American Christians, A Thanksgiving Sermon Preached on Thursday the 24th of November 1803* (Hartford: Hudson and Goodwin, 1804); Isaac Backus, *An Appeal to the Public for Religious Liberty* (Boston: John Boyle, 1783); etc.

42. *See* "Our Founding Fathers Were Not Christians," BibleTrash.com, July 4, 2000, accessed June 13, 2011, http://freethought.mbdojo.com/foundingfathers.html; Jim Walker, "Thomas Jefferson of Christianity and Religion," Nobeliefs.com, accessed October 25, 2011, http://nobeliefs.com/jefferson.htm.

43. Lorenzo Dow, *Biography and Miscellany* (Norwich, CT: William Faulkner, 1834), 242–243.

44. Thomas Jefferson, *Memoir, Correspondence, and Miscellanies*, ed. Thomas Jefferson Randolph, vol. 3 (New York: G. & C. & H. Carvill, 1830), 441.

45. Thomas Jefferson, *The Writings of Thomas Jefferson*, ed. Andrew A. Lipscomb, vol. 15 (Washington, DC: The Thomas Jefferson Memorial Association, 1904), 60.

46. Samuel Knox, *A Vindication of the Religion of Thomas Jefferson* (Baltimore: W. Pechin, 1800); Thomas E. Buckley, "Thomas Jefferson and Myth of Separation," Religion and American Presidency, accessed July, 14, 2011, http://www.thedivine conspiracy.org/Z5212U.pdf.

47. Fred Hood, *Reformed America: The Middle and Southern States, 1783–1837* (Tuscaloosa, AL: The University of Alabama, 1980), 83.

48. Elias Smith, *The Whole World Governed by a Jew, or, The Government of the Second Adam as King and Priest* (Exeter: Henry Ranlet, 1805), 34–35, 76–77.

49. Thomas Jefferson, *The Papers of Thomas Jefferson; Jefferson's Memorandum Books*, eds. James A. Bear Jr. and Lucia C. Stanton (Princeton: Princeton University Press, 1997), 1:402, 403, 407; 2:1093, 1177, 1196, 1403, 1068, etc.

50. Thomas Jefferson, *The Papers of Thomas Jefferson; Jefferson's Memorandum Books*, eds. James A. Bear Jr. and Lucia C. Stanton, vol. 2 (Princeton: Princeton University Press, 1997), 1070, 1144, 1146, 1180, 1403.

51. Thomas Jefferson, *The Papers of Thomas Jefferson; Jefferson's Memorandum Books*, eds. James A. Bear Jr. and Lucia C. Stanton, vol. 2 (Princeton: Princeton University Press, 1997), 884.

NOTES

52. Thomas Jefferson, *The Papers of Thomas Jefferson; Jefferson's Memorandum Books*, eds. James A. Bear Jr. and Lucia C. Stanton (Princeton: Princeton University Press, 1997), 1:285; 2:837, 1057, 1062, 1071, 1095, 1111, 1130, 1154, 1348, etc.

53. Mark A. Beliles, *"Religion and Republicanism in Jefferson's Virginia"* (PhD diss., Whitfield Theological Seminary School, 1993), 143. *See also* Thomas Jefferson, *Memoir, Correspondence, Miscellanies*, ed. Thomas Jefferson Randolph, vol. 3 (Charlottesville: F. Carr and Co., 1829), 463.

54. John Leland, "Which Has Done the Most Mischief in the World, The Kings-Evil or Priest-Craft?" in *The Writings of the Late Elder John Leland, Including Some Events in His Life, Written by Himself, with Additional Sketches*, ed. L. F. Greene (New York: G. W. Wood, 1845), 484.

55. David Ramsay, *The History of the American Revolution*, vol. 1 (Dublin: William Jones, 1795), 212.

56. Thomas Jefferson, *The Works of Thomas Jefferson*, ed. Paul Leicester Ford, vol. 9 (New York: G. P. Putnam's Sons, 1905), 393.

57. Thomas Jefferson, *Memoir, Correspondence, and Miscellanies*, ed. Thomas Jefferson Randolph, vol. 3 (New York: G. & C. & H. Carvill, 1830), 3:304–305, 377–378, 461–462; 4:204–206, 274–277; Thomas Jefferson, *The Works of Thomas Jefferson*, ed. Ford, vol. 11 (New York: G. P. Putnam's Sons, 1905), 51, 491.

58. Thomas Jefferson, *The Writings of Thomas Jefferson*, ed. Andrew A. Lipscomb, vol. 14 (Washington, D.C.: The Thomas Jefferson Memorial Association, 1907), 119.

59. Farrell Till, "The Christian Nation Myth," the Secular Web, accessed June 7, 2011, http://www.infidels.org/library/modern/farrell_till/myth.html.

60. Thomas Jefferson, *The Works of Thomas Jefferson*, ed. Paul Leicester Ford, vol. 11 (New York: G. P. Putnam's Sons, 1905), 204.

61. Ibid., 11:358–359.

62. "The Constitution of Virginia," *The Constitution of the Sixteen States* (Boston: Manning and Loring, 1797), 212 ". . . all ministers of the gospel, of every denomination, be incapable of being elected members . . ."

63. Jefferson, *The Papers of Thomas Jefferson*, ed. Boyd, 8:470.

64. Thomas Jefferson, *The Works of Thomas Jefferson*, ed. Paul Leicester Ford, vol. 9 (New York: G. P. Putnam's Sons, 1905), 14.

LIE # 7: THOMAS JEFFERSON WAS AN ATHEIST AND NOT A CHRISTIAN

1. Joseph J. Ellis, *Founding Brothers* (New York: Vintage Books, 2000), 139 quoted in Mark A Gifford, "Country Mouse and Town Mouse," hyerliterature.com, May 18, 2010, accessed October 25, 2011, http://www.hyperliterature.com/?p=1763.

2. "Cloudy Judgment," Minds Alike, April 18, 2011, accessed October 25, 2011, http://mindsalike.co/2011/04/18/cloudy-judgement/.

3. Paul O'Brien, "Jefferson," Paul O'Brien's Web, accessed May 12, 2011, http://home.comcast.net/~pobrien48/jefferson_Letters.htm.

4. "An Interview with Michael Weinstein of Military Religious Freedom Foundation," Pagan + Politics, February 26, 2010, accessed October 25, 2011, http://www.facebook.com/note.php?note_id=360240177811.

5. John E. Remsburg, *Six Historic Americans* (New York: The Truth Seeker Company, 1906), 65.

6. *See* "Freethinker," Thesaurus.com, accessed June 20, 2011, http://thesaurus com/browse/freethinker; "Freethinker," Dictionary.com, accessed June 20, 2011, http://dictionary.reference.com/browse/freethinker; "Freethinker," synonyms.net, accessed June 20, 2011, http://www.synonyms.net/synonym/freethinker; "Freethinker," thesaurus.yourdictionary.com, accessed June 20, 2011, http://thesaurus.yourdictionary.com/freethinker.

7. "Atheist," *Merriam-Webster Dictionary*, accessed May 11, 2011, http://www.merriam-webster.com/dictionary/atheist?show=0&t=1305132077.

8. "Atheist," About.com, accessed May 11, 2011, http://atheism.about.com/library/glossary/general/bldef_atheist.htm.

9. "Atheist," Dictionary.com, accessed May 11, 2011, http://dictionary.reference.com/browse/atheist.

10. Benjamin Franklin, *The Works of Benjamin Franklin*, ed. John Bigelow, vol. 5 (New York: G. P. Putnam's Son, 1904), 325–326.

11. Jefferson, *The Writings of Thomas Jefferson*, ed. Lipscomb, 12:405.

12. Claude G. Bowers, *The Young Jefferson* (Boston: Houghton Mifflin Company, 1945), 312.

13. Rosalie David, ed., *Fredericksville Parish Vestry Book, 1742–1787* (Manchester, Missouri, 1978), 88.

14. Thomas Jefferson, *The Works of Thomas Jefferson*, ed. Paul Leicester Ford, vol. 2 (New York: G. P. Putnam's Sons, 1904), 255.

15. Sarah Randolph, *The Domestic Life of Thomas Jefferson* (New York: Harper & Brothers, 1871), 343–345.

16. William Stoddard, *The Lives of the Presidents: John Adams and Thomas Jefferson*, vol. 2 (New York: White, Stokes, & Allen, 1887), 270.

17. Randolph, *The Domestic Life of Thomas Jefferson*, 62–63.

18. Ibid.

19. Henry S. Randall, *The Life of Thomas Jefferson*, vol. 3 (New York: Derby & Jackson, 1858), 101–103.

20. William H. B. Thomas, *Faith of Our Fathers: Religion and the Churches in Colonial Orange County* (Orange, VA: Orange County Bicentennial Commission, 1975), 8.

21. John Leland, *The Writings of the Late Elder John Leland, Including Some Events in His Life, Written by Himself, with Additional Sketches*, ed. L. F. Greene (New York: G. W. Wood, 1845), 98.

22. William Maxwell, *A Memoir of the Rev. John H. Rice, D. D.* (J. Whetham: Philadelphia, 1835), 50–51.

23. Ibid.

24. Edgar Woods, *Albemarle County in Virginia* (Charlottesville: Michie Company, 1901), 131.

25. W. Hopkins, "The Literature of the Disciples of Christ," in W. T. Moore, ed., *The Christian Quarterly* (Columbia, MO: G. A. Hoffman, 1897), 498.

26. Elias Smith, *The Life, Conversion, Preaching, Travels and Sufferings of Elias Smith*, vol. 1 (Boston: 1840), 275.

27. "Christianity on the Early American Frontier: A Gallery of Trendsetters in the Religious Wilderness," *Christian History Magazine* 45 (1995), 23.

28. Michael G. Kenny, *The Perfect Law of Liberty: Elias Smith and the Providential History of America* (Washington, DC: Smithsonian Institution Press, 1994), 93.

29. Wilburn E. MacClenny, *The Life of Rev. James O'Kelly and the Early History of the Christian Church in the South* (Suffolk: Edwards & Broughton Printing Company, 1910), 217–221.

30. Thomas Campbell, *On Religious Reformation*, accessed June 6, 2011, http://www.mun.ca/rels/restmov/texts/tcampbell/etc/ORR.HTM.

31. Michael G. Kenny, *The Perfect Law of Liberty: Elias Smith and the Providential History of America* (Washington, DC: Smithsonian Institution Press, 1994), 128. *See also* William B. Erdman, *Erdman's Handbook to Christianity in America*, ed. Mark Noll (Grand Rapids: William B. Erdmans Publishing Co., 1983), 210.

32. William Maxwell, *A Memoir of the Rev. John H. Rice* (Philadelphia: J. Wetham, 1835), 51–52.

33. Alexander Campbell, "To Timothy," Memorial University, March 1, 1827, accsessed October 25, 2011, http://www.mun.ca/rels/restmov/texts/acampbell/tcb/TCB410.HTM#Essay5.

34. Douglas Allen Foster, *The Encyclopedia of the Stone-Campbell Movement* (Grand Rapids: William B. Eerdmans Publishing, 2004), 356.

35. J. F. Burnett, *Elias Smith: Reformer, Journalist, Doctor; Horace Mann: Christian Statesman and Educator* (Dayton: The Christian Publishing Association, 1921), accessed October 25, 2011, http://www.mun.ca/rels/restmov/texts/jburnett/eshm/ESHM.HTM.

36. Thomas Jefferson, "Thomas Jefferson Papers, to Francis A. Van Der Kemp on July 9, 1820" Library of Congress, accessed October 25, 2011, http://hdl.loc.gov/loc.mss/mtj.mtjbib023864.

37. Thomas Jefferson, *Memoir, Correspondence, and Miscellanies*, ed. Thomas Jefferson Randolph, vol. 4 (New York: G. & C. & H. Carvill, 1830), 35–354.

38. Ibid., 4:360–361.

39. Thomas Jefferson, "Thomas Jefferson Papers, to Salma Hale on July 26, 1818," Library of Congress, accessed October 25, 2011, http://hdl.loc.gov/loc.mss/mtj.mtjbib023250.

40. Thomas Jefferson, *Memoir, Correspondence, and Miscellanies*, ed. Thomas Jefferson Randolph, vol. 4 (New York: G. & C. & H. Carvill, 1830), 349.

41. Ibid. 4:358.

42. Ibid.

43. Thomas Jefferson, "Thomas Jefferson Papers, to Ezra Styles Ely on June 25, 1819," Library of Congress, accessed October 25, 2011, http://hdl.loc.gov/loc.mss/mtj.mtjbib023541.

44. Thomas Jefferson, *The Adams-Jefferson Letters*, ed. Lester J. Cappon, vol. 2 (Chapel Hill: The University of North Carolina Press, 1959), 421.

45. Thomas Jefferson, *Memoir, Correspondence, and Miscellanies*, ed. Thomas Jefferson Randolph, vol. 4 (New York: G. & C. & H. Carvil, 1830), 321.

46. Thomas Jefferson, *The Writings of Thomas Jefferson*, Henry A. Washington, vol. 7 (New York: Derby & Jackson, 1859), 395.

47. Thomas Jefferson, "The Thomas Jefferson Papers, to Martha (Patsy) Jefferson on December 11, 1783," Library of Congress, accessed October 25, 2011, http://hdl.loc.gov/loc.mss/mtj.mtjbib000839.

48. Thomas Jefferson, *Memoir, Correspondence, and Miscellanies*, ed. Thomas Jefferson Randolph, vol. 4 (New York: G. & C. & H. Carvill, 1830), 326.

49. Ibid., 327.

50. Thomas Jefferson, *The Works of Thomas Jefferson*, ed. Paul Leicester Ford, vol. 1 (New York: G. P. Putnam's Sons, 1904), 69.

51. Thomas Jefferson, "The Thomas Jefferson Papers, to Ezra Styles Ely on June 25, 1819," Library of Congress, accessed October 25, 2011, http://hdl.loc.gov/loc.mss/mtj.mtjbib023541.

52. Thomas Jefferson, *The Works of Thomas Jefferson*, ed. Paul Leicester Ford, vol. 2 (New York: G. P. Putnam's Sons, 1904), 260, "Notes on Religion," October 1776.

53. Thomas Jefferson, *Memoir, Correspondence, and Miscellanies*, ed. Thomas Jefferson Randolph, vol. 4 (New York: G. & C. & H. Carvill, 1830), Vol. IV, p. 322, to William Short on April 13, 1820.

54. Thomas Jefferson, "The Thomas Jefferson Papers, to Thomas B. Parker on May 15, 1819," Library of Congress, accessed October 25, 2011, http://hdl.loc.gov/loc.mss/mtj.mtjbib023495.

55. Thomas Jefferson, "The Thomas Jefferson Papers, to Salma Hale on July 26, 1818," Library of Congress, accessed October 25, 2011, http://hdl.loc.gov/loc.mss/mtj.mtjbib023250.

56. Thomas Jefferson, *Memoir, Correspondence, and Miscellanies*, ed. Thomas Jefferson Randolph, vol. 4 (New York: G. & C. & H. Carvill, 1830), 358.

57. Ibid.

58. Ibid., 4:363.

59. Thomas Jefferson, *The Writings of Thomas Jefferson*, ed. Paul Leicester Ford, vol. 10 (New York: G. P. Putnam's Sons, 1899), 144n.

60. Thomas Jefferson, *Memoir, Correspondence, and Miscellanies*, ed. Thomas Jefferson Randolph, vol. 4 (New York: G. & C. & H. Carvill, 1830), 366.

61. Thomas Jefferson, *The Writings of Thomas Jefferson*, ed. Paul Leicester Ford, vol. 9 (New York: G. P. Putnam's Sons, 1898), 412.

62. Judith S. Levey, ed., *The Concise Columbia Encyclopedia* (New York: Avon Books, 1983), 872.

63. *See* Rev. Charles Buck, *A Theological Dictionary Containing Definitions of All Religious Terms* (Philadelphia: Edwin T. Scott, 1823), 582; *An Answer to the Question, Why Do You Attend a Unitarian Church?* (Christian Register Office, circa 1840); Daniel Rupp, *An Original History of the Religious Denominations at Present Existing in the United States* (Philadelphia: J. Y. Humphrys, 1844), 711; etc.

64. Daniel Rupp, *An Original History of the Religious Denominations at Present Existing in the United States* (Philadelphia: J. Y. Humphrys, 1844), 711.

65. James Truslow Adams, ed., *Dictionary of American History* (New York: Charles Scribner's Sons, 1940), s.v. "Unitarians."

66. John Quincy Adams, *Memoirs of John Quincy Adams*, ed. Charles Francis Adams, vol. 7 (Philadelphia: J. B. Lippincott & Co., 1875), 324.

67. Ibid.

68. Eliakim Littell, ed., "The Antislavery Revolution in America," in *The Living Age*, vol. 86 (Boston: Littell, Son, and Company, 1865), 200.

69. Samuel J. May, *Some Recollections of Our Antislavery Conflict* (Boston: Fields, Osgood, & Co., 1869), 335.

70. Including Benjamin Rush, Charles Clay, John Adams, William Short, and Thomas Cooper.

NOTES

71. *See* Thomas Jefferson, *Memoir, Correspondence, and Miscellanies*, ed. Thomas Jefferson Randolph, vol. 4 (New York: G. & C. & H. Carvill, 1830), 206; Jefferson, *The Writings of Thomas Jefferson*, ed. Lipscomb, 15:1; etc.

72. *See* Thomas Jefferson, *The Works of Thomas Jefferson*, ed. Paul Leicester Ford, vol. 9 (New York: G. P. Putnam's Sons, 1905), 459n; Thomas Jefferson, *Memoir, Correspondence, and Miscellanies*, ed. Thomas Jefferson Randolph, vol. 4 (New York: G. & C. & H. Carvill, 1830), 320; Benjamin Rush, *Letters of Benjamin Rush*, ed. L. H. Butterfield, vol. 2 (Princeton: Princeton University Press, 1951), 863–864; Thomas Jefferson, *Memoir, Correspondence, and Miscellanies*, ed. Thomas Jefferson Randolph (New York: G. & C. & H. Carvill, 1830), 4:44–49, 3:413; Thomas Jefferson, *The Works of Thomas Jefferson*, ed. Paul Leicester Ford, vol. 4 (New York: G. P. Putnam's Sons, 1904), 413; Thomas Jefferson, *The Writings of Thomas Jefferson*, ed. Paul Leicester Ford, vol. 8 (New York: G. P. Putnam's Sons, 1897), 130; etc.

73. Thomas Jefferson, "Syllabus of an Estimate of the Merit of the Doctrines of Jesus, Compared with Those of Others," in *The Works of Thomas Jefferson*, ed. Paul Leicester Ford, vol. 9 (New York: G. P. Putnam's Sons, 1905), 459n.

74. Thomas Jefferson, *Memoir, Correspondence, and Miscellanies*, ed. Thomas Jefferson Randolph, vol. 4 (Boston: Gray and Bowen, 1830), 361.

75. Ibid., 4:360.

76. Ibid., 4:350.

77. Wilburn E. MacClenny, from "The Prospect Before Us," in *The Life of Rev. James O'Kelly and the Early History of the Christian Church in the South* (Suffolk: Edwards & Broughton Printing Company, 1910), 217.

78. Jefferson, *The Writings of Thomas Jefferson*, ed. Lipscomb, 14:385.

79. Thomas Jefferson, *Memoir, Correspondence, and Miscellanies*, ed. Thomas Jefferson Randolph, vol. 3 (Boston: Gray and Bowen, 1830), 506.

80. Thomas Jefferson, *The Writings of Thomas Jefferson*, ed. Henry A. Washington, vol. 7 (New York: Derby and Jackson, 1859), 127.

81. Dumas Malone, *Jefferson the President, First Term 1801–1805*, vol. 4 (Boston: Little Brown & Co., 1970), 205.

82. Ibid., 202.

83. Benjamin Rush, *The Autobiography of Benjamin Rush* (Princeton: Princeton University Press, 1948), 152.

84. Benjamin Rush, *Letters of Benjamin Rush*, ed. L. H. Butterfield, vol. 2 (Princeton: Princeton University Press, 1951), 864.

85. Thomas Jefferson, *The Writings of Thomas Jefferson*, ed. Henry A. Washington, vol. 7 (New York: H. W. Derby, 1861), 281.

86. *American Heritage Dictionary* (1983), *2nd College Edition*, s.v. "Deism"; *American College Dictionary* (1947), s.v. "Deism."

87. *See* Thomas Jefferson, "Query XVIII The particular customs and manners that may happen to be received in that state?" *Notes of the State of Virginia* (Philadelphia: Matthew Carey, 1794), 236–237; Thomas Jefferson, *The Works of Thomas Jefferson*, ed. Paul Leicester Ford, vol. 11 (New York: G. P. Putnam's Sons, 1905), 419–420; Thomas Jefferson, *The Works of Thomas Jefferson*, ed. Paul Leicester Ford, vol. 11 (New York: G. P. Putnam's Sons, 1905), 471; and others.

88. Thomas Jefferson, "Second Inaugural Address on April 4, 1805," *The Writings of*

Thomas Jefferson, ed. Paul Leicester Ford, vol. 8 (New York: G. P. Putnam's Sons, 1897), 348.

89. *See* Thomas Jefferson, *Memoir, Correspondence, and Miscellanies*, ed. Thomas Jefferson Randolph (Charlottesville: F. Carr and Co., 1829), 3:439, 4:23; Thomas Jefferson, *The Works of Thomas Jefferson*, ed. Paul Leicester Ford, vol. 12 (New York: G. P. Putnam's Sons, 1905), 474n; etc.

90. *See* Thomas Jefferson, *Memoir, Correspondence, and Miscellanies*, ed. Thomas Jefferson Randolph (New York: G. & C. & H. Carvill, 1830), 4:349–350, "Syllabus of an Estimate of the Merits of the Doctrines of Jesus, Compared with Those of Others," 3:514–517; Jefferson, *The Writings of Thomas Jefferson*, ed. Lipscomb, 10:376–377, 12:315; Thomas Jefferson, *Memoir, Correspondence, and Miscellanies*, ed. Thomas Jefferson Randolph (Charlottesville: F. Carr and Co., 1829); etc.

91. See, for example, Thomas Jefferson, *Memoir, Correspondence, and Miscellanies*, ed. Thomas Jefferson Randolph, vol. 4 (New York: G. & C. & H. Carvill, 1830), 23–24, 176.

92. Randall, *The Life of Thomas Jefferson*, 672.

CONCLUSION: THOMAS JEFFERSON: AN AMERICAN HERO

1. Jack M. Balkin, "Tradition, Betrayal, and the Politics of Deconstruction—Part II," Yale University, 1998, accessed October 25, 2011, http://www.yale.edu/lawweb/jbalkin/articles/trad2.htm.

2. Henry S. Randall, *The Life of Thomas Jefferson*, vol. 3 (New York: Derby & Jackson, 1858), 673.

3. Paul Vitz, *Censorship; Evidence of Bias in our Children's Textbooks* (Ann Arbor: 1986), 77.

4. Ibid., 80.

5. John Adams, *The Works of John Adams*, ed. Charles Francis Adams, vol. 2 (Boston: Little, Brown and Co., 1850), 17.

6. See, for example, B. L. Rayner, *Life of Thomas Jefferson* (Boston: Lilly, Wait, Colman, & Holden, 1834); Sarah Randolph, *The Domestic Life of Thomas Jefferson* (New York: Harper & Brothers, 1871); John T. Morse, Jr., *Thomas Jefferson* (Boston: Houghton, Mifflin Company: 1885); Andrew Allison, *The Real Thomas Jefferson* (Washington, DC: National Center for Constitutional Studies, 1983); Dumas Malone, *Jefferson and His Time*, vols. 1–6 (Boston: Little, Brown & Company, 1951–1981); etc.

7. Randall, *The Life of Thomas Jefferson*, vol. 1 (New York: Derby & Jackson, 1858), http://books.google.com/books?id=TRxCAAAAIAAJ&printsec=frontcover&dq=editions: Q73dCAMDp8QC&hl=en&ei=T1X_TdfhBMuutwfGyIy-Dg&sa=X&oi=book_result&ct=result&resnum=1&ved=0CC0Q6AEwAA#v=onepage&q&f=false); Henry S. Randall, *The Life of Thomas Jefferson*, vol. 2 (New York: Derby & Jackson, 1858), http://books.google.com/books?id=lxxCAAAAIAAJ&printsec=frontcover&dq=editions:Q73dCAMDp8QC&hl=en&ei=T1X_TdfhBMuutwfGyIy-Dg&sa=X&oi=book_result&ct=result&resnum=2&ved=0CDIQ6AEwAQ#v=onepage&q&f=false); Henry S. Randall, *The Life of Thomas Jefferson*, vol. 3 (New York: Derby & Jackson, 1858), http://books.google.com/books?id=a9NQEl4jfP8C&printsec=frontcover&dq=editions:Q73dCAMDp8QC&hl=en

&ei=T1X_TdfhBMuutwfGyIy-Dg&sa=X&oi=book_result&ct=result&resnum=4&
ved=0CDwQ6AEwAw#v=onepage&q&f=false).

8. Margaret Thatcher, "Lady Margaret Thatcher at Monticello, on the Occasion of the 253rd Anniversary of the Birth of Thomas Jefferson and the Presentation of the First Thomas Jefferson Medal for Statesmanship," document from Monticello, April 13, 1996.

9. *The Debates, Resolutions, and Other Proceedings, in Convention, on the Adoption of the Federal Constitution*, ed. Jonathan Elliot, vol. 2 (Washington, DC: Printed for the Editor, 1828), 281.

10. Jefferson, *Writings of Thomas Jefferson*, ed. Lipscomb, 14:384.

11. "Take the Quiz: What We Don't Know," Newsweek.com, accessed June 21, 2011, http://www.*newsweek*.com/2011/03/20/take-the-quiz-what-we-don-t-know.html.

12. *Scopes v. State*, 289 S.W. 363 (Tenn. 1927).

13. Clarence Darrow, as quoted in *The World's Most Famous Court Trial: Tennessee Evolution Case* (Cincinnati: National Book Company, 1925), 74.

14. Robert Byrd, "A Failure to Produce Better Students," Library of Congress, June 9, 1997, accessed November 11, 2011, http://www.gpo.gov/fdsys/search/citation. result.CREC.action?congressionalRecord.volume=143&congressionalRecord.page Prefix=S&congressionalRecord.pageNumber=5393&publication=CREC.

15. D. Salahu-Din, H. Persky, and J. Miller, "The Nation's Report Card: Writing 2007," National Center for Education Statistics, 2008, accessed October 25, 2011, http:// nces.ed.gov/nationsreportcard/pdf/main2007/2008468.pdf.

16. Sheldon and Jeremy Stern, "The State of State U. S. History Standards in 2011," Thomas Fordham Institute, February 2011, accessed October 25, 2011, http:// www.edexcellencemedia.net/publications/2011/20110216_SOSHS/SOSS_History_ FINAL.pdf. These findings are based on the published scope and sequence of history standards for the various states. States that require students to learn only from 1900 forward are California, Connecticut, Nevada, North Dakota, Oregon, and Washington. States that require students to learn from Reconstruction forward are Colorado, Delaware, Florida, Hawaii, Indiana, Kansas, Kentucky, Louisiana, Maryland, Michigan, Missouri, New Mexico, Ohio, South Dakota, Tennessee, Texas, and Utah.

17. "Losing America's Memory: Historical Illiteracy in the 21st Century," American Council of Trustees and Alumni, August 4, 2003, accessed October 25, 2011, https://www.goacta.org/publications/downloads/LosingAmerica%27sMemory.pdf.

18. Peter Wood, "Vanishing Act," *The Chronicle of Higher Education*, May 19, 2011, accessed October 25, 2011, http://chronicle.com/blogs/innovations/vanishing-act/ 29479.

19. Sean Alfano, "Poll: Majority Reject Evolution," CBS, February 11, 2009, accessed October 25, 2011, http://www.cbsnews.com/stories/2005/10/22/opinion/polls/main 965223.shtml.

20. Google Books, http://books.google.com/; Project Gutenberg, http://www.gutenberg. org/wiki/Main_Page; Page By Page Books, http://www.pagebypagebooks.com/author list.html; Online Books (Monergism), http://www.monergism.com/free_online_ books.php; Read Print, http://www.readprint.com/; Internet Archive, http://www. archive.org/details/texts); etc.

21. Mark Noll, Nathan Hatch, and George Marsden, *The Search for Christian America* (Colorado Springs: Helmers & Howard, 1989).

22. Thomas Paine, *The Writings of Thomas Paine*, ed. Moncure Daniel Conway, vol. 3 (New York: G. P. Putnam's Sons, 1894), 68, "Letter Addressed to the Addressers on the Late Proclamation [Royal Proclamation Against Seditious Writings]," 1792.

23. Noah Webster, *An American Dictionary of the English Language*, vol. 1 (New York: S. Converse, 1828), 101, s.v. "History."

24. Randolph, *The Domestic Life of Thomas Jefferson*, 38.

25. Randall, *The Life of Thomas Jefferson*, 3:675; Randolph, *The Domestic Life of Thomas Jefferson*, 337.

26. Randolph, *The Domestic Life of Thomas Jefferson*, 289–290.

27. Ibid.

28. "Social Hours of Daniel Webster," *Harper's Magazine* (July, 1856), as quoted in Randall, *The Life of Thomas Jefferson*, 1:490–491.

29. Randall, *The Life of Thomas Jefferson*, 3:671

30. Randolph, *The Domestic Life of Thomas Jefferson*, 344–345.

31. Ibid.

32. Randall, *The Life of Thomas Jefferson*, 3:671.

33. Ibid., 3:673.

34. Randolph, "Dr. Dunglison's Memoranda," in *The Domestic Life of Thomas Jefferson*, 394–395.

35. Calvin Coolidge, "Address Before the Congress Sitting in Joint Session in the House of Representatives," *American Presidency Project*, February 22, 1927, accessed October 25, 2011,, http://www.presidency.ucsb.edu/ws/index.php?pid=418&st=&st1=#ixzz1PNL7rdMJ.

Acknowledgments

Anytime that a work of this magnitude is produced—a work that includes hundreds of footnotes from thousands of historical sources—there are many who must be acknowledged. After all, the Scriptures remind us that we should give honor to whom it is due (Romans 13:7) and among those worthy of public recognition are:

- Early American historians (such as Jared Sparks, Benson Lossing, George Bancroft, Richard Frothingham, Charles Coffin, John Fiske, and others) who believed that they should objectively report history without spin or personal opinion—that it was their duty to record everything that occurred, including not only the bad and the ugly (which is too often the limit of historical examination today) but also the good.

- Current websites that invested extensive time and money in placing thousands of original unedited historical documents online so that they can now be read in their entirety by any citizen without the extraneous personal opinions with which many scholars seek to bias readers. Such praiseworthy websites include the Avalon Project, the Library of Congress, the American Presidency Project, a Century of Lawmaking, and many others.

- Jefferson scholars such as Dr. Mark Beliles, who in 1993 not only researched Jefferson's faith by reading scores of

Jefferson's own writings but also studied countless letters, writings, diaries, and memoirs from scores of clergymen who personally interacted with Jefferson. Beliles thus presents remarkable insight into Jefferson's complex relationship with the clergy, reaching conclusions that, although consistent with primary source historical data, are dramatically different from the opinions of many today who call themselves Jefferson scholars but have read few of Jefferson's own writings. Others worthy of mention who demonstrate the same sound historical approach include Dr. Daniel Dreisbach and Dr. Philip Hamburger.

- My own research staff who took hundreds of tedious questions I posited them and provided answers from primary source documents. Among the many who were vital in the research and writing of this book were Sarah Freeman, Caroline Henry, Tim Stackpole, Kristy Stedman, Brian Freeman, Damaris Schuler, Timothy Barton, Gabriella Franks, Derringer Dick, and Jennifer Farley.

- Also, my sincere appreciation is due my wife, Cheryl, who graciously and flexibly accommodated the countless hundreds of hours I spent researching and writing this work, often at irregular times and in unusual settings.

- Of course, my highest gratitude is humbly offered to my Creator and Redeemer without Whose daily sustenance and mercy my life would not even exist. It is only in His loving Providence that we live, move, and have our very being.

I offer my heartfelt thanks to each of these; their contributions, most of which will never be fully known by the public, have been indispensable.

DAVID BARTON

Spring 2012

About the Author

David Barton is the founder and president of WallBuilders, a national profamily organization that presents America's forgotten history and heroes with an emphasis on our moral, religious, and constitutional heritage. He is the author of many best-selling books, including *Original Intent, The Bulletproof George Washington, American History in Black and White, The Question of Freemasonry and the Founding Fathers*, and many others. He also addresses more than four hundred groups each year. David and his wife, Cheryl, have three grown children.

Barton was named by *Time* magazine as one of America's twenty-five most influential evangelicals, and he has received numerous national and international awards, including Who's Who in Education and DAR's highest award, the George Washington Honor Medal.

Index

INDEX

INDEX

Cornett, Daryl, 31
Corruption, Age of, 119
Coutts, W., 158
Creationist view of Newton, 40
Curtis, William Eleroy, xv
Cutler, Manasseh, 133, 151–152
Czechoslovakia, xiii

D
Dabney, Robert, 57
Danbury, Connecticut Baptist Association, 123–125
Darrow, Clarence, 204
Dartmouth, 45
De Interpretatione Naturae Prooemium (Bacon), 38–39
Dearborn, Henry, 43
Declaration of Independence
  acknowledgments of God in, 131
  Jefferson's assertion on, 36–37
  Jefferson's draft, 100–101
  painting of signers, xi, xvii
  Scottish Common Sense philosophy and, 35
Deconstructionism, xvi–xviii, 77, 149, 162, 196
  avoiding effects, 199–202
definition of history and, 209
deists, 191
  Jefferson's language and, 155
  Locke as, 40
Democratic-Republicans, 142
denominational nonpreferentialism, 178, 194
  as University of Virginia goal, 48–51, 56
denominations, Jefferson's views of conflict from, 179
Disciples of Christ, 45, 189
Dissenting (non-Anglican) churches, 172
Divine Providence, 35
DNA testing, 1, 193
  news articles on Jefferson and Hemings, 6–7
  retraction of story about Jefferson and Hemings, 3–4
documentation
  need for verifiable, 15

primary source, xxiii, 207
primary source, vs. modern experts, 209
Douglass, Frederick, 87, 111–112
Douglass, William, 33
Dow, Lorenzo, 156
Dowse, Edward, 71
Dreisbach, Daniel, 207
Dunglison, Robley, 51
Dutch Reformed, 45

E
Early, John, 172
Eclectics, 77, 235n50
Eliot Bible, 69
Elizabeth I (Queen of England), 121
Elliott, Robert, 44
Ellis, Edward, xv
Ellis, Joseph, 1–2, 6, 12–13
Elson, Henry William, xv
emancipation, 89
  Jefferson as advocate, 94, 194–195
  Jefferson's actions and writings on, 99
  Jefferson's bill emancipating all slaves born after act passage, 101
  Unitarians and, 186–187
Emancipation Proclamation, 111
Emerson, Ralph Waldo, 185
Emmons, Nathanael, opposition toJefferson, 147–148
end times, Jefferson opinion on, 181
English, teaching methods, 205
Enlightenment
  Christian vs. secular viewpoint, 37
  European, and Jefferson's thinking, 36
Epictetus, 74, 76, 77
Epicurus, 74, 76, 77
Epistles of Paul, de-emphasizing, 179–182
equality, Jefferson's actions and writings on, 99
establishment clause, in First Amendment, 122
Estabrook, Prince, 88
ethics, professorships with responsibility for religious teaching, 49
European Enlightenment, and Jefferson's thinking, 36
European witch trials, xvii–xviii

INDEX

INDEX

INDEX

INDEX

JEFFERSON, THOMAS

B — JEF

Barton, David

The Jefferson lies